WHITMAN, SLAVERY,
AND THE EMERGENCE OF
LEAVES OF GRASS

Martin Klammer

WHITMAN, SLAVERY, AND THE EMERGENCE OF *LEAVES OF GRASS*

The Pennsylvania State University Press
University Park, Pennsylvania

Library of Congress Cataloging-in-Publication Data

Klammer, Martin, 1957–
    Whitman, slavery, and the emergence of Leaves of grass / Martin
Klammer.
        p.   cm.
    Includes bibliographical references (p.) and index.
    ISBN 0-271-01315-X (cloth)   ISBN 0-271-01642-6 (paper)
    1. Whitman, Walt, 1819–1892—Political and social views.   2. Slavery
and slaves in literature.   3. Whitman, Walt, 1819–1892. Leaves of
grass.   4. Race relations in literature.   5. Afro-Americans in
literature.   6. Literature and society—United States—History—19th
century.   I. Title.
PS3242.S56K53   1995
811'.3—dc20   93-33495
                                                                              CIP

Published by The Pennsylvania State University Press,
University Park, PA 16802-1003

Second printing, 1996

It is the policy of The Pennsylvania State University Press to use acid-free paper
for the first printing of all clothbound books. Publications on uncoated stock
satisfy the minimum requirements of American National Standard for Information Sciences—Permanence of Paper for Printed Library Materials, ANSI
Z39.48–1984.

For Joy

Contents

Acknowledgments

One person far above all others deserves my thanks for help in bringing this text about. Ed Folsom introduced me to Walt Whitman in a summer course some years ago, and he has nurtured my interest and scholarship in Whitman ever since. His enthusiasm for Whitman has stirred my enthusiasm, and his encouragement and generous assistance over the years have been invaluable. It is simply true that this text would not have been brought to fruition without his help. Thanks, Ed.

I would also like to thank Jerry Loving, Kathleen Diffley, Wynn Thomas, and Jimmie Killingsworth for their thoughtful criticism and advice. I thank Philip Winsor and Cherene Holland of Penn State Press for editorial support, as well as Linda McCurdy, Head of Public Services in the Special Collections Library at Duke University in Durham, North Carolina, and Alice Birney, American Literature Specialist at the Library of Congress, who each were quite helpful in providing me with copies of Whitman manuscripts.

Finally, I would like to thank my wife, Joy Conrad, who did nothing special except put up with me throughout the production of this text, which is probably enough.

Abbreviations

CG   *Congressional Globe.*

Essays   Ralph Waldo Emerson. *Essays and Lectures.* Ed. Joel Porte. New York: Library of America, 1983.

CP   Walt Whitman. *Complete Poetry and Collected Prose.* Ed. Justin Kaplan. New York: Library of America, 1982.

EPF   ———. *The Early Poems and the Fiction.* Ed. Thomas L. Brasher. New York: New York University Press, 1963.

GF   ———. *The Gathering of the Forces.* Ed. Cleveland Rodgers and John Black. 2 vols. New York: G. P. Putnam's Sons, 1920.

NUPM   ———. *Notebooks and Unpublished Prose Manuscripts.* Ed. Edward F. Grier. 6 vols. New York: New York University Press, 1984.

UPP   ———. *The Uncollected Poetry and Prose of Walt Whitman.* Ed. Emory Holloway. 2 vols. Garden City, N.J.: Doubleday, Page & Company, 1921.

Introduction

On July 4, 1953, Langston Hughes published a column on Walt Whitman in the popular African American newspaper, the *Chicago Defender.* In the column, subtitled "Calls Whitman Negroes' First Great Poetic Friend, Lincoln of Letters," Hughes praised Whitman as the "greatest of American poets," one whom "Negroes should read and remember." *Leaves of Grass,* Hughes wrote, "contains the greatest poetic statements of the real meaning of democracy ever made on our shores." Hughes cited passages from Whitman's poetry that denounce slavery and proclaim the equality of all people; he asserted of a passage from the poem "Says" that "certainly there has been no clearer statement made on equality or civil or political rights than this statement"; and he noted the numerous references in Whitman's poetry "to Negroes, to Africa, to Asiatics and to darker peoples in general," all of whom Whitman includes within "the amplitude of his democracy and his humility."[1]

Two weeks later Hughes printed in its entirety a letter from Lorenzo D. Turner, a professor of English at Roosevelt College in Chicago, who disagreed with Hughes's praise of Whitman's racial attitudes. Turner wrote: "From a careful study of all Whitman's published works I am convinced that he was not a friend of the Negro, and had very few contacts with Negroes, and thought that they were inferior to other human beings." Turner quoted a number of passages, mostly drawn from Whitman's journalism, in which Whitman attacked abolitionists, proposed a colonization scheme for blacks, admired the South and proslavery Senator John C. Calhoun, and expressed his reluctance to endorse Northern interference with the institution of slavery. Turner concluded: "*Leaves of Grass* was Whitman's show-piece, and, unfortunately, is the only one of his works that the average readers see. But to

1. Langston Hughes, "Calls Whitman Negroes' First Great Poetic Friend, Lincoln of Letters," *Chicago Defender,* 4 July 1953, 11.

get a true picture of Whitman one has to read his writings that are not included in *Leaves of Grass*."[2]

In another two weeks, Hughes responded with a column entitled "Like Whitman, Great Artists Are Not Always Good People." Turner's "provocative letter," Hughes wrote, "still does not deter me from maintaining that *Leaves of Grass* is a very great book, and one which Negroes or anyone else, for that matter, should read and remember." It is by Whitman's poems that "the whole world knows him," and his poems "came out of the greatest of the man himself." If Whitman in his "workaday editorials" contradicted "his own highest ideals"—as did Jefferson, the owner of slaves—then it is "the best of him that we choose to keep and cherish, not his worst," Hughes said. Many great artists and leaders "have not always been great men and women in their every day thoughts, speech or ways of living." Great people, Hughes said, are not gods: "They are mortal human beings, subjected to all the currents and evils, sins and stupidities of their times."[3]

This simple exchange of letters in 1953 effectively captures the variety of Whitman's statements and the critical debate that has ensued as scholars and biographers seek to understand Whitman's baffling and seemingly contradictory attitudes toward African Americans.[4] Commentators have repeatedly noted what Newton Arvin once called Whitman's "vacillations and inconsistencies on the slavery question."[5] On one hand Whitman *is,* as Hughes said, the great champion of democracy and equality, one who in *Leaves of Grass* consistently includes blacks and other people of color in his vision of an ideal republic and one who has had an enormous influence on African American poets. According to George Hutchinson, "Probably no white American poet has had a greater impact upon black American literature than Walt Whitman."[6] But on the other

2. Langston Hughes, "An English Professor Disagrees on Whitman's Racial Attitudes," *Chicago Defender,* 18 July 1953, 11.

3. Langston Hughes, "Like Whitman, Great Artists Are Not Always Good People," *Chicago Defender,* 18 July 1953, 11.

4. Turner himself seems to have had a different view of Whitman years earlier. In a book published in 1929, *Anti-Slavery Sentiment in Literature* (Washington, D.C.: The Association for the Study of Negro Life and History, 1929), Turner cited Whitman and melodramatist Dion Boucicault as "the best" examples of writers who "showed no hostility to the slaveholder, but allowed the strength of their opposition to slavery to be determined by their depth of sympathy for the slave." Whitman expressed "keen sympathy" for the slave in "Song of Myself," Turner noted. Such "sentimental arguments" were attempts to move the people "to action" (89).

5. Newton Arvin, *Whitman* (New York: Macmillan, 1932), 31.

6. George B. Hutchinson, "Whitman and the Black Poet: Kelly Miller's Speech to the Walt Whitman Fellowship," *American Literature* 61 (1989): 46.

hand, a number of Whitman texts show that he thought blacks inferior to whites and that his opposition to the extension of slavery had little, if anything, to do with sympathy for slaves.

Over the years critics have described and tried to account for Whitman's contradictions between his conservative, prejudiced views as a journalist, rooted in the mainstream Northern attitudes of his day, and his visionary, egalitarian ideas as a poet, inspired by the hope of a multiracial and inclusive America.[7] Yet none has understood this polarity as a *historical* phenomenon—something that evolves in response both to historical events and to other contemporary discourses on slavery—nor have critics described the convergence of these forces in Whitman's initial and revolutionary work, the 1855 *Leaves of Grass*.

This study complicates the models of Whitman's thinking about race offered by earlier critics, both in its argument and in its historical approach. My central argument is that Whitman's thinking about African Americans and slavery—largely ignored in Whitman scholarship as significant to his poetry—is, in fact, essential to the development and the poetry of the 1855 *Leaves of Grass*. More specifically, I seek to understand Whitman's emergence as a poet through a detailed, historical analysis of his thinking about African Americans and slavery from the beginning of his career through the 1855 edition. In carefully tracing his thinking and writing about race, I aim to achieve several goals: to understand how Whitman's attitudes toward African Americans and slavery evolve over time; to demonstrate how Whitman's focus on slavery is a compelling force behind his quest for a new form of expression that culminates in *Leaves of Grass*; and to show the ways in which Whitman's representations of African Americans and slavery make *Leaves of Grass* a major text dealing with race relations in the mid-

7. Roger Asselineau, for example, seeks to resolve the inconsistencies by proposing a distinction between Whitman's philosophical assent to egalitarianism and his personal, racist attitudes rooted in his grandparents' slaveholding past: "Much as he approved of Rousseau's declarations on the fundamental equality of all men beyond racial differences, he nevertheless continued to behave and to react like a Long Island peasant whose grandparents had owned slaves" (*The Evolution of Walt Whitman* [Cambridge: Harvard University Press, 1960–62], 2:191). Another critic assigns the "disparity of views" to the difference between Whitman's public and private writings (Reginald Martin, "The Self-Contradiction Literatus: Walt Whitman and His Two Views of Blacks in America," *Calamus: Walt Whitman Quarterly: International* 27 [1986]: 13). And yet others sense a sharp dichotomy between Whitman's poetic ideals and the "everyday realities of his society," distinguishing between what Whitman said and what he "actually fought for and achieved" (see Ken Peeples, Jr., "The Paradox of the 'Good Gray Poet' [Walt Whitman on Slavery and the Black Man]," *Phylon* 35 [1974]: 31, and Mary-Emma Graham, "Politics in Black and White: A View of Walt Whitman's Career as a Political Journalist," *CLA Journal* 17 [1973]: 270).

nineteenth century. No previous study has focused on the significance of slavery in understanding the development of Whitman's poetry, and I believe the perspective offered here will provide a new point of entry to Whitman and will stimulate discussions about the relationship of race and rhetoric in Whitman's poetry.

Throughout the early course of Whitman's career his thinking on slavery evolves in several stages. In his early years as a writer Whitman is essentially a pro-slavery apologist, as evidenced by a section in his temperance novel *Franklin Evans* that mimics the narrative conventions of contemporary plantation romances and subverts those of abolitionist fiction. As victory in the war with Mexico opens up new western territories in the late 1840s, Whitman in his journalism takes a strong "Free Soil" position opposed to the extension of slavery. This position is motivated more by his concern for the opportunities of white laborers than by sympathy for African Americans. At the same time, however, Whitman begins to read the essays of Ralph Waldo Emerson and to conceive of himself, his vocation, and slavery in radically different ways. Sensing the transcendent possibilities within himself, he begins a series of new and unusual poetry experiments in his notebooks—the same poetry that would emerge, revised, eight years later in *Leaves of Grass*. At the heart of these experiments is a deeply humanitarian concern for the suffering of slaves, completely unlike anything Whitman had expressed in his slavery editorials.

From 1848 on, I argue, Whitman holds these two attitudes in an unresolved tension, never dissolving the distinction between his Free Soil journalism and his radically new and sympathetic poetry about slaves, nor, apparently, finding an audience that would simultaneously be receptive to both views. While repeated political defeats quiet but do not altogether silence Whitman's central concern for Free Soil, he continues in his poetry to develop images of African Americans that emphasize their dignity, equality, and humanity. My thesis is that the historical events of 1854 not only resolve these tensions within his position on slavery but also liberate and in fact compel Whitman to revise and publish the twelve poems known as *Leaves of Grass*. Northern indignation about the 1854 Kansas-Nebraska Act (which threatened to repeal the 1820 Compromise) and about the Anthony Burns case (which returned a Boston black man to the South under force of federal law) so radicalize and galvanize opposition to slavery that Whitman is suddenly guaranteed what he had not thought possible: an audience vehemently opposed to slavery *and* compelled by both of Whitman's concerns—Free Soil and humanitarian sympathy for the slave. Thus regenerated, Whitman at last publishes *Leaves of Grass* in 1855, his eloquent passages about African

American dignity and suffering not only expressive of an inner voice he had been responding to since 1847 but also useful toward the political goals of advancing Free Soil and opposing the Fugitive Slave Law. The final two chapters of this study interpret the 1855 *Leaves of Grass* as a stunning and novel portrayal of African Americans and a modeling for whites of the response of imaginative entry into the slave's experience.

Throughout this work I seek to understand Whitman's thinking on race within a complex set of factors, including national and local political developments on the issue of slavery, racial attitudes and ideologies that were prevalent in American culture, Whitman's own growth as a writer who was constantly seeking new ways to make himself known to his readers, and the specific rhetorical goals Whitman attempted in all of his writings through 1855. Moreover, the study highlights the way in which Whitman responded to various texts about slavery: abolitionist and pro-slavery fictional narratives, the essays of Emerson, the *Congressional Globe* during debates over the Wilmot Proviso (1846–48) and the 1850 Compromise, and the wealth of newspaper editorials and other public reactions to the 1854 Kansas-Nebraska Act and enforcement of the Fugitive Slave Law. While I leave to others a comprehensive discussion of the career of Whitman's attitudes toward African Americans, my focus raises new and important questions about the influence of one of America's most powerful and painful institutions—slavery—on the development of one of its most important writers.

A note about terminology: throughout the text I use interchangeably the terms "blacks" and "African Americans." The latter might be challenged since the slaves' American-ness was very much the point of dispute in Whitman's time. American citizenship for blacks, after all, was not granted until after the Civil War. I use the term, however, not only because of its contemporary resonance, but because it reflects both the historical origin and the rightful place of free and slave blacks in antebellum America, despite the law's failure to recognize that place. "Each belongs here or anywhere just as much as the welloff," Whitman writes, "just as much as you."[8]

---

8. Walt Whitman, *Complete Poetry and Collected Prose*, ed. Justin Kaplan (New York: Library of America, 1982), 122. Subsequent references will be cited in the text as *CP*.

1

THE CONSTRUCTION
OF A PRO-SLAVERY APOLOGY

Most discussions of Whitman's attitudes toward African Americans begin with his journalism of the late 1840s in which he opposed the extension of slavery into the new western territories. But such approaches overlook a much earlier text and what is by far Whitman's longest writing involving an African American: the eight curious chapters of the 1842 temperance novel *Franklin Evans, or The Inebriate* (hereafter *Franklin Evans*), written when Whitman was twenty-three. Briefly summarized, in this part of the novel the narrator, Franklin Evans, a young, alcoholic Northerner, travels south from New York to a Virginia plantation. Almost immediately upon arrival he is sexually attracted to a female Creole slave. Franklin lets his desire be known to the slave owner, and, in a fit of drunkenness (and with the slave owner's help), he marries the woman and simultaneously has her manumitted. Upon sobering up he discovers to his disgust what has happened, but he is "saved" from his own actions by the sudden appearance of a sexually aggressive Northern white woman who, after arriving on the plantation, targets him as her next romantic conquest. The Creole wife then becomes violently jealous and in a mad frenzy murders the woman and commits suicide, leaving young Franklin to ponder—and reject—any sense of responsibility.

Whitman was not especially proud of *Franklin Evans*, telling Horace Traubel that it was "damned rot—rot of the worst sort" and claiming that he wrote it in three days with "the help of a bottle of port or what not."[1] Yet it was by far Whitman's most popular work, selling in his estimation around twenty thousand copies.[2] Most critics agree with Whitman that the novel is a hackneyed piece of tractarian temperance fiction, and yet the absence of critical commentary about the unusual "Creole episode" is surprising. What critical discussions there are of *Franklin Evans* often ignore, or at the very least minimize, the issues of race in the novel.[3] The few commentators who speak at all about the mulatto narrative in *Franklin Evans* treat it as a sexual rites-of-passage for young Franklin (and, by association, for Whitman) apart from any considerations of race.[4] What is missing from all of these discussions are essential issues: why, for example, one-fourth of Whitman's temperance novel is devoted to a biracial relationship, or how that portion of the narrative allows the speaker—and perhaps Whitman, too, through the writing of fiction—to pursue sexual fantasies about a slave woman within the bounds of conventional Victorian morality, using bouts of alcoholism as a psychic and moral "cover" for his desire, manipulation,

1. Horace Traubel, *With Walt Whitman in Camden* (Boston: Small Maynard and Co., 1906), 1:93. For a sampling of critical responses to *Franklin Evans,* see Jean Downey's Introduction to *Franklin Evans* (New Haven: College and University Press, 1967), 21; Gay Wilson Allen, *The Solitary Singer* (Chicago: University of Chicago Press, 1985), 58; and Paul Zweig, *Walt Whitman: The Making of the Poet* (New York: Basic Books, 1984), 115.

2. Traubel, *With Walt Whitman in Camden,* 1:93.

3. For discussions of *Franklin Evans* that entirely overlook the Creole episode, see Anne Dalke, "Whitman's Literary Intemperance," *Walt Whitman Review* 3 (1985): 17–22, and Barton Levi St. Armand, *"Franklin Evans:* A Sportive Temperance Novel," *Books at Brown* 24 (1971): 136–47. Conversely, for criticism that focuses on Whitman's attitudes toward blacks and yet ignores *Franklin Evans,* see Oscar Cargill, "Walt Whitman and Civil Rights," *Essays in American Literature Presented to Bruce Robert McElderry* (Athens: Ohio University Press, 1970), 48–58, and Reginald Martin, "The Self-Contradiction Literatus: Walt Whitman and His Two Views of Blacks in America," *Calamus: Walt Whitman Quarterly: International* 27 (1986): 13–22.

4. See, for example, Allen, *The Solitary Singer,* 59–60. Alone among a previous generation of critics to at least acknowledge that the woman is of a different race, Leslie Fiedler in *Love and Death in the American Novel* (New York: Criterion Books, 1960), 286, nonetheless sees the Creole woman as simply another type among various shades of "dark" and "fair" ladies whom American writers symbolically employ.

Among more recent readings, Betsy Erkkila briefly examines *Franklin Evans* in the context of the temperance movement in *Whitman the Political Poet* (New York: Oxford University Press, 1989), 29–32. Erkkila locates *Franklin Evans* within what she defines as the broad themes of all of Whitman's writing—his commitment to "regenerating . . . the American people in the purity, strength, and power of republican principle" (29)—but she does not, however, mention the extended Creole episode. See also Zweig, *Walt Whitman,* 63–64, and Justin Kaplan, *Walt Whitman: A Life* (New York: Simon and Schuster, 1980), 105.

and domination of the woman. Moreover, *Franklin Evans* is singularly revealing not only in what it indicates about a young Walt Whitman's racial attitudes, but especially about how these attitudes are constructed from an eclectic gathering of various "texts" and ideologies then prevalent in both Northern *and* Southern antebellum culture. Most revealing is the way in which Whitman replicates the conventions of pro-slavery fiction and subverts those of abolitionist literature to create a thoroughgoing apology for slavery, all within a temperance tract. On one hand, Whitman's essentially pro-slavery posture is not entirely surprising, given the predominant racial attitudes of the nineteenth century when most white Americans viewed persons of African descent as inferior beings and, in the words of historian George Fredrickson, as a "permanently alien and unassimilable element of the population."[5] Yet the very presence of the Creole episode in *Franklin Evans* is striking when one considers both the expectations of Whitman's reform-minded audience—sympathizers of abolition as well as temperance—and the absence of any need for such an episode.[6]

Moreover, *Franklin Evans* was published during a period of relative calm in the history of the volatile slavery question in antebellum America. For many Americans, slavery had simply not yet become an issue. The constitutional compromises and the 1820 Missouri Compromise appeared to have settled the disputes between North and South for the time being.[7] *Franklin Evans* suggests not only Whitman's heightened interest in race relations but also a direct relationship between Whitman's racial attitudes and his reliance on conventional discursive strategies, a relationship that remains constant from early in his career through the publication of the 1855 *Leaves of Grass*. The conventionality of

5. George Fredrickson, *The Black Image in the White Mind: The Debate on Afro-American Character and Destiny, 1817–1914* (New York: Harper and Row, 1971), 1.

6. The novel is unusual in other ways, too. In *Amalgamation!: Race, Sex, and Rhetoric in the Nineteenth-Century American Novel* (Westport, Conn.: Greenwood Press, 1985), James Kinney lists *Franklin Evans* as one of only ten American novels of miscegenation from the late eighteenth century until 1850 (236). Kinney also cites *Franklin Evans* as a rare pre-1850 Northern novel about Southern blacks and as a plantation story that openly talks of miscegenation (39, 46).

7. The three compromises on slavery in the United States Constitution to which the North agreed in order to gain Southern acceptance of the Constitution are the famous Three-fifths Clause, which counted each slave as three-fifths of a person for the basis of representation in the lower house and the electoral college (Article I, Section 2), a clause forbidding for twenty years the passage of a federal law that would prohibit the importation of slaves (Article I, Section 9), and the Fugitive Slave Clause, which required the return of slaves who escaped into free states (Article IV, Section 2).

The Missouri Compromise admitted Missouri as a slave state but prohibited slavery in the rest of the Louisiana Purchase that lay north of 36°30′.

Whitman's racial prejudices is reflected in the degree to which Whitman borrows from other discourses to create his own discourse—that is, the degree to which his text is constructed of other texts. So long as his own racial attitudes reflect the racial prejudices of a mainstream segment of American culture, his discursive strategies will largely be the imitation of what he has seen and read. In other words, his discursive strategies will always be as orthodox as his racial assumptions. When Whitman begins to liberate himself, he does so simultaneously with respect to both race and rhetoric: his radical new thinking about blacks demands radical new discursive strategies, and vice versa. The process and dynamic of these interactions will be explored throughout this study. A close and contextualized reading of his most popular work suggests that nowhere is Whitman more conventional or more racist, even by nineteenth-century standards, than in *Franklin Evans*.

For the first three-fourths of the novel, *Franklin Evans* appears to be a conventional mid-century temperance novel born of the evangelical reform movement. The narrator's claim to be telling a true and factual story, the cause-and-effect chain of first drink leading to degradation, and the loose, episodic structure are all characteristics of conventional temperance literature.[8] Yet with the advent of the Creole episode in chapter 15, the text changes from a conventional temperance novel into another type of conventional antebellum literature, that of the pro-slavery romance.[9] The episode begins when Franklin wanders onto the plantation of Bourne, a character modeled after the aristocratic Southern gentleman sentimentalized in pro-slavery novels and, even to some degree, after Thomas Jefferson. Bourne is gracious and intelligent, solicitous of his new guest and clearly kind to his slaves. Like Jefferson, Bourne owns a Virginia plantation home that stands at the top of a hill, adorned with exotic plants.[10] After only two days of visits with Bourne,

8. For a useful discussion of the conventions of temperance literature in the nineteenth century, see Herbert Brown, *The Sentimental Novel in America, 1789–1860* (Durham: Duke University Press, 1940), 201–40.

9. That Whitman was himself aware of such a change and of the improbability of the tale he was about to tell is evident from a paragraph he inserted in a revised version of *Franklin Evans*, printed serially in the *Brooklyn Eagle*, November 16–30, 1848. Whitman writes: "What I have now to relate—a train of events quite out of the method of my hitherto adventures—bears somewhat the air of romance. And yet, reader! when we look around us in the course of our every day lives, or go out among our neighbors, and investigate what is transacted there, you might come to the knowledge of things far more improbable and inconsistent." See Walt Whitman, *The Early Poems and the Fiction*, ed. Thomas L. Brasher (New York: New York University Press, 1963), 202–3n46. Subsequent references will be cited in the text as *EPF*.

10. According to Fawn Brodie in *Thomas Jefferson: An Intimate History* (New York: W. W. Norton, 1974), 88, Jefferson's Monticello (meaning "little mountain") was adorned

and before the action of the Creole episode begins, Franklin is moved by his host's considered, humanitarian view of slavery, which he describes at length in the only discussion of slavery in the novel:

> Perhaps it may hardly be the appropriate place here, to remark upon the national customs of this country; but I cannot help pausing a moment to say that Bourne, as he saw with his own eyes, and judged with his own judgment, became convinced of the fallacy of many of those assertions which are brought against slavery in the south. He beheld, it is true, a large number of men and women in bondage; but he could not shut his eyes to the fact, that they would be far more unhappy, if possessed of freedom. He saw them well taken care of—with shelter and food, and every necessary means of comfort: and he wondered in his own mind, as he remembered what misery he had seen in his travels through various countries of Europe, that the philanthropists of the Old World should wish to interfere with the systems of the New— when the merely nominal oppression of the latter is overbalanced, so many hundred times, by the stern reality of starvation and despotism in the former. (*EPF*, 202)

After repudiating as "fallacy" abolitionist assertions about slavery, Bourne advances arguments that were dear to both pro-slavery apologists and to the nascent Northern labor movement, of which Whitman and his father had been ardent followers. Bourne asserts, for example, that slavery is a beneficial institution, a source of sustenance and happiness for the slaves: "He beheld, it is true, a large number of men and women in bondage; but he could not shut his eyes to the fact, that they would be far more unhappy, if possessed of freedom." Such a view reflected the slaveholding South's emerging justification for slavery and mimicked the strategy of pro-slavery novelists. Prior to the rise of abolitionism in the 1830s, the major cotton-producing states argued that slavery was both economically necessary and a vital system of control over a potentially dangerous African population. These justifications rested on the notion that servitude was an essential stage in human progress and that black behavior, both by reason of circumstance and

---

with Mediterranean plants not native to Virginia—"figs, acacia, pomegranates, almonds, olives, nectarines, and oranges." Even Jefferson's slight differences from Bourne are suggestive: Bourne is a bachelor and Jefferson a widower; Bourne is French by birth and Jefferson by affection—he was a Francophile whose years in Paris as foreign minister were among the fondest he would remember (Brodie, 185).

nature, demonstrated that blacks were ill-equipped for freedom.[11] By the middle of the 1830s, however, in response to charges from the nascent abolitionist movement that slavery was inherently sinful, the South increasingly emphasized the so-called moral argument that slavery was a "positive good." Africans were said to be not only unfit for freedom but ideally suited to slavery. Far from being degraded, slaves were said to be better off in a safe and civilized society that provided food, shelter, and clothing than in the wildly dangerous and cannibalistic Africa of their roots. Moreover, black character—thought to be inherently unstable, savage, and brutish—was supposedly civilized or refined by the institution of slavery. Whitman's Bourne articulates just such views: "He saw them well taken care of—with shelter and food, and every necessary means of comfort."

The notion of the "happy slave" who finds fulfillment in serving a white master was frequently translated into popular stories and pictures. The South Carolina novelist and critic William Gilmore Simms, whom Whitman read later in his career, wrote that the African came from a continent where he was "a cannibal, destined . . . to eat his fellow, or be eaten by him." Southern slavery "brought him to a land in which he suffers no risk of life or limb other than that to which his owner is equally subjected," and had increased "his health and strength," improved "his physical symmetry and animal organization," elevated "his mind and morals," and given him "better and more certain food, better clothing, and more kind and valuable attendance when he is sick."[12] Whitman's portrayal of Bourne's slaves adds one more text to the pro-slavery canon. The supposed happiness of Bourne's slaves is one of the first things Franklin notices when he arrives in Virginia, even before he meets Bourne. He spends part of his time "chatting with the slaves, from whose liveliness and cheerful good-humor, I derived no small share of mirth myself" (*EPF,* 201).

Moreover, the comparison Bourne makes between the "stern reality" of life for laborers in the "Old World" (Europe) and the "merely nominal oppression" of slave life in the United States was employed not only in pro-slavery novels but by the emerging labor movement in the 1830s

11. For a discussion of the evolution of pro-slavery arguments, see George Fredrickson, *The Black Image in the White Mind,* 44–46.

12. William Gilmore Simms, "The Morals of Slavery," in *The Pro-Slavery Argument,* 273. (Originally published in *The Southern Literary Messenger* 3 [November 1837]: 637.) Quoted in Fredrickson, *The Black Image in the White Mind,* 52. Gay Wilson Allen writes that Whitman notated a passage on composition from Simms's *Views and Reviews* in the late 1840s (*The Solitary Singer,* 134). Whether Whitman was familiar with Simms's fiction at the time he was composing *Franklin Evans* cannot be ascertained.

and 1840s.[13] Recent work by M. Wynn Thomas has demonstrated the significance of labor on Whitman's life and writings, and Thomas's arguments need not be repeated here.[14] It is useful, however, to review briefly the influence of labor on Whitman's early life, especially since his writing on slavery in the late 1840s is largely driven by his insistence on opportunity for the working classes, as we shall see.

Whitman's father, a carpenter, was one of thousands of disaffected independent artisans in a rapidly industrializing New York in the 1820s and 1830s. As New York became the most productive manufacturing city in the United States and the fastest-growing industrial center in the world from 1825 to 1850, the process of subcontracting and subdivision of labor alienated independent artisans from their craft and devalued their work. Many felt that the dignity and independence of their work had been undermined by what Sean Wilentz calls "self-evident inequalities of power and material expectations at every level of production," manifested by the intensification of labor, underpayment, and subordination to the rule of another.[15]

Walt Whitman Sr. seems to have had a particularly difficult time in the late 1820s when he moved his family from home to home and began working for wages.[16] Like many others, Whitman Sr. turned to the radical political philosophy of Frances Wright and Robert Dale Owen—and later, William Leggett—to give expression to his frustrations, fears, and hopes. The freethinking Wright drew large crowds as she railed against the inequalities perpetuated by the growth of market capitalism and against a banking system that favored the privileged. Whitman Sr. often took young Walt to these meetings, which inspired the rise of the first Workingmen's associations in Eastern cities in the late 1820s and 1830s. In the 1830s William Leggett, an editorial writer for New York–area newspapers, forcefully articulated the principles of the radical wing of Jacksonian Democracy, giving vent to workers' demands for higher wages and to their anger against banks that refused to extend credit to all but the privileged classes. Walt Whitman, then, was raised on a politics deeply rooted in the Jeffersonian ideals of self-sovereignty and equal

13. For use of the comparison between slavery and "wage slavery" in pro-slavery novels, see Brown, *The Sentimental Novel in America*, 254–73.

14. For Thomas's discussion of how the rapid changes toward mass production and industrialization affected the livelihood and politics of Walter Whitman Sr., see *The Lunar Light of Whitman's Poetry* (Cambridge: Harvard University Press, 1987).

15. Sean Wilentz, *Chants Democratic: New York City and the Rise of the American Working Class, 1788–1850* (New York: Oxford University Press, 1984), 129.

16. Gay Wilson Allen, *The Solitary Singer*, 7.

rights—including economic rights—articulated for him by Wright and Leggett.

Thus it is not surprising that when Whitman first writes of slavery, he focuses on the "wage slavery" of Northern white labor and not on the "peculiar institution" of the South. As Eric Foner points out, with conditions deteriorating in New England factories and in the artisan workshops of New York and Philadelphia, the emerging Northern labor movement had begun to appropriate slavery as its central metaphor. The status of the Northern worker was compared to that of the Southern slave and found to be essentially similar. "Wage slavery" meant long working hours and extremely low pay, but even beyond this, it evoked fears of the poor social conditions of many European laborers and of further class stratification in America. Working for wages was itself considered a form of slavery—an assault on the "traditional artisanal ideal of economic and personal independence."[17]

Whitman, a fledgling journalist at the time, made this same argument in his first extant editorial on slavery in the April 2, 1842, issue of *The New York Aurora*, written six months prior to the publication of *Franklin Evans*. In the editorial Whitman criticizes English abolitionists who denounce American slavery. He does so by describing a lithograph of two pictures, inscribed "Black and White Slaves." One picture depicts an impoverished English laborer and his family—"his wife lying dead upon a heap of straw, an infant endeavoring to draw moisture from her breast"—while a parish officer announces that they are going to the workhouse. The other picture shows a Southern gentleman, lady, and their two children calling on a family of their slaves: "Every thing bears the impress of cheerfulness and content." Whitman draws the obvious moral for the English abolitionists: "Let our transatlantic neighbors take the beam out of their own eyes—and then they can reasonably find fault with the mote in ours."[18]

These two anti-abolitionist, pro-slavery arguments (the "happy slave" and "wage slavery") gain additional force in *Franklin Evans* by their setting within a context with which many of Whitman's readers would have been familiar. A common literary convention of pro-slavery novels was the "conversion" to slavery experienced by a respectable person from outside the South. Herbert Brown writes that "by far the most popular method" to offset abolitionist claims of the horrors of slavery was to send "an ardent abolitionist to the South for a visit with a college

17. Eric Foner, *Politics and Ideology in the Age of the Civil War* (New York: Oxford University Press, 1980), 60.

18. Walt Whitman, *Walt Whitman of the New York Aurora*, ed. Joseph J. Rubin and Charles H. Brown (State College, Pa.: Bald Eagle Press, 1928), 126–27.

friend or a favorite cousin. Once across the line, Northern prejudices were made to melt like snow beneath Dixie's sun."[19] Franklin does not explicitly remark on his "conversion," yet immediately after his summary of Bourne's apologia he mentions he was "constant in my visits to my new acquaintance" whom he found to be "an intelligent and very affable companion" (EPF, 202). Moreover, Franklin's subsequent actions make clear that he shares Bourne's views. He even fantasizes about being the plantation owner. His walks about the plantation "made me familiar with all its affairs; and I even took upon myself, at times, the direction of things, as though I were upon my own property. I cannot look back upon this period of my life without some satisfaction" (EPF, 203). Such "narcotic effects" of the plantation setting were by then a "well-established" tradition in pro-slavery novels, according to Brown.[20] The narrator of J. P. Kennedy's 1832 novel Swallow Barn, for example, soliloquizes that "'I only want a thousand acres of good land, an old manor-house, on a pleasant site, a hundred negroes, a large library, a host of friends . . . with some few et ceteras not worth mentioning.'"[21]

Franklin's plantation fantasy begins to take shape when he first lays eyes on Margaret, the Creole slave. He is immediately attracted to her "large, soft, voluptuous eyes," "beautifully cut lips," and "complexion just sufficiently removed from clear white, to make the spectator doubtful whether he is gazing on a brunette, or one who has indeed some hue of African blood in her veins" (EPF, 204). These traits are not simply random details, but rather the specific characteristics associated with the "tragic mulatto" archetype from abolitionist fiction.[22] Like Margaret, the tragic mulatto is a beautiful young woman who possesses only the slightest evidence of Negro blood and one whose sensuality is highlighted by the narrator's attention to her lips and eyes.[23] The typical abolitionist story of the tragic mulatto (or tragic "octoroon") is of a woman who was raised and educated "white" by a kind patrician father, but who discovers at her father's death that she is actually a slave whom he has failed to properly free. Sold into slavery, she is victimized, usually by a lower-class slave-dealer or overseer attempting to violate her. She

19. Herbert Brown, The Sentimental Novel in America, 246.

20. Ibid., 246.

21. Quoted in ibid., 250.

22. For a discussion of the mixed-race woman in mid-century fiction, see Jules Zanger, "The 'Tragic Octoroon' in Pre–Civil War Fiction," American Quarterly 18 (1966): 63–70.

23. Ibid. See also Werner Sollors, "'Never Was Born': The Mulatto, An American Tragedy," The Massachusetts Review 27 (1986): 293–316, and Barbara Christian, "Shadows Uplifted" in Feminist Criticism and Social Change, ed. Judith Newton and Deborah Rosenfelt (New York: Methuen, 1985), 181–215.

is then rescued by a high-born Northerner who wishes to marry her. The story ends when she escapes with her lover or, more often, commits suicide or dies of shame. Because a white, especially female, readership could identify physically with the tragic mulatto, the convention elicited sympathy and moral indignation from antebellum Northern audiences.[24] In *Franklin Evans,* however, Whitman borrows the convention of the tragic mulatto only to subvert it for pro-slavery ends.

As the narrative begins, Margaret is, like the tragic mulatto, abused by the overseer Phillips. When she must explain to Bourne why she knocked Phillips unconscious with a heavy instrument in order to resist his advances, Franklin plays the role of the rescuing Northerner and intercedes on her behalf. While Margaret pleads for mercy—perhaps for her life—Franklin "could not help being struck by her beauty" (*EPF,* 205), a feeling he attributes in part to the influence of liquor. In temperance fiction intemperance is of course the parent of all sins, but here intemperance not only explains but excuses Franklin's desire for Margaret. Moreover, Franklin's willingness to advocate her rights ("she would at least have one defender and advocate" [*EPF,* 205]) becomes the means by which she becomes indebted to him and by which he may exercise his desire. Whitman thus maneuvers his protagonist into a position that would likely appeal to his white male readers: Franklin is able to possess a mulatto woman as the object of his sexual desire not by force but by the cover of alcoholism and the moral certainty that he has earned the woman's gratitude and affection.[25] Initially Franklin's feelings of "prudence and self-respect" contravene his desire, yet soon enough his mind becomes confused by "strong drink" and he arranges to both marry and manumit Margaret in a remarkable double ceremony.[26] Franklin is confident of Margaret's affection. He says of Margaret: "I have no doubt

24. Zanger, "The 'Tragic Octoroon,'" 63–64.

25. Whitman's narrative contortions were also perhaps influenced by the South's changing attitudes toward miscegenation. While sexual liaisons between white men and slave women gradually increased until about 1850, violent hostility against miscegenation began in the 1830s, when the South felt more and more compelled to justify slavery—and thus the separation of races—in response to attacks by abolitionists. For this reason, Southern antebellum novels did not stress miscegenation or an image of the loose black woman. With or without the sanction of marriage, Whitman's narrator could have legally exercised his sexual desire without the woman's consent: at this time the rape of black women by men of either race did not exist under Virginia law. See Kinney, *Amalgamation!,* 12–15, and Christian, "Shadows Uplifted," 190.

26. Such an occurrence was not as "absurd" as Whitman's narrator claims (144). Eugene Genovese writes: "The Supreme Court of Kentucky refused to judge insane a white man who wanted to marry the slave he had just emancipated. However repugnant, the court declared, such concubinage occurred too often to permit denial of the attraction." See *Roll, Jordan, Roll: The World the Slaves Made* (New York: Random House, 1976), 415.

she had loved me tenderly, ever since the time of my interference in her behalf when she was arraigned for striking Phillips" (*EPF,* 210). But one might also suggest that Margaret has only been liberated from one form of bondage to another, since at the time of the ceremony and throughout the wedding night Franklin is "quaffing bottle after bottle" (*EPF,* 207).

Whitman's readers might well interpret this double ceremony as a metaphor for emancipation and racial coexistence; that is, only a fool or a drunkard would allow such a thing to happen. For the very next day Franklin awakens from his drunken lethargy, repulsed by what he discovers has taken place. "What disgust with myself filled my mind at view of the conduct I had been pursuing!" (*EPF,* 207). Whitman's self-disgusted narrator echoes the thoughts of men in other popular novels involving miscegenation, such as the speaker in Mayne Reid's *The Quadroon* who laments: "You can ill comprehend the horrid feeling . . . the positive disgust and horror felt for the 'white' who would ally himself *in marriage* with a *slave*!—No matter how white *she* be, no matter how beautiful."[27] Moreover, such repentant self-loathing was also a fact of life in the contorted biracial relationships of nineteenth-century America. As Eugene Genovese writes: "Individual exceptions aside, blacks and whites were not free to love each other without considerable emotional confusion, marked in part by a self-contempt projected onto the other." The tragedy of miscegenation, Genovese suggests, lay not so much in "lust and sexual exploitation" as in "the terrible pressure to deny the delight, affection, and love that so often grew from tawdry beginnings. Whites as well as blacks found themselves tortured as well as degraded, but not always for the reasons they thought."[28]

Realizing his enormous social transgression, Franklin suddenly begins to hate Margaret—the one "whom but a little while before I had looked on with the deepest admiration" (*EPF,* 207)—and he seeks a way out. Whitman mechanically and self-consciously provides one ("The course of my narrative needs now that another character should be introduced") in the person of Mrs. Conway, a handsome, cultured, yet sexually aggressive young widow from the North. She arrives out of nowhere and pursues Franklin with a zeal that he cannot resist.

If Whitman were aware of the stereotypical images of women in Southern ideology and antebellum literature, he did not consistently follow them. As a number of historians and critics of black women's writing have recently pointed out, the sexual ideology of the slaveholding South

27. Mayne Reid, *The Quadroon; or, Adventures in the Far West,* "War Trail" edition (London: Routledge, 1856). Quoted in Sollors, "'Never Was Born,'" 301.
28. Genovese, *Roll, Jordan, Roll,* 419.

created a "virgin/whore dichotomy" that demanded moral superiority from white women and sexual availability from black women.[29] White women were characterized by delicate constitutions, sexual purity, and moral superiority to men, while black women were cast by Southern mythology into the roles of subhuman creatures who were, by nature, strong and sexual. The black woman's supposed lewdness and impurity—and even her blackness—kept intact the image of the white woman as chaste and pure. And, as Hazel Carby has argued, while white women were to "repress all overt sexuality" in order to qualify as paragons of virtue, the supposedly overt sexuality of black women—connected to the "dark forces of evil and magic"—also functioned to relieve the white male of responsibility for his own advances, since he was represented "as being merely prey to the rampant sexuality of his female slaves."[30]

While Margaret's subsequent actions confirm the black woman stereotype, Mrs. Conway is no paragon of virtue. Beyond her physical similarity to chaste Southern heroines—light hair, blue eyes, and delicate skin—she has more in common with the black woman stereotype than she does with that of the Southern belle.[31] She is "a woman of the world" who has "but one aim, the conquest of hearts. And seldom did she determine to make any individual addition to her adorers, but what her efforts were crowned with triumph." Franklin, then, becomes yet one more conquest for her: "she made up her mind to bring *me* to her feet" (*EPF*, 208).

Whatever Whitman's sexual proclivities may have been at the time, it seems striking that his protagonist becomes the object of desire of both women—one white, one black—and that both are reduced to stereotypes. Moreover, Mrs. Conway functions not only as one more female element in the expanding male fantasy, but also to displace Margaret's anger toward Franklin. For spurned and treated abusively by Franklin,

29. For useful discussions of the portrayal of black and white women in pre–Civil War Southern literature, see Christian, "Shadows Uplifted," 190; Minrose C. Gwin, "Green-Eyed Monsters of the Slavocracy: Jealous Mistresses in Two Slave Narratives," in *Conjuring*, ed. Marjorie Pryse and Hortense J. Spillers (Bloomington: Indiana University Press, 1985), 39–52; and Katherine Fishburn, *Women in Popular Culture: A Reference Guide* (Westport, Conn.: Greenwood Press, 1982).

30. *Reconstructing Womanhood* (New York: Oxford University Press, 1987), 26–27.

31. The image of the chaste Southern woman is typified by this description from the 1852 novel *Eoline, or Magnolia Vale* by Caroline Lee Hentz: "Eoline, with her fair hair, and celestial blue eyes bending over the harp . . . really seemed 'little lower than the angels,' and an aureola of purity and piety appeared to beam around her brow." Quoted in Hazel Carby, *Reconstructing Womanhood*, 26.

Margaret now seeks revenge—not on Franklin, but on her white rival.[32]
Mrs. Conway adds to Margaret's fury by successfully imploring Franklin
to give her possession of Margaret's younger brother, Louis. In one of
the more bizarre twists of the narrative, Margaret and Louis plot to kill
Mrs. Conway by luring her to the house of a family struck by a plague
that has suddenly gripped the plantation. When that strategy fails, Margaret literally takes matters into her own hands and strangles Mrs. Conway in her sleep. At this point Whitman's narrator, conscious that "I
have already dwelt long enough, and too long, on this part of my history" (*EPF*, 229), dispatches Margaret rather quickly with the generic
"tragic mulatto" ending—her confession and suicide in a jail cell:[33]

> From some train of motives which the great Heart-Viewer alone
> can fathom, the creole soon after sent for Phillips and myself,
> and made a full confession. Upon her story as she told it to me,
> and her own acknowledgment, I have given many of the incidents
> in the previous two chapters, which, at the time they took place,
> were totally unknown to me. That very night she committed sui-
> cide in her cell. I never saw her again. (ibid.)

Margaret's violent turn reinforces the images of blacks advanced by
pro-slavery apologists beginning in the 1820s—namely, that blacks are
inherently unstable, violent, and vengeful, and surely unfit for freedom.
Throughout the narrative, Margaret's emotionalism is highlighted: she
has "strong passions" bent on revenge (*EPF*, 210), "a sharp and bitter
tongue" (213), and a heart that "had still a remnant of the savage"
(224). Her inhumanity is further emphasized by the way in which Franklin demonizes her. Even as Franklin apparently sympathizes with the
woman whom he victimizes ("Poor Margaret!"), he describes her as
having a "fiery disposition," "most devilish" traits (210), "devilish self-
incitements" (224), "the spirit of her fiery race" (213), and eyes that
appear as "two bright small orbs, fixed, and yet rolling in fire" as she

32. The transference of Margaret's anger from Franklin to Mrs. Conway reverses (or
at least distorts) what actually happened in plantation life when it was the mistress of the
plantation who blamed the slave woman instead of her husband for illicit sexual relations.
Catherine Clinton writes that "when [male] slaveowners sexually harassed or exploited
female slaves, mistresses sometimes directed their anger, not at their unfaithful husbands,
but toward the helpless slaves." See *The Plantation Mistress: Woman's World in the Old
South* (New York: Pantheon, 1982), 188.

33. Werner Sollors writes that suicide by the "tragic mulatto" is "the cultural given in
American settings; Quadroon and Octoroon lovers survive only if they remove themselves
to Europe with their white suitors or spouses." See "'Never Was Born,'" 300.

waits to enter the room of her victim (225). At no point does Franklin stop to recount what has happened to Margaret to incite this supposedly demonic disposition, or how he himself is implicated in her mad vengeance. In her murderous rage, Margaret becomes the object not of the readers' sympathy but of their fear. On a small scale she epitomizes the image of the revolting slave that captured the imagination and fed the anxiety of the South, especially in the years following Nat Turner's 1831 rebellion.

Whitman's characterization of Margaret may also have been influenced by an unusual and highly debated "finding" about blacks from the 1840 United States census that Southern congressmen used to promote the benefits of slavery. Released in 1841, just a year prior to publication of *Franklin Evans*, the census enumerated for the first time the number of mentally ill persons—or "insane and idiots," as they were then officially described—and contained the startling revelation that mental illness among free blacks was about eleven times higher than among slaves.[34] In the Southern states, the ratio of supposedly mentally ill blacks was one to every 1,558, but in the Northern states, it was one to every 144.5. The gross errors in defining and recording mental illness were revealed by Dr. Edward Jarvis, a physician and specialist in mental disorders and a founder of the American Statistical Association—but not until January 1844. For three years, then, these statistics were interpreted by slavery apologists as official evidence of the peculiar suitability of blacks for slavery and the dangerous consequences of emancipation. Seizing upon the census for political profit, Southern congressmen contrasted the happy, well-fed, and healthy moral condition of Southern slaves with the condition of free blacks of the North. The *Southern Literary Messenger* asked its readers: "Let us ... suppose a half of a million of free negroes suddenly turned loose in Virginia, whose propensity it is, constantly to grow more vicious in a state of freedom. ... Where should we find Penitentiaries for the thousands of felons? Where, lunatic asylums for the tens of thousands of maniacs? Would it be possible to live in a country where maniacs and felons met the traveller at every cross-road?"[35] Seen in this light, Whitman's tale of lunacy and vengeance even more so affirms the rhetoric of slavery. Margaret's suddenly violent and deranged condition following her emancipation (despite what brought it on) could be interpreted by Whitman's readers as

34. For a discussion of the 1840 census and the supposed level of mental illness among blacks, see Leon F. Litwack, *North of Slavery: The Negro in the Free States, 1790–1860* (Chicago: University of Chicago Press, 1961), 40–50.

35. "Reflections on the Census of 1840," *Southern Literary Messenger* 9 (1843): 342–47. Quoted in Litwack, *North of Slavery*, 42.

a typical example of the black person's propensity "to grow more vicious in a state of freedom."

Thus throughout the Creole episode Whitman has mimicked or transformed separate pro-slavery rhetorical and fictional conventions (the conversion experience, the plantation owner's fantasy, the "virgin/whore" paradigm, the violent, emotional, and "insane" black woman) and concurrently subverted separate conventions from reform literature (the tragic mulatto, miscegenation as a drunken mistake). The tragic denouement of Margaret's suicide takes this pattern one step further. As Anne Dalke points out, "Although Evans is the oblique cause of his wife's degradation, Margaret herself takes the final steps so common in temperance literature: those of unrestrained rage, murder, and suicide."[36] Thus, in this violent ending Whitman remarkably *combines* the formulae from temperance and abolitionist fiction to achieve a decidedly unreformed result. While in temperance fiction the behavior of the drunkard inevitably leads to his own suicide, here the function of suicide brought on by one's self-degradation is assumed by the "tragic mulatto" from abolitionist fiction. This extraordinary subversion of conventions is even more strange when one considers Whitman's intended audience. Reform-minded Northerners would be familiar with both temperance fiction and the tragic mulatto, but surprised—if not shocked—to recognize these conventions manipulated in a way which defends the institution of slavery. Margaret, not Franklin, bears the brunt of Whitman's moral condemnation, though intemperance perfunctorily serves as the cause of the whole, sordid affair:

> The true explanation of the mystery is, I think, to be found in my former, and present habits of drinking spiritous liquors. Those habits were of the most insidious, sly, and fatal detriment to me. They relaxed my energy of character, what little I had, and left me like a ship upon the ocean, without her mainmast. (*EPF*, 213)

In the end, Franklin quickly puts Margaret out of his mind, returns to New York, and, upon the inheritance of "a comfortable property" and with his friends' encouragement, successfully becomes abstinent.

One must be cautious about drawing broad conclusions from *Franklin Evans*, especially considering Whitman's immaturity as well as his seeming contempt for the project (as evidenced by his claim to have written it in three days while drinking port). The use of various popular literary conventions in *Franklin Evans* suggests at the very least that Whitman

36. Dalke, "'Whitman's Literary Intemperance,'" 18.

was grasping at what was available from contemporary discourses to fashion quickly a readable—and marketable—temperance novel. And in this he succeeded. For whatever reasons—the liveliness of the episodic story, the popularity of temperance fiction, the appeal of stereotypical characters and situations—*Franklin Evans* sold far more copies than any single printing of Whitman's poems. It is difficult to ascertain how much narrative control Whitman had over his material, and so it may be less accurate to speak of Whitman manipulating the conventions than of the conventions manipulating *him*. Yet, consciously or not, Whitman's adaptation of the conventions of pro-slavery plantation romances and subversion of those of abolitionist and temperance literature betray a sympathy for the arguments advanced by slave-owning Southerners and their literary apologists.

One should not altogether be surprised by the text's pro-slavery stance and formulaic approaches to race, however, especially considering the types of racial thinking within Whitman's political circles, his personal experience with blacks, and his history as a writer up until this time.[37] Although the Democratic response to slavery was by no means monolithic, most Jacksonian Democrats enthusiastically asserted white superiority and argued for black exclusion from political life. Sociologist Pierre van den Berghe has termed this ideology as "Herrenvolk democracy"— that is, the equal superiority of all who belong to the Herrenvolk (master race) over all who do not.[38] Thus, Jacksonian democratic ideology carried the rhetoric of popular democracy to an extreme "almost unparalleled in American political history," according to George Fredrickson, and at the same time condoned a form of "anti-Negro demagoguery that anticipated the Southern race baiters of a later era." This pattern was especially apparent in Whitman's home state of New York, where, Fredrickson says, "extreme disparagement of local blacks was often combined with fervent assertions of Jacksonian principle."[39] Even the most radical spokespersons for the common laborer, including those associated with Workingmen's movements, emphasized that democracy was for whites only.[40]

37. For a useful discussion of Whitman's early political influences, see Betsy Erkkila's *Whitman the Political Poet*, 1–24.

38. Pierre van den Berghe, *Race and Racism: A Comparative Perspective* (New York: Wiley, 1967), 18. Quoted in James M. McPherson, *Ordeal by Fire: The Civil War and Reconstruction* (New York: Alfred A. Knopf, 1982), 33. See also John Ashworth, *"Agrarians" and "Aristocrats": Party Political Ideology in the United States, 1837–1846* (Urbana: University of Illinois Press, 1986), 223.

39. Fredrickson, *The Black Image in the White Mind*, 90.

40. Despite the dominance of a Herrenvolk ideology within the Democratic party, Democrats expressed a variety of responses that ranged from pro-slavery apologetics to

The combination of Northern white egalitarianism and black proscription was more than rhetoric. In 1821 the suffrage of blacks in New York was constitutionally restricted to those who owned at least $250 of property. The measure was initiated by the state's Democrats and chiefly supported by voters who feared black economic competition and wanted to make the state unattractive to African American immigration.[41] Moreover, there is considerable evidence that during the rise of radical egalitarianism in New York in the 1830s Jacksonians used anti-black prejudice as a weapon against their Whig opponents. As John Ashworth has tersely put it: "The Democratic commitment to racism was almost as intense as the Democratic commitment to democracy."[42] Not only Democrats held such views. George Fredrickson asserts that after the 1830s "widespread, almost universal agreement" existed on the beliefs that blacks were intellectually and temperamentally inferior to whites and that full equality for blacks in the foreseeable future was virtually unthinkable.[43] In this context, Whitman's portrayal of Margaret in *Franklin Evans* is hardly surprising.

Whitman's own lack of actual experience with blacks surely contributed to his naive and stereotypical views. Whitman's contact with African Americans, like that of most white Northerners at the time, was extremely limited. Both sides of Whitman's family—the Whitmans and the Van Velsors—had been slave owners for more than a century.[44] Near the end of his life Whitman claimed that he could "almost remember" the slaves of his grandfather and great-grandfather in New York who owned "a number." In *November Boughs,* written in 1888, he recalled:

> The hard labor of the farm was mostly done by them, and on the floor of the big kitchen, toward sundown, would be squatting a

---

abolitionism. James Kirke Paulding, a New York writer and staunch Jacksonian, defended slavery on the basis of the "natural inequalities" of the races. (For a discussion of Paulding's views, see Lorman Ratner, *Powder Keg: Northern Opposition to the Antislavery Movement, 1831–1840* [New York, Basic Books, 1968], 59–64.) On the other hand, a number of Jacksonians took the abolitionist position that slavery was "evil." Fanny Wright, for example, who was occasionally heard by Whitman, lectured against slavery in the mid-1830s in New York City. The largest group of Democratic radicals, however, were, according to Bruce Laurie, "strangely silent on the question, neither openly taunting abolitionists nor resorting to the racist diatribes of Democratic politicians." See Laurie, *Artisans into Workers* (New York: Hill and Wang, 1989), 71.

41. See Foner, *Politics and Ideology,* 79.

42. John Ashworth, *"Agrarians" and "Aristocrats,"* 95. See also Lee Benson, *The Concept of Jacksonian Democracy* (Princeton: Princeton University Press, 1961), 319.

43. Fredrickson, *The Black Image in the White Mind,* 321.

44. See Kaplan, *Walt Whitman: A Life,* 131.

circle of twelve or fourteen "pickanninies," eating their supper
of pudding (Indian corn mush) and milk . . . I remember "Old
Mose," one of the liberated West Hills slaves, well. He was very
genial, correct, manly, and cute, and a great friend of mine in
childhood. (*CP,* 174)

Whitman's notebooks of the 1850s show that, in fact, the "memory"
of blacks eating their supper was a story told to his mother by his
Grandmother Whitman.[45] "Old Mose" may have been the black person
Whitman knew best in his life, at least until the Civil War when he met
with black soldiers during his hospital visits.

Whitman's boyhood home, Brooklyn, was a village where blacks com-
prised about ten percent of the population in the 1820s and 1830s and
were employed mostly as coachmen, gardeners, or cooks. Whites and
blacks led separate lives, and it is unlikely that Whitman had more than
a passing acquaintance with blacks. The school that young Whitman
attended was segregated by race, with whites in the basement and first
floor, and blacks on the second. Whitman's impression of African Americans also may have been affected by the large number who were unem-
ployed. Barred from many occupations, many blacks were forced to beg
or scrape for a living in the best way they knew how.[46]

Without any firsthand knowledge of blacks, then, Whitman constructed images and stories of them culled from popular literature, a
source he had turned to frequently in his early career as a writer. Up
until this time Whitman had consistently been a derivative writer. His
thoughts and ways of expression were largely imitations of what he had
read in the popular newspapers and magazines of the day. None of the
ten poems he had published from 1834 to 1840 or the twenty-two short
stories published before and shortly after *Franklin Evans,* from 1841 to
1848, "was in the least original" in the judgment of Gay Wilson Allen.
Whitman's early poetry and fiction, Allen writes, mimicked popular
magazine accounts of "virtue betrayed . . . romantic Indians, patriotic
love for old sights, relics, traditions, and sentimental folk tales."[47] His

45. Walt Whitman, *Notebooks and Unpublished Prose Manuscripts,* ed. Edward F.
Grier (New York: New York University Press, 1984), 1:12, 20. Subsequent references will
be cited in the text as *NUPM.*
46. For Whitman's early experiences with blacks, see Jerome Loving, *Walt Whitman's
Champion: William Douglas O'Connor* (College Station: Texas A & M University Press,
1978), 98ff., and Joseph Jay Rubin, *The Historic Whitman* (University Park: The Pennsylvania State University Press, 1973), 15–18.
47. Allen, *The Solitary Singer,* 66.

early poetry was conventional in subject matter as well as in meter and in rhyme (usually iambic tetrameter with a simple *abab* or *abcb* rhyme scheme). His central poetic theme—the melancholy fact of mortality and the contemplation of life after death—was borrowed from the eighteenth-century "graveyard" poets. Allen writes that "the mawkish sentiment was that of the poetry columns of the various weekly newspapers on which Whitman had worked; and the didacticism was labored."[48]

Whitman's early fiction, though generally considered more distinctive and successful than his early poems, was also largely imitative. No single model dominated the composition of his stories, but critics have detected in his fiction the influences of Poe, Hawthorne, Cooper, Scott, and lesser-known writers.[49] As Justin Kaplan notes, the themes and situations of these stories—harsh fathers (or father figures), adoring mothers, the contrast between the city and the innocent country—appear in the "conventional cheap fiction of Whitman's day, a lot of which is hardly more mawkish, melodramatic, and hackneyed than these stories."[50] In this context it is useful to remember that Whitman's first jobs in journalism were as a typesetter or "compositor," one who literally takes the letters and words of others and sets them down in print. His early poetry and fiction—indeed, much of his writing up until the 1855 *Leaves of Grass*—was more or less an extension of this process.

Whitman's early representation of blacks and slavery in *Franklin Evans*, therefore, is perhaps no more one-dimensional and stereotypical than his depiction of much of life in his fiction and poetry. Without belaboring the obvious, he was an immature writer. And yet the particular choices he makes in his first foray into writing about race suggest both a heightened awareness or interest in issues of race and a pro-

48. Ibid., 38. In "The Love That Is Hereafter," for example (published in the *Long Island Democrat,* May 19, 1840), the speaker laments his lonely, unloved life and hopes for affection from another person in the afterlife. The popularity of William Cullen Bryant's "Thanatopsis" in 1821 had made this kind of theme and tone popular. See also Rubin, *The Historic Whitman,* 47.

49. See Rubin, *The Historic Whitman,* 86, and Kaplan, *Whitman,* 116–17.

50. Justin Kaplan, "Nine Old Bones: *Walt Whitman's Blue Book,*" *The Atlantic Monthly* 221, no. 5 (1968), 62. Though Whitman would later claim a "serious wish . . . to have all those crude and boyish pieces dropp'd in oblivion" (*CP,* 927), at the time of their publication they met with a fair degree of success. Joseph Jay Rubin writes that in 1841 Whitman became the leading contributor of fiction to the *Democratic Review,* and by autumn of 1842, when he had placed at least ten tales in magazines, the stories were considered fairly popular and were extracted liberally. When a prospectus for a weekly *Tatler* was circulated, "the name Walter Whitman stood with Hawthorne and Bryant in the list of the ablest American authors promised to subscribers" (*The Historic Whitman,* 86).

slavery position whose themes and strategies were largely taken from Southern literature.

Franklin Evans locates young Walt Whitman as deeply embedded in popular conventions of writing and racial thinking. How Whitman would become an original writer, how he would develop the startling voice of the 1855 *Leaves of Grass*, has much to do with the liberation of his vision and writing about blacks and slavery. In the next four years (1842–46) Whitman worked for several New York–area newspapers but had little to say about blacks or slavery as compromise agreements between North and South were not contested. With American victory in the war with Mexico in 1846, however, questions about the extension of slavery into the new territories once again thrust the issue onto the nation's center stage. Whitman's passionate involvement in these questions began in response to heated debates in Congress that would not be resolved until 1850, and then only tentatively.

2

THE FAILURE
OF BORROWED RHETORIC

The years 1846–50 mark a pivotal passage in the nation's fateful course toward civil war. Beginning with the Wilmot Proviso in 1846 and ending with the 1850 Compromise, these four years witnessed the first serious rupture in North-South relations as members of Congress engaged in rancorous, even violent, debate over the future of slavery in new territories gained from American victory in the war with Mexico. Regional divisions intensified and the general tone of public discourse changed from amicable, if guarded, respect to outright hostility between North and South. For the first time the nation's political divisions were drawn along sectional rather than party lines. One major party, the Whigs, would soon die and another be born as the nascent "Free Soil" movement captured the aspirations—or fed the fears—of many Northerners. By 1850 North and South reached an uneasy truce with a compromise bill that made concessions to each side but satisfied neither.

These same years mark a pivotal turning point in the development of Walt Whitman as a poet. Throughout this time Whitman actively participated in the public debate over slavery through his editorials in New York–area newspapers and his political activism on behalf of the Free Soil cause. Like his earlier temperance tract *Franklin Evans,* Whitman's slavery editorials reveal a writer who is deeply imbedded in the rhetoric of his age, one whose compositions are largely a matter of recomposition, a piecing together of the arguments of others, rather than anything striking or original. In response to the controversy over the extension of slavery into new territories, Whitman's position on slavery shifts from the pro-slavery apologetics of *Franklin Evans* toward a Free Soil position based on his concern for the opportunities of white laborers, but not on any sympathy for the plight of slaves. Yet whereas the conventionally racist rhetoric of *Franklin Evans* seemed to "work"—if only to sell books—the very failure of Whitman's conventional Free Soil rhetoric to affect change so frustrates Whitman that he is compelled by late 1847 in a new direction as a thinker and writer. At the same time, however, political defeats to the Free Soil cause only strengthen Whitman's resolve. He continues to argue vehemently against the extension of slavery until Northern acceptance of the 1850 Compromise leads him toward a retreat from public writing and a reconsideration of his vocation.

This chapter traces Whitman's writings in response to the slavery debates of 1846 and 1847 in various political forums—Congress, the Democratic party at national and state levels, and the New York state legislature, among others—and sets the context for understanding the beginning of his evolution toward becoming the poet of *Leaves of Grass*. Whereas the first chapter located Whitman's early position as a racial thinker by an analysis of his first extant "racial text," the following chapters will trace the historical development of Whitman's racial thinking in the context of the slavery debates of the late 1840s and early 1850s. It is only with close attention to detail, and in subtle ways, that we begin to see the direct relationship between the development of Whitman's racial thinking and his emergence as a poet.

The year 1846 is a key turning point in the life of Whitman and of the United States. In late February of that year, Whitman, who continued to work as a journalist in the New York City area following the publication of *Franklin Evans,* accepted the editorship of the Brooklyn *Eagle,* the official Democratic newspaper of Kings County and, according to Ezra Greenspan, "one of the party's most important organs in the region."[1] The two years of Whitman's editorship at the *Eagle* coincided with a dynamic and tumultuous period both locally and nationally. On the local scene, Whitman reported on Brooklyn's churches, schools, shops, streets, and cultural events. Nationally, he responded to such issues as territorial expansion, the Mexican War, sectionalism, free trade,

1. Ezra Greenspan, *Walt Whitman and the American Reader* (Cambridge: Cambridge University Press, 1990), 54.

states' rights, worker discontent, and especially the extension of slavery as these issues increasingly threatened to dissolve the Union.[2] Already like the poet of the 1855 *Leaves of Grass,* Whitman had democratic designs on his readers: he sought not merely to inform or entertain, but to educate his readers on all matters so that they might become self-sufficient, democratic citizens of the national polis. In one of his earliest editorials, Whitman describes his hope of establishing a close "communion" with his readers:

> We really feel a desire to talk on many subjects, to *all* the people of Brooklyn; and it *ain't* their ninepences we want so much either. There is a curious kind of sympathy (haven't you ever thought of it before?) that arises in the mind of a newspaper conductor with the public he serves. He gets to *love* them. Daily communion creates a sort of brotherhood and sisterhood between the two parties . . . And we want as many readers of the Brooklyn *Eagle*— even unto half of Long Island—as possible, that we may increase the number of such friends. For are not those who daily listen to us, friends?[3]

The issue over which Whitman would make his most fervent appeals to his "friends"—though he did not yet know it—would be the argument over the extension of slavery into new territories. Just two months after Whitman assumed the editorship, a young congressional representative from Pennsylvania sponsored an amendment that would change forever the way the nation discussed and "resolved" the issue of slavery. In August 1846 the controversy came to a head with the introduction of what came to be known as the Wilmot Proviso. When President Polk asked Congress for an appropriation of two million dollars for territory that might be acquired from Mexico after the war, Representative David Wilmot of Pennsylvania introduced an amendment stating that "as an express and fundamental condition to the acquisition of any territory from the Republic of Mexico . . . neither slavery nor involuntary servitude shall ever exist in any part of said territory."[4]

2. For Whitman's concerns and topics as editor of the *Eagle,* see Erkkila, *Whitman the Political Poet,* 25–26.

3. Walt Whitman, "Ourselves and the *Eagle*," Brooklyn *Eagle,* 1 June 1846; *The Uncollected Poetry and Prose of Walt Whitman,* ed. Emory Holloway, 2 vols. (Garden City, N.J.: Doubleday, Page & Company, 1921), 1:115. Subsequent references will be cited in the text as *UPP.*

4. *Congressional Globe,* 29th Cong., 1st sess., 1217. Subsequent references will be cited in the text as *CG.*

That the Wilmot Proviso quickly divided Congress along sectional rather than party lines was an ominous sign for the nation's future. The Constitutional compromises and the Missouri Compromise of 1820 had supposedly settled territorial disputes about slavery, and abolitionism had not proved effective in moving Congress toward a reconsideration of the issue. But with a vast new territory opened up by the results of the Mexican War, the debate over slavery exploded into a controversy over sectional power. Northern Democrats, angered about their loss of power to Southern Democrats in the previous two years over such issues as tariff duties and the Oregon boundary, joined Northern Whigs who had consistently opposed slavery. The House passed the Wilmot Proviso along sectional lines in both 1846 and 1847, but the Senate, in which the South had greater power, blocked the proviso in March of 1847 and Polk's appropriations bill was eventually passed by both houses without it.[5]

Despite the proviso's defeat, debate over the bill gave rise to the "free soil" sentiment that would profoundly affect the nation's future, finding institutional form in the Free Soil party in 1848 and later in the Republican party. Following the proviso's introduction, Whitman wrote about a dozen editorials in support of it from December 1846 until his departure from the *Eagle* in January 1848. Whitman's arguments eventually echo the Free Soilers' position that the introduction of slavery into new territories would discourage, if not prohibit, white laborers from migrating to those areas because white labor, in competition with slave labor, would be "degraded." "The voice of the North proclaims that *labor must not be degraded,*" Whitman writes in April 1847. "The young men of the free States must not be shut out from the new domain (where slavery does not exist now) by the *introduction* of an institution which will render their honorable industry no longer respectable."[6] In contrast to abolitionists who opposed slavery on moral and humanitarian grounds, Free Soilers cared more about the rights of whites than about the rights of blacks.[7] Wilmot himself said that the purpose of the proviso was to defend the rights and opportunities of white laborers: "I would preserve for free white labor a fair country, a rich inheritance,

5. For an excellent discussion of the debate over the Wilmot Proviso, see James M. McPherson, *Battle Cry of Freedom: The Civil War* (New York: Oxford University Press, 1988), 47–76.

6. Walt Whitman, *The Gathering of the Forces*, ed. Cleveland Rodgers and John Black, 2 vols. (New York: G. P. Putnam's Sons, 1920), 1:205–6. Subsequent references will be cited in the text as *GF*.

7. See Foner, *Politics and Ideology*, 82, and McPherson, *Ordeal*, 42.

where the sons of toil, of my own race and color, can live without the disgrace which association with negro slavery brings upon free labor."[8]

Free Soilism became popular among a segment of the Northern population in part because of what George Fredrickson calls its "overtly Negrophobic or exclusionist" element. Those Free Soilers who opposed not only slavery but also "the presence of Negroes on any basis whatsoever" gave expression, Fredrickson says, to a "deep-seated and long-existing desire on the part of many white Americans for a racially homogeneous society."[9] Whitman's writings in the late 1840s do not exhibit such exclusionist sentiments, yet the leading organizers of the Free Soil movement came from Whitman's own New York state Democratic party, a party whose position on slavery, as we saw earlier, was strongly rooted in an anti-black ideology. When at the 1846 New York Democratic convention the issue of black suffrage was again raised, the Democratic press staunchly opposed reduction of the $250 property requirement for blacks. One paper asserted that blacks were inferior to whites and insisted that blacks be given no political rights at all. William Cullen Bryant's Evening Post, soon to become the state's chief Free Soil newspaper, worried that black suffrage would dramatically increase Whig power in the state. Bryant advocated the right of white citizens to place limits on black citizenship. During the election of convention delegates, Democrats blatantly appealed to racial prejudice. Although the New York Democratic party had been split throughout the 1840s into two factions—the conservative Hunkers and the radical Barnburners—both stood together at the 1846 convention to block any extension of black suffrage.[10]

The Free Soil movement's "practical" response to slavery thus attracted more Northerners than did the appeals of abolitionists. According to Eric Foner, when the Free Soil party formed in 1848, it was broad enough to include "the most vulgar racists and the most determined supporters of Negro rights, as well as all shades of opinion between these extremes."[11] Free Soilism, Foner says, marked a "vital turning point" in the anti-slavery crusade: in representing anti-slavery

8. CG, 29th Cong., 2d sess., appendix, 314–17.

9. Fredrickson, The Black Image in the White Mind, 130–31, 140.

10. See Foner, Politics and Ideology, 79–80. "Barnburners" were named by their intra-party rivals after the Dutch farmer who burned down his barn to rid it of a few rats. Barnburners were supposedly doing the same thing to the Democratic party. In turn Barn-burners called their antagonists "Hunkers" because they kept to their homes or "hunks" and were said by their rivals to rarely know what was going on in the world. See Rubin, The Historic Whitman, 140.

11. Foner, Politics and Ideology, 92.

in its "least radical form," it provided a vehicle by which anti-slavery became, for the first time, "a truly mass movement in the North."[12]

Free Soilism marked a "vital turning point" in the career of Walt Whitman as well. Whitman's editorials on the Wilmot Proviso are much more telling than his critics and biographers generally recognize—not only for the position he espouses but also for the way in which the conventionalism of his views, coupled with a series of political and personal losses relating to the Wilmot Proviso, seem to have pushed him toward experimentation with the kind of free-verse poetry that would emerge eight years later in *Leaves of Grass*. Far from being either radical or original as some critics suggest, Whitman in his anti-slavery editorials essentially parrots the various arguments of Northern congressmen during the debates over the proviso in February and March of 1847, just as he parroted the fictional strategies of plantation romances a few years earlier.[13] Like Free Soil Northerners in Congress, Whitman bases his argument on the economic opportunities of white labor, and nowhere does he mention concern for the slave. And like his political counterparts, Whitman invokes the memory of Thomas Jefferson as the prototypical Free Soiler, characterizes the debate as an issue not of race but of class between the "grand body of white workingmen" and the "aristocratic owners of slaves," and sharply distinguishes between abolitionist "interference" with slavery in the South and the question of the extension of slavery into the West. Whitman closely followed the heated debates between John Calhoun and the South on one side and a host of Northerners, including David Wilmot and Whitman's own Free Soil Senator, John Dix, on the other. In reading Whitman's editorials in light of arguments by Northern congressmen, one senses from their close similarity not only a duplication bordering on plagiarism, but a yearning on the young editor's part to participate in this urgent national discourse.

Whitman's position on the Wilmot Proviso did not emerge full-blown, however. It gradually evolved over the course of little more than a year, from December 1846 to January 1848, as the proviso was debated at the national and state levels. In the early stages Whitman exudes a confidence that the Wilmot Proviso can be negotiated by North and South in a spirit of openness, moderation, and respect for Constitutional remedies. Whitman had demonstrated this confidence even before the

12. Ibid., 72, 93.
13. For the view that Whitman's editorials were revolutionary in their thrust, see Erkkila, *Whitman the Political Poet*, 44–51. Erkkila argues that Whitman's political journalism spoke "the egalitarian and millennial language of the revolutionary enlightenment" (48), though she does qualify that judgment by saying these editorials "swung between the antislavery rhetoric of the American Revolution and the anti-Negro phobia of his age" (47).

proviso was introduced. On August 7, just hours before Wilmot proposed his amendment, Whitman sided with legislators in the House who had opposed the extension of slavery into Oregon, feeling that "the slow but sure and steady spread of political and moral truth [would] do its work among the people, [and] all that ought to be done in reference to slavery, would be done."[14]

In his first editorial written after the introduction of the Wilmot Proviso (hereafter "Wilmot"), dated December 5, 1846, Whitman confidently urges the full participation of all sides. Though he condemns the "mad fanaticism" of the "ultra Abolitionists," he yet calls slavery an "evil" and celebrates the free expression of all sides in the debate as a "holy right," the very foundation of democracy without which "we might *all* become a nation of slaves":

> It is to the discoveries and suggestions of free thought, of "public opinion," of liberal sentiments, that we must at this age of the world look for quite all desirable reforms, in government and any thing else. (GF 1:193)

Two weeks later Whitman urges the Democratic members of Congress to "plant themselves quietly, without bluster, but fixedly and without compromise, on the requirement that *Slavery be prohibited in them* [the new territories] forever" (GF 1:194).

The following month Whitman embraces the principles behind the "State Address" of the Democratic party of Massachusetts, which regards slavery as "'a great evil, a direct, practical denial of the essential truths of Democracy,'" but recognizes the right of slavery to exist in the South (GF 1:195). The "Address" denounces the "cowardice" of "dough faces"—those Northern congressmen who dare not oppose the extension of slavery "'lest the slave-holding States take offense.'" And it urges that a middle path might be found between abolitionists and "dough faces" through the "bold and honest" expression of opinion, adherence to constitutional rights and remedies, and a "constant regard for each and all of the great doctrines of Republicanism" (GF 1:196). That virtually all of Whitman's editorial consists of quotations from the Massachusetts address suggests how little he had to say on the subject that was original.

Whitman's faith in the democratic process was soon tested when in

14. Quoted in Rubin, *The Historic Whitman*, 147. Rubin's valuable and detailed reading of Whitman's life within the context of his age unfortunately suffers from a lack of citations to quotations and other historical material. In such places I cite Rubin directly, as above.

early February 1847 congressional debates exploded into vitriolic exchanges and threats by the South of disunion. By February 10 one member of Congress was already recalling "a memorable occasion, a few weeks since, when all was calm and quiet; when no cloud of domestic discord obscured the horizon; when no man dreamed of the renewal of these hostilities."[15] Senator John C. Calhoun of South Carolina led the Southern charge, claiming that if slavery were prohibited from new territories and the balance between the two sections of the country were destroyed, "a day . . . will not be far removed from political revolution, anarchy, civil war, and widespread disaster."[16] Northerners countered that there was no danger of disunion, but if the South threatened disunion, then "we will not consent that the power, the patronage, the arms, and the blood of the nation shall be used to propagate slavery over a free soil— . . . let dissolution come."[17]

Clearly concerned about the repercussions of such exchanges, Whitman in his pro-Wilmot editorials takes on a new, more urgent tone marked by a sort of desperate hopefulness. In a February 3 piece entitled "The Most Emphatic Expression of Opinion on an Important Subject Ever Given By The Empire State!" Whitman celebrates the passage of anti-slavery resolutions by a wide majority in both New York state houses, and he concludes—wrongly, it will turn out—that as to the slavery issue "the Northern Democracy show *one solid unbroken phalanx*" (GF 1:197–98). Whitman also reminds his readers that the *Eagle* was the first Democratic paper "to take an unalterable stand against the allowance of slavery in any new territory, under any circumstances, or in any way" (GF 1:197).

Three days later Whitman writes what is surely one of his most passionate journalistic tributes to the American republic: "The Next Blessing to God's Blessing—Shall It Be Jeopardized?" Suggesting the transcendent importance of the slavery issue by employing religious imagery and language, Whitman claims the Union is a "political blessing" that deserves to stand "in the near neighborhood of the great common blessings vouchsafed us by God—life, light, [and] freedom"—and that not only the "happiness" of the nation's citizens but also "the perpetuity of the sacred fire of freedom" anxiously await the Union's fate. Hearing with "alarm" the "angry recriminations and threats" in Congress and denouncing those who "flippantly" speak of disunion, Whitman clings to the hope that the slavery issue might be peaceably resolved. He sug-

15. James C. Dobbin, a Democratic representative from North Carolina, in CG, 29th Cong., 2d sess., 383.
16. CG, 29th Cong., 2d sess., 454.
17. Jacob Brinkerhoff, a Democratic representative from Ohio, in ibid., 380.

gests that there is no need to discuss Wilmot *"with any more angry tone, with any more retorts, or any more harsh allusions, than two men might use in discussing a point of mathematics"* (GF 1:229–32). At this point, then, slavery is for Whitman an abstract political question that threatens to overtake the greater national interest—preservation of the Union. Whitman concludes the editorial with a harsh, apocalyptic judgment: never in history would an act "damn its author to the hatred of his race" as would "the deed of him who should provoke . . . the dissolution of the American Union. . . . Well might after ages invent new epithets of ignominy and hatred for him and his most wicked conduct" (233–34).

Contrary to Whitman's appeals, both houses of Congress continued the fractious debates that further drove a wedge between North and South. Calhoun claimed, for example, that the effect of Wilmot "would be to give to the non-slaveholding states monopoly of the public domain, to the entire *exclusion* of the Slaveholding states" (my emphasis).[18] Northerners countered this "exclusionist" argument by asserting that the proviso excluded from the disputed territory neither the Southern free laborer nor the slaveholder who chose to employ free labor. The only exclusion, said New York Senator John Dix, existed in "slave territory" where the free laborer of the North would not go "where he is compelled to toil side by side with the slave."[19]

With this further exacerbation of differences, Whitman appears to give up hope of a peaceful resolution. He eschews his conciliatory rhetoric, advocating instead the Free Soil position which he will zealously adhere to throughout the 1840s and into the 1850s. He stakes out his position by repeating, almost verbatim at times, the various arguments and rhetorical strategies with which pro-Wilmot Northern congressmen countered the South. In a March 11 editorial, for example, he writes "The Opinions of Washington and Jefferson on an Important Point." In it he asserts that these founding fathers "looked with anxious solicitude to the period when even the soil of the slave States should become free, as has actually occurred in New York." Directly rebutting Calhoun's claim of constitutional right to "engraft slavery" on the new territories, Whitman states that Jefferson, the "great apostle of liberty," looked with hope to the time when the "words which he put forth in the Declaration of Independence, 'that all men are born free and equal,' should be as true in fact as self-evident in theory" (GF 1:199–200).[20] Despite his

18. Ibid., 453.
19. Ibid., 543.
20. Referring to Jefferson as "the [great] apostle of liberty" was apparently common among Free Soilers. In a speech before the House on February 9, Representative Brinkerhoff of Ohio referred to Jefferson as "the Apostle of American democracy" (CG, 29th

stronger moral tone, Whitman's arguments have nothing to do with the condition of slaves.

Whitman's rhetorical strategy directly mimics that of the pro-Wilmot forces in Congress, who were especially adamant to establish that the South's native son, Thomas Jefferson, opposed the extension of slavery and looked for its ultimate abolition. When one Virginia congressman objected, several Northerners quoted at length from Jefferson's *Notes on the State of Virginia* and private letters and stressed his authorship of the provision in the 1787 Northwest Ordinance banning slavery from the northwest territories.[21] The Wilmot group was also eager to include the anti-slavery thoughts of Washington and Madison in an attempt to settle the question of the framers' intent.

One month later, after a string of stunning American victories in Mexico intensified the Wilmot debates, Whitman continues to echo congressional speeches in editorials dated April 22 and April 27. His writings seek to preserve the compact of the Union while making clear his adamant opposition to the extension of slavery. He sharply distinguishes between interference with the status quo of slavery in the South—the "unquestionable folly" of abolitionists with which "we have nothing to do"—and the establishment of slavery in "fresh land," an issue that is among "our highest duties as Christians, as men, and as Democrats" to discuss. He again appeals to the memory of "Washington, Jefferson, Madison, and all the old fathers of our freedom" who "sought the extinction of" slavery. And again implying the almost religious significance of the slavery debate, Whitman asserts that the North has been and will continue to be "faithful" to the Constitutional compromise. Whitman also rebuts Calhoun's "exclusion" argument by reversing the rhetoric and asserting that the only ones excluded if the slave interest had its way would be free men in new slave land (*GF* 1:200–208).

Most important, however, Whitman's editorials make increasingly clear that his chief interest is in advocating the rights of white laborers in conflict with the privileged slaveholding class of the South. In refuting a recent speech by Calhoun, Whitman distinguishes "white freemen" from the "*aristocracy* of the South—the men who work only with other men's hands" (*GF* 1:203–4). He exalts the "brave, industrious and energetic freemen" of the "East, North *and* South" who will flow into the new territory "if they can go and not find themselves the equals only of negro slaves." Whitman says simply: "Where the land is cultivated by

---

Cong., 2d sess., 378). The term appears in quotation marks, suggesting its common and borrowed usage.

21. See, for example, the speech of Senator William Upham, a Vermont Whig, on March 1, 1847 (*CG*, 29th Cong., 2d sess., 546–51).

slaves it is *not* also cultivated by freemen," adding that in the slave states it is not "respectable" for white men to labor on the land (204).

Whitman's ideas could have been lifted from the texts of any number of Northern congressmen, and in fact they copy many of the arguments made by his own Senator John Dix six weeks earlier on the floor of the Senate. Whitman may have been familiar with Dix's speech, or Dix himself may have simply been articulating the common themes of Free Soilers that ran throughout their speeches and editorials. Dix begins by distinguishing between, on the one hand, Southern states where slavery will remain "unmolested," and, on the other, the "consideration of admitting new States into the Union with slavery."[22] He repeatedly invokes Jefferson, comparing the Wilmot Proviso to Jefferson's 1787 provision and claiming for Free Soilers "the ground taken by Jefferson more than sixty years ago."[23] And, like Whitman, he passionately champions as the *sine qua non* of America's glorious future the opportunity of the free white laborer—"in the South as well as the North"—to go into new territory unhindered by black competition:

> Wherever free labor has gone forth on this continent, the forest has bowed before it; towns and villages have sprung up like magic in its track; canals, railroads, and busy industry, in all its imaginable forms, have marked its progress; civilization, in its highest attributes, follows it; knowledge and religion go with it hand in hand.[24]

By September 1847, just prior to an important state Democratic convention that would attempt to resolve the slavery issue, Whitman's position has found its focus. He eschews some of his earlier arguments and gets right to the point: slavery is "destructive to the dignity and independence of all who work, and to labor itself" (*GF* 1:208–9). His opening comments in a September 1, 1847, editorial make clear that the issue of slavery is one of class, not race.

> The question whether or no there shall be slavery in the new territories which it seems conceded on all hands we are largely to get through this Mexican War, is a question between *the grand body of white workingmen, the millions of mechanics, farmers, and operatives of our country,* with their interests on the one

22. *CG*, 29th Cong., 2d sess., 541.
23. Ibid., 542.
24. Ibid.

side—and the interests of the few thousand rich, 'polished,' and aristocratic owners of slaves at the South, on the other side. (*GF* 1:208)

"Respectable workingmen," Whitman adds, "cannot exist, much less flourish, in a thorough slave State." He repeatedly warns that white laborers might be "put down to an equality with slaves," degraded to the "miserable level of what is little above brutishness—sunk to be like owned goods, and driven cattle!" And he exhorts *the workingmen of the North, East, and West, to come up, to a man, in defence of their rights, their honor, and that heritage of getting bread by the sweat of the brow, which we must leave to our children"* (*GF* 1:210–11). As Wynn Thomas notes, Whitman's focus here on labor as the key to his stance on slavery articulates the essential position he will hold "through all the turbulence of the succeeding years" up until the Civil War.[25]

This focus on the rights of whites and seeming indifference to the plight of blacks reflects a fairly standard attitude of many white Northerners, including the Barnburner faction of the New York Democratic party, of which Whitman was a member. The Barnburners made it clear that their support of Wilmot was based on concern for the free white laborer of the North and opposition to the prospect of blacks—slaves *or* free—in the new territories. As Representative George Rathpun put it:

> I speak not of the condition of the slave. I do not pretend to know, nor is it necessary that I should express an opinion in this place, whether the effect of slavery is beneficial or injurious to him. I am looking to its effect upon the white man, the free white man of this territory.[26]

Moreover, among the degrading effects of slavery, the Barnburners generally felt association of the white laborer with the black slave to be most important. They tended not to distinguish between the free black and the slave, seeing the competition and "degradation" resulting from any form of black labor as anathema to their cause.[27] While Whitman emphasizes that "the influence of the slavery institution is to bring the dignity of labor down to the level of slavery" (*GF* 1:209), he does not, like his Barnburner colleagues, invoke white anxiety about associating with blacks. Neither, however, does he mention concern for the slave.

25. Thomas, *The Lunar Light*, 180.
26. George Rathpun, at Utica Convention, *Proceedings of the Utica Convention* (Albany, 1848), 25. Quoted in Foner, *Politics and Ideology*, 82.
27. Foner, *Politics and Ideology*, 81–82.

Whitman's lack of sympathy for slaves in his Wilmot editorials is not surprising, given his other editorials on blacks and slavery. Thomas Brasher points out that generally "Whitman had little to say in the *Eagle* about slavery" and that he "temperately avoided drawing a moral from news stories of incidents involving slaves." On April 8, 1846, when the *Eagle* described the execution in New Orleans of a female slave for "cruelty to her mistress," Whitman's focus, according to Brasher, was on the "barbarity of public hangings, not the evils of slavery." On July 11, when the *Eagle* reported what seemed like cruel punishments for blacks involved in the supposed poisoning of an overseer—one was to be hanged and another to wear a five-pound collar on his neck for a year and be whipped every month—Whitman again had nothing to say.[28]

Only regarding the horror of the "middle passage" on the slave ships from Africa does Whitman sympathize with the slave. In one of his earliest *Eagle* editorials in March 1846, Whitman scathingly attacks the slave trade, still legal in Brazil and practiced illegally in the United States and Europe, as "that most abominable of all men's schemes for making money" (*GF* 1:187). Whitman voices a righteous anger at "the crowding of a mass of compact human flesh into little more than its equal of space" on slave ships, carefully detailing the wretched conditions aboard the ship and repeatedly asking his readers to "imagine" the suffering of *"three hundred and thirty-six men and women"* in a space forty by twenty-one feet with a three-foot ceiling (*GF* 1:187–88).[29] He laments how "the negro is torn from his simple hut—from his children, his brethren, his parents, and friends—to be carried far away and made the bondman of a stranger" and how the "negro mother's heart" is filled with anguish over "this wicked business!" (189).

Despite Whitman's abhorrence, however, his attitude toward slavery is curiously ambiguous:

> It is not ours to find an excuse for slaving, in the benighted condition of the African. Has not God seen fit to make him, and leave him so? Nor is it our fault because the chiefs of that barbarous land fight with each other, and take slave prisoners. The whites encourage them, and afford them a market. Were that market destroyed, there would soon be no supply. (*GF* 1:189–90)

28. Thomas L. Brasher, *Whitman as Editor of the Brooklyn Daily Eagle* (Detroit: Wayne State University Press, 1970), 163.

29. Whitman's invitations to his readers to imaginatively enter the slave's experience anticipate a similar rhetorical strategy in "Song of Myself." See Chapter 6.

He seems here to endorse the popular notion that Africans were naturally "benighted," but to reject that idea as a justification for slavery as he indicts both African chieftains and white slave owners. He concludes the editorial by calling for more stringent enforcement of the slave-trade laws, which should "pry out every man who helps the slave-trade—not merely the sailor on the sea, but *the cowardly rich villain, the speculator on the land*—and punish *him*" (GF 1:190).

This editorial suggests that Whitman sharply distinguished between the conditions of slaves in ships and those working on Southern plantations. As we saw in *Franklin Evans,* he may not have taken seriously the abolitionist accounts of slavery. His repugnance at the slave trade may also be mixed up with a desire not to have blacks in America at all, given what we know of his zeal for white labor. Most likely, Whitman's opposition to the slave *trade* had the double rhetorical appeal of joining abolitionists' moral opposition to slavery at its roots with a reluctance to alienate the South by challenging slavery's status quo.

Whitman's editorials, taken as a whole, suggest some movement from his seemingly pro-slavery stance in *Franklin Evans* toward a central concern for the freedom and "dignity" of white labor, though, as noted, his labor orientation to the slavery issue is already evident in the "wage slavery" argument of the earlier text. Moreover, like *Franklin Evans,* much of his newspaper writing on slavery was derivative, constructed by ideas wholly unoriginal to him, though composed (or recomposed) in ways he hoped would be effective.[30] The close similarity between Whitman's arguments and those of the Wilmot contingent in Congress do not necessarily diminish Whitman's opinions and writing: the nature of political debate is that members of one position repeat and reformulate arguments they think most effective. Rather, the similarities show that Whitman was deeply immersed in the rhetoric of his age, so much so that it is sometimes difficult to distinguish his voice from that of others.

And yet, despite the conventionalism of his anti-slavery prose, at least one passage suggests that Whitman's writing about slavery moves him—consciously or not—toward a new form of writing. One of the few

---

30. At one point it appears that Whitman was even copying a ten-year-old editorial by William Leggett, almost word for word. Whitman occasionally reread Leggett's editorials and appears to have gathered from them some of his material on slavery. On July 29, 1837, Leggett wrote: "Every American who, in any way, authorizes or countenances slavery, is derelict to his duty as a Christian, a patriot, and a man." (See William Leggett, *Democratick Editorials: Essays in Jacksonian Political Economy,* ed. Lawrence H. White [Indianapolis: Liberty Press, 1984], 229.) Writing ten years later, Whitman said that "we should all be derelict to our highest duties as Christians, as men, and as Democrats" (GF 1:202).

truly original notes to Whitman's slavery writings is a catalogue in his
September 1, 1847, editorial that appears to anticipate the catalogues
of his 1855 poetry. When Whitman exhorts "every mechanic" to assert
that they "are not willing to be put on the level of negro slaves," he
breaks into a catalogue of artisan trades. Refiguring the catalogue as
poetry shows more clearly this nascent form:

> . . . The carpenter, in his rolled up sleeves,
> the mason with his trowel,
> the stonecutter with his brawny chest,
> the blacksmith with his sooty face,
> the brown fisted shipbuilder, whose strokes
>   rattle so merrily in our dock yards—
> . . . shoemakers, and cartmen, and drivers,
> and paviers, and porters, and millwrights,
> and furriers, and ropemakers, and butchers,
> and machinists, and tinmen, and tailors,
> and hatters, and coach and cabinet makers—
> upon the honest sawyer and mortar-mixer,
>   too, whose sinews are their own—
> and every hard-working man . . .
>
> (*GF* 1:210)

The catalogue quality of this sentence must be noted with caution.
Elsewhere in his journalism Whitman writes long, cumulative sentences;
and here, the long line that is characteristic of his mature poetry is
absent. But the focus on artisans and workers, the use of the definite
article to create representative figures, and the repeated use of "And" to
connect different occupations all remind one of later Whitman catalogues. The emergence of this catalogue may be telling, for, as we shall
see, it appears just prior to the time Whitman began poetic experiments
in his notebooks, and it suggests, perhaps, that in both journalism and
poetry Whitman's struggle to articulate his slavery views produces new
forms of expression. Yet whereas in *Leaves of Grass* catalogues will
include portraits of slaves as part of his all-encompassing experience,
here the vision is not inclusive, but exclusive: Whitman celebrates the
white freemen in hopes that they will speak with one voice *against* being
put "on the level of negro slaves."

Despite Whitman's various rhetorical strategies to make Free Soil
popular among the mass of voters, the last months of 1847 brought
repeated political losses that eventually drove Whitman out of his job.
In September, Whitman's hopes for a peaceful resolution to the slavery

debate within the state Democratic party were dashed when the Hunker-controlled State Democratic Convention meeting at Syracuse tabled a resolution demanding that slavery be excluded from new territories. In response to that action, the Barnburners walked out. Meeting on their own at Herkimer in October, the Barnburners endorsed the Wilmot Proviso—some calling it the "White Man's Proviso"—and picked their own slate of candidates.[31] By November, with the New York Democratic party badly split, Whitman turned conciliatory and pragmatic, urging his readers just before the state election to put aside differences over the Wilmot Proviso and vote a straight party ticket. "What have the officers to be chosen next week—the lieutenant governor, the comptroller, the State treasurer, &c.,—what have they, in their official capacity, to do with the bearings of that proviso?" he asks (*GF* 1:215). Concerned about the party's future, he suppresses his more radical sentiments, simply hoping for a Democratic victory. All issues, he says, "subside" before the central one: "*Shall the Democratic ticket succeed, or shall the Whig ticket succeed?*" (214–15).

The results could not have been more devastating as the Democratic party lost overwhelmingly. In an editorial several days after the election, an embittered Whitman sounds almost militant, charging (somewhat hypocritically, it seems) that the Democratic party deserved to lose because it had failed to endorse the Wilmot Proviso at Syracuse and had not been, of late, "sufficiently bold, open and radical":

> *We must plant ourselves firmly on the side of freedom, and openly espouse it.* The late election is a terrific warning of the folly of all half-way policy in such matters—of all compromises that neither receive or reject a great idea to which the people are once fully awakened. (*GF* 1:222)

Rather than defeat him, then, the losses seem to have fortified Whitman's resolve in fighting for Free Soil. His claim that "the people are now fully awakened to this matter of enacting slavery into new and free ground" suggests his *own* awakening and radicalization on what he now called "*the* topic" (*GF* 1:222). He concludes by exhorting his party to be "true"—"true to itself, and to its great duties—true to the memory of the Revolutionary Fathers who fought for freedom, and not for slavery," and true especially to Thomas Jefferson, who, in the Declaration of Independence, charged King George III and the British parliament

31. For the Barnburner-Hunker conflict in New York State, see Foner, *Politics and Ideology*, 84, and Rubin, *The Historic Whitman*, 176.

with not taking "measures to prevent the extension of slavery in the Colonies."

Whitman's new and more radical posture proved costly. In January 1848, he was fired for an editorial he wrote in opposition to the "popular sovereignty" idea promulgated by Michigan Senator Lewis Cass. Cass's notion that settlers in the territories be allowed to decide for themselves whether to have slavery gained popularity in late 1847 and replaced the Wilmot Proviso in the eyes of Northern Democrats as a solution to the slavery problem. With the support of many Southern Democrats, the idea propelled Cass to the 1848 Presidential nomination. As simple and fair as Cass's idea sounded, it of course opened the possibility of slave owners (and potential slave owners) flooding a territory, commandeering its political system, and creating a slave-owning state.

The brief editorial for which Whitman was fired merely states Cass's position, as revealed in a recent letter made public, then asserts that the idea "might come with a better show of sense" if Cass understood an essential fact about territorial sovereignty, namely, that Congress is the local government for territories, and that introducing slavery as a matter of "profit and loss" would not be "profitable" (GF 1:227–28). Throughout the Wilmot debates of 1847, Whitman's employer, Isaac Van Anden, a Hunker Democrat, had patiently tolerated Whitman's pro-Wilmot views. But now Whitman seems to have crossed the line. Whatever else might have transpired is not known—there were rumors that in a fit of anger Whitman kicked a prominent politician down a flight of stairs—but by January 21 Van Anden admitted he had "dispensed" with his editor.[32] At least two rival papers suggested that Whitman's dismissal was due to his angering the local conservative Democrats by his "bold denunciation of slavery and advocacy of the Wilmot Proviso."[33] While Whitman's opposition to the extension of slavery was becoming more adamant, it had also cost him his job. And yet it had also prepared him, in ways that he himself could not predict, to begin to seek out new forms of expression on race and slavery. That new expression could only be compelled by an entirely different force on his life, one as far removed from conventional politics and journalism as Whitman now found himself to be.

32. For a brief recounting of Whitman's leavetaking from the Eagle, see Rubin, The Historic Whitman, 180.

33. The New York Atlas, 23 January 1848. Quoted in Rubin, The Historic Whitman, 180.

3

EMERSON, NEW ORLEANS, AND
AN EMERGING VOICE

While Whitman's commitment to the cause of Free Soil only became more firmly entrenched in the face of Democratic election losses and his dismissal from the *Eagle*, at the same time he was pulled in a new and altogether different direction. Sometime during these years Whitman began reading Emerson, though it is impossible to say precisely when. The first time Whitman *writes* about reading Emerson, however, occurs in late 1847, just after the Democratic defeat in the New York State election. At approximately the same time he also begins to explore and create a wholly new and different voice—that of "the poet." Notebooks in which he began his experiments can fairly accurately be dated to 1847 (*NUPM* 1:54). Whitman himself later said that he began "elaborating the plan of my poems . . . and shifting it in my mind through many years (from the age of twenty-eight to thirty-five)," thus confirming a date of 1847 (*CP*, 1002). The peculiar combination of Whitman's increasing radicalization over slavery, on one hand, and the inspirational influence of Emerson, on the other, encouraged—even compelled—Whitman to begin his poetic explorations. And it is perhaps no coincidence that at the heart of this new poetry is a focus on slaves and slavery.

Whitman first became acquainted with Emerson's thinking in 1842, when he attended and reported on at least one of Emerson's lectures in New York City. In March 1842 Emerson delivered six lectures he had earlier given in Boston: "The Times," "The Poet," "The Conservative," "The Transcendentalist," "Manners," and "Prospects." Whitman reviewed the lecture on "The Poet" in the March 7 *Aurora* but appears not to have understood what he heard. As Joseph Jay Rubin points out, Whitman's report indicates that he spent as much time in "scouting the full house" as in listening to Emerson.[1] Whitman notes at the beginning of his piece that there were "a few beautiful maids—but more ugly women, mostly blue stockings; several interesting young men with Byron collars, doctors, and parsons; Grahamites and abolitionists," several editors and other "species of literati." He pokes fun at Horace Greeley's eager enthusiasm, saying "he would flounce like a fish out of water, or a tickled girl" whenever Emerson said anything good. But the most that Whitman seems to have digested from the talk was Emerson saying that "the first man who called another an ass was a poet." Whitman at least grasps that "the business of the poet is expression—the giving of utterance to the emotions and sentiments of the soul; and metaphors." But he backs off from any deeper interpretation, concluding:

> It would do the lecturer great injustice to attempt anything like a sketch of his ideas. Suffice it to say, the lecture was one of the richest and most beautiful compositions, both for its matter and style, we have ever heard anywhere, at any time.[2]

Whitman was clearly moved, but not yet in a way that would compel anything more than admiration.[3]

After 1844, Emerson's ideas were readily accessible both in published essays and in reviews and articles in magazines that Whitman read regularly.[4] It was not until 1847, however, that Whitman's close reading of Emerson can be clearly documented. In May of that year he clipped an article on Emerson's poetry from the *Democratic Review,* making several comments in the margins demonstrating his agreement with Emerson's—and not the reviewer's—ideas about poetry, such as Emerson's statement that "the perfect poet must be *unimpeachable* in manner as well as matter."[5]

1. Rubin, *The Historic Whitman*, 70.
2. Whitman, *Walt Whitman of the New York Aurora*, 105.
3. Another view of how well Whitman comprehended Emerson in this first encounter is offered by Jerome Loving, who concludes that Whitman "did not miss the salient points of Emerson's lecture." See Jerome Loving, *Emerson, Whitman, and the American Muse* (Chapel Hill: University of North Carolina Press, 1982), 10.
4. Floyd Stovall, *The Foreground of "Leaves of Grass"* (Charlottesville: University of Virginia Press, 1974), 285.
5. Ibid., 286–87.

The first documented evidence of Whitman writing about Emerson's essays occurs in a December 15, 1847, *Eagle* editorial, just one month after the election losses. Whitman's brief editorial on Emerson's essay "Spiritual Laws" reads as follows:

> In one of Ralph Waldo Emerson's inimitable lectures, occurs the following striking paragraph, which every heart will acknowledge to be as truthful as it is beautiful:
>> When the act of reflection takes place in the mind, when we look at ourselves in the light of thought, we discover that our life is embosomed in beauty. Behind us, as we go, all things assume pleasing forms, as clouds do afar off. Not only things familiar and stale, but even the tragic and terrible, are lures of memory. The river bank, the weed at the water side, the old house, the foolish person, however neglected at the passing, have a grace in the past. Even the corpse that has lain in the chambers, has added a solemn ornament to the house.[6]—The soul will not know either deformity or pain. (*GF* 2:270–71)

After the disappointments of late 1847—the violent Congressional debates, the loss of the Wilmot Proviso at the national and state levels, the fracturing and diminishment of the state Democratic party, and Whitman's own increasing political isolation on the slavery issue—Whitman perhaps took some comfort in the thought that the soul "will not know either deformity or pain."

Many critics have pointed to the influence of Emerson's essay "The Poet" on Whitman's conception of himself, his world, and his poetic vocation. Passages from *Leaves of Grass* seem to be taken directly from Emerson's essay. As we shall see, by late 1847 Whitman appears to have already been affected by Emerson's view of "the Poet," though in ways that are not always direct or apparent. But Whitman was also, if less obviously, influenced by Emerson's essays drawn from the 1841 volume, *Essays: First Series,* which did not include "The Poet." Whitman calls these essays "Shrewd and wise reflections . . . plentiful flowing rivulets of fine thought epigrammatic expressions of the first water."[7] A number

6. The lasting influence of this essay on Whitman is suggested by Whitman's use of this trope in the opening lines of the Preface to the 1855 *Leaves of Grass:* "America . . . perceives that the corpse is slowly borne from the eating and sleeping rooms of the house" (*CP,* 5).

7. Quoted in Stovall, *Foreground,* 290. Stovall relates that this undated manuscript, a paragraph praising Emerson's *Essays: First Series,* may have been intended for a review of Emerson's essays in the Brooklyn *Eagle.* The manuscript is part of the Berg Collection of the New York Public Library.

of Emersonian themes in these essays would directly influence Whitman: the primacy of the self, the divine potential within, the evolutionary process of life, the dual nature of the universe, and the vitality of the present and the future, to name a few.[8] But the immediate thrust of Emerson's influence on Whitman in these essays lies in his exhortation to trust one's instincts and principles over and against the demands and expectations of society. In the opening paragraph of "Self-Reliance," Emerson writes:

> To believe your own thought, to believe that what is true for you in your private heart is true for all men,—that is genius. Speak your latent conviction, and it shall be the universal sense.[9]

Emerson urges his readers to see that individuals can be directly known only by what they autonomously say and do, and not through the filter of social and political organizations. Identity based on imitation or group identification obscures the real person. "Insist on yourself. Never imitate," Emerson writes. "Your own gift you can present every moment with the cumulative force of a whole life's cultivation; but of the adopted talent of another you have only an extemporaneous half possession" (*Essays*, 278–79). Emerson tells his readers that "under all the screens" of religious and political affiliation "I have difficulty to detect the precise man you are: and of course so much force is withdrawn from your proper life" (263). Likewise, in "Spiritual Laws" Emerson warns about the dangers of losing one's self to the "machine" of contemporary institutions, habits, and expectations.

> The common experience is that the man fits himself as well as he can to the customary details of that work or trade he falls into, and tends it as a dog turns a spit. Then is he a part of the machine he moves; the man is lost. Until he can communicate himself to others in his full stature and proportion, he does not yet find his vocation . . . Whatever he knows and thinks, whatever in his apprehension is worth doing, that let him communicate, or men will never know and honor him aright. (*Essays*, 310–11)

8. For a brief but useful summary of Emerson's *Essays: First Series*, see Donald Yannella, *Ralph Waldo Emerson* (Boston: Twayne Publishers, 1982), 36–56. For more thorough discussions of Emerson's influence on Whitman, see Loving, *Walt Whitman's Champion* and *Emerson, Whitman, and the American Muse* or Stovall, *Foreground*.

9. Ralph Waldo Emerson, *Essays and Lectures*, ed. Joel Porte (New York: Library of America, 1983), 259. Subsequent references will be cited in the text as *Essays*.

Did Whitman identify with Emerson's diagnosis or respond to his exhortations? Any direct connection is, of course, speculative, yet the circumstances of Whitman's life (and his writings) suggest a strong and immediate link. Whitman's writing had always been derivative and his identity constructed of the "filter" of affiliation with the Democratic party and various newspapers in New York. Whitman had hoped from the beginning of his tenure with the *Eagle* that he might intimately reach his readers. But the very nature of journalistic discourse—its insistence on the "party line," on coalescing the ideas of others and not speaking from one's own voice—seems to have prohibited direct communication. As we have seen, little if anything that Whitman had written was original; the ideas, even the very words, were culled from the voices of others. In Emerson's phrase, Whitman had too often relied on "the adopted talent of another." Whitman was already beginning to feel a deep sense of frustration, as this 1847 notebook entry suggests:

> Every soul has its own individual language, often unspoken, or lamely feebly haltingly spoken; but a true fit for that man, and perfectly adapted to his use.—The truths I tell you or any other, may not be plain to you, because I do not translate them fully from my idiom into yours.—If I could do so, and do it well, they would be as apparent to you as they are to me; for they are truths. (*NUPM* 1:60–61)

Whitman had not yet succeeded in making plain the "individual language" of his soul. Moreover, the problem of translating "the truths" from "my idiom into yours" was further compounded by Whitman's new and mysterious understanding of a divided self. Perhaps influenced by Emerson's notion of the over-soul and the dualism of nature, Whitman writes: "I cannot explain the mystery, but I am always conscious of myself as two—as my soul and I; and I reckon it is the same with all men and women" (*NUPM* 1:63). Whitman's sense of a divided and not fully articulated self is captured in Emerson's line: "We but half express ourselves, and are ashamed of that divine idea which each of us represents" (*Essays*, 260). Half of Whitman—the material, quotidian, derivative "I"—is expressed through his journalistic writings. But his other half—the unique, divine soul that Whitman begins to discover in these early notebooks—continues to go publicly unexpressed.

As Whitman passionately struggled, in Emerson's phrase, to "communicate himself to others in his full stature and proportion," his reading of Emerson may have provided the inspiration to begin a wholly new type of writing. Emerson exhorts his readers to recognize their tran-

scendent potential—the "influx of the Divine mind into our mind"—
and encourages them to follow the "secret impulse" of their character
(*Essays*, 392).

> Each man has his own vocation. The talent is the call ... He
> inclines to do something which is ... good when it is done, but
> which no other man can do. He has no rival. For the more truly
> he consults his own powers, the more difference will his work
> exhibit from the work of any other. (*Essays*, 310)

Whether Whitman was moved by Emerson's call to "do something
... which no other man can do" by creating a work different "from the
work of any other," he undeniably began to create something new in
late 1847 with the free-verse experiments that can be documented as
having been written at this time. Moreover, this new poetry makes com-
pellingly clear the vital link between a new self and Whitman's own
emerging, idiosyncratic attitudes toward blacks and slavery. For at the
very start of Whitman's writing experiments are radical proclamations
about the equality and humanity of slaves. When Whitman first breaks
into poetry in these notebooks, his first poetic fragment proclaims an
inclusive and egalitarian concern for slaves:[10]

> I am the poet of slaves and of the masters of slaves
> I am the poet of the body
> And I am
> > > (*NUPM* 1:67)

These lines project a wholly new and different self and a new voice
about African Americans startlingly unlike anything Whitman had written about blacks in *Franklin Evans* or in his editorials for the Brooklyn
Eagle. The very foundation of Whitman's poetic vocation, these lines
say, is a speaker who embraces, absorbs, and treats equally "slaves and
the masters of slaves." While Whitman's journalistic writings on slavery
emphasize race and class differences, in his first recorded poetic lines
Whitman levels all social distinctions by including both slaves and masters in the same syntactic and spatial unit. Furthermore, he unites these
most extreme classes—white and black, owners and owned—in the
definition of the poet's central concerns.

10. I am indebted to Betsy Erkkila for this observation. See Erkkila, *Whitman the
Political Poet*, 50–51.

The riskiness of such notions is suggested by the fact that this first attempt at poetry is broken off in mid-line. But the poet begins again:

> I am the poet of the body
> And I am the poet of the soul
> I go with the slaves of the earth equally with the masters
> And I will stand between the masters and the slaves,
> Entering into both so that both will understand me alike.
>
> (*NUPM* 1:67)

Here the two sides of the divided self—body and soul—are reconciled, and that reconciliation seems to make possible the poet's egalitarian joining of himself with both slaves and masters. The slaves and masters cannot, however, be brought together themselves because of the history of their relationship, and so, as Betsy Erkkila points out, the poet must "stand between" them, imaginatively "entering into both" of their experiences.[11] Complete reconciliation will be achieved only in a fully inclusive and multiracial democracy, the type of society envisioned and modeled in the 1855 *Leaves of Grass*.

These initial images give startling voice to the transcendent possibilities at the heart of Whitman's emerging poetic vision. Foremost among his concerns are the resolution of the slavery issue and the equal treatment of all people. Whitman the poet enters the lives of slaves and masters, desiring to be understood by them and to project his readers into their lives as well. Moreover, he proclaims a radical egalitarian vision and an identification with slaves that are altogether absent from his journalism.

Following these opening lines are more than two hundred lines of poetry in which Whitman further defines his poetic vocation and aesthetic. He is the poet of "Strength and Hope," reviving the dying man with "tremendous breath" (*NUPM* 1:67–68). He is the poet who absorbs all things, understanding that a "leaf of grass" is not less than "the journeywork of suns and systems of suns" (70–71). But most important, he is the poet of all people, a poet whose inclusive vision embraces "women as well as men" and "sinners and the unlearned" (70, 73). He will not have "a single person" left out: "I will have the prostitute and the thief invited. . . . I will make no difference between them and the rest" (80). That this radical egalitarianism is the focal point of his vocation is underscored by the one line that Whitman intended to stand out by his use of italics: "*I am the poet of Equality.*" This single-line entry

11. Ibid., 51.

occurs just below the note, "Amount rec'd from Mr. V. A./ 1847" (71), suggesting that he may have arrived at this understanding of the poet's vocation at precisely the same time he was settling accounts with his employer, Isaac Van Anden, at the *Eagle*.

This stunning and radical enunciation of poetic principles from a conventional, workaday, Democratic journalist raises a number of puzzling questions, few of which Whitman scholars have been able to answer satisfactorily. How did Whitman arrive at this poetic aesthetic? How could he contain the disparate beliefs and voices of his "poetic" self and his "journalistic" self? Was the Free Soil journalist the "real" Walt, housed in the flesh of a mortal body and the ideologies of a flawed world, and the egalitarian poet the "ideal" Walt, that transcendent being he longed to become? And how seriously does one attach the language of his rhetorics—either poetry *or* journalism—to what he "really" believed? This study does not claim to unravel such mysteries, but it is possible to move nearer to understanding Whitman's sources of inspiration, his peculiar focus on slaves, and, ultimately, his emergence as a poet.

The most likely source for Whitman's definition of "the poet" would of course be Emerson's essay "The Poet," which Whitman heard—but did not understand—in 1842 and may have read sometime after its first publication in 1844. There is some scholarly disagreement about when Whitman was first influenced by this essay: Floyd Stovall has "no doubt that Whitman read the essay with great care in 1854 and perhaps also earlier"; Jerome Loving assumes an earlier date, saying Whitman "quite possibly" read Emerson's *Essays: Second Series,* which included "The Poet," shortly after it appeared in 1844.[12] Even accepting Loving's earlier date, the influence of "The Poet" in 1847 seems not to have been as direct as it would be in *Leaves of Grass*. By 1855 Whitman was veritably lifting lines out of Emerson's essays and revising them slightly before placing them in "Song of Myself."[13] In these 1847 notebooks, however, Whitman seems to have eclectically chosen only certain key ideas from "The Poet" and transformed them to fit his broader, democratic purpose.

Emerson's central idea, simplified greatly, is that the poet uniquely possesses the gift of being able to listen to nature and translate its beauty into language for others. The poet's "office" is to announce and affirm "the beauty of things, which becomes a new and higher beauty when expressed. Nature offers all her creatures to him as a picture-language"

12. Stovall, *Foreground,* 296; Loving, *Emerson, Whitman,* 62.
13. For examples, see Stovall, *Foreground,* 295–96.

(*Essays*, 452). The poet is the interpreter, the sayer, and the namer of Nature's beauty. Whitman's notes and poem fragments show that he is already accepting this role, representing the beauty of nature in all its divinity: he seeks to show, for example, that "all grains of sand, and every egg of the wren" is "perfect" (*NUPM* 1:71). But Whitman's concern surpasses Emerson's. For he will translate not only nature, but the language of all human beings:

> No two have exactly the same language, and the great translator and joiner of the whole is the poet. He has the divine grammar of all tongues, and says indifferently and alike How are you friend? to the President in the midst of his cabinet, and Good day my brother, to Sambo, among the hoes of the sugar field, and both understand him and know that his speech is right. (*NUPM* 1:61)

Thus Whitman adopts Emerson's theory of the poet but socializes his role as translator to become the voice and expression of all people, including that of slaves (even if stereotypically rendered).

Furthermore, Emerson states that "the Universe is the externisation of the soul": "All the facts of the animal economy, sex, nutriment, gestation, birth, growth, are symbols of the passage of the world into the soul of man to suffer there a change and reappear a new and higher fact" (*Essays*, 453, 456). Again, Whitman agrees: "The soul or spirit transmutes itself into all matter." Yet Whitman does not stop there. His poet enters not only into nature, but into all of humanity—especially those elements of humanity separated by the institution of slavery. As we have seen, one of his primary acts is that of "entering into both [masters and slaves] so that both shall understand me alike" (*NUPM* 1:67).

Finally, Emerson's poet "re-attaches things to nature and the Whole— re-attaching even artificial things . . . to nature, by a deeper insight" (*Essays*, 455). Again, Whitman applies to nature this notion of joining. The 1847 notebook includes three Whitmanesque catalogues of nature's elements attached to each other by the conjunction "And" at the beginning of the poetic line. But Whitman moves beyond nature into the social world, specifically the world that he knew was increasingly fragmented by the slavery debates. The "joiner of the whole" is identified by his ability to greet president and slave alike and to walk "with the slaves of the earth equally with the masters." The "Whole" for Whitman the poet was not only the natural, cosmic whole, but the united members of a multiracial and egalitarian United States.

Whitman's vision of "the poet," then, is rooted in Emerson but flowers in its own unique ways. Whitman translates Emerson's key ideas—the poet as interpreter of nature, as joiner, as one who externalizes the soul—into his own idiom, an idiom that includes nature but also encompasses human beings, especially American slaves. That Whitman should focus on slaves is not altogether surprising, given his and the nation's obsession with the question of slavery. But that he should *begin* his new poetry with a word about slaves, and that he should speak so radically about them, treating them "equally" and incarnating himself into their experience ("Entering into" them)—these things are more difficult to comprehend.

W. E. B. DuBois, in his classic series of essays, *The Souls of Black Folk* (1903), provides a key to understanding how Whitman's reading of Emerson would lead naturally to a focus on slaves. Without referring to Emerson or Whitman, though seeming to be familiar with both, DuBois points out that one's sense of one's own divinity, an idea first promulgated in the nineteenth century, radically transforms one into being deeply compassionate for others:

> The nineteenth was the first century of human sympathy,—the age when half wonderingly we began to descry in others that transfigured spark of divinity which we call Myself; when clod-hoppers and peasants, and tramps and thieves, and millionaires and—sometimes—Negroes, became throbbing souls whose warm pulsing life touched us so nearly that we half gasped with surprise, crying, "Thou too! hast Thou seen Sorrow and the dull waters of Hopelessness? Hast Thou known Life?" And then all hopelessly we peered into those Other-Worlds, and wailed, "O World of Worlds, how shall man make you one?"[14]

DuBois's analysis helps us understand the personal transformation in Whitman that led to his poetic concern for slaves. Inspired by Emerson to discover in himself "that transfigured spark of divinity which we call Myself," Whitman for the first time recognized that his own divinity was connected to all others'. Their sorrow was his sorrow, their humanity his humanity. Together, they sought to be made "one." This, of course, is the discovery of Whitman's speaker in section 5 of "Song of Myself":

> Swiftly arose and spread around me the peace and
> knowledge that pass all the argument of the earth,

14. W. E. B. DuBois, *The Souls of Black Folk* (New York: New American Library, 1982), 235–36.

And I know that the hand of God is the promise of my own,
And I know that the spirit of God is the brother of my own,
And that all the men ever born are also my brothers,
     and the women my sisters and lovers. . . .

                                                    (*CP*, 30–31)

In his first lines of poetry in the 1847 notebooks ("I am the poet of slaves and of the masters of slaves"), Whitman demonstrates that *he* will be the agent of this unity, sympathizing with that group of people most distant from his own experience—the "Negroes" for whom DuBois says one "sometimes" finds compassion—and bringing them together both with himself and their natural enemies, the slave owners.

Whitman's radical new vision, however, did not, and would not, carry over into his journalism. For in this Whitman was always consistent: even after the 1855 *Leaves of Grass* made public the radically inclusive vision of blacks first expressed in these 1847 notebooks, Whitman remained in his journalism conventionally racist and segregationist, with little public sympathy or concern for blacks. These sharp distinctions between the Free Soil journalist and the radically new and sympathetic poet are already apparent as early as 1848. For in his next journalistic writings, Whitman falls back on the conventions and perceptions regarding blacks that he expressed in *Franklin Evans*.

Shortly after he was fired from the *Eagle*, Whitman accepted a position in New Orleans, thus giving him a chance to see and live among blacks and other people of color in ways that were not possible in Brooklyn. Whitman's brief stay in New Orleans in 1848 would be his only visit to the South, and it would leave a lasting, though not immediately apparent, impression on his life and work. That he went to New Orleans at all was a matter of luck, or circumstance. On February 9, while attending the Broadway Theatre in New York, Whitman met J. E. McClure, a Southern entrepreneur planning to start a newspaper called the *Crescent* in New Orleans. Within fifteen minutes they had negotiated a contract. Two days later Whitman left New York with his fourteen-year-old brother Jeff for a two-week journey by train, stagecoach, and boat across an American landscape he had previously only imagined.[15]

New Orleans at this time was a lively city, teeming with troops returning from the recent defeat of Mexico. Whitman said later that New Orleans was the nation's "channel and *entrepot* for everything, going and returning. It had the best news and war correspondents; it had the

15. For accounts of Whitman's trip to New Orleans, see Allen, *The Solitary Singer*, 91–94; Rubin, *The Historic Whitman*, 185–205; and Zweig, *Walt Whitman*, 65–78.

most to say, through its leading newspapers . . . and its voice was readiest listen'd to" (*CP*, 1200). New Orleans was also an ethnically diverse city. Its population of African Americans, Creoles, Native Americans, and Spanish Americans among others was new to Whitman, a fairly provincial New Yorker who had little experience with people of color.

Whitman at first enjoyed his work as the "exchange editor" of the *Crescent*. He went through dozens of out-of-town newspapers that arrived by mail every morning, "making up the news," as he said, "with pen and scissors" (*NUPM* 1:87). The central news event of these months was the revolution in France. Living in a city full of French-speaking peoples and European refugees, Whitman was caught up in the excitement. Slavery was of course also a central concern, and the *Crescent*, like other Southern papers, took a strong pro-slavery view. It listed those arrested for harboring fugitive slaves and in the daily summary of crime it branded accused persons with racially signifying acronyms, such as "f.w.c."—free woman of color. The paper editorialized that the sixty thousand blacks of the city had "too much latitude in the way of vice and amusement" and called for the arrest of those found in grog shops (thirty-three were soon arrested).[16] The *Crescent* also ran advertisements of slave auctions to be held at Banks' Arcade, which also served as a news-gathering center. Whitman likely attended one or more of these auctions where planters lounged at a bar sipping brandy and water and the slaves filled the benches in small rooms. Although he records no impressions of them at the time, the slave auctions were to become the material for one of his most important passages on slavery and blacks in *Leaves of Grass*, as we shall see.[17]

Whitman would make known his ideas about blacks and slavery not in editorials, as before, but in prose sketches of people he met on long walks through the city. He spent hours strolling on Lafayette Square or along the levees, recording his impressions in a series of articles for the *Crescent*. One of his favorite amusements, he recalled later, was going to the old French Market on Sunday mornings.

16. Quoted, without citation, in Rubin, *The Historic Whitman*, 203.

17. Though Whitman showed no indignation in his writing about the treatment of slaves, his brother Jeff expressed himself otherwise. In a letter to Walt Whitman Sr. dated March 14, 1848, Jeff wrote: "On Sunday morning we took a walk down to the old French church [The St. Louis Cathedral] and an old looking thing it is too. Every one would go up and dip their fingers in the holy water and then go home and *whip* their *slaves*. One old black took a bottle home to wash the sins out of her family." (*Dear Brother Walt: The Letters of Thomas Jefferson Whitman*, ed. Dennis Berthold and Kenneth M. Price [Kent, Ohio: Kent State University Press, 1984], 6.)

The show was a varied and curious one; among the rest, the Indian and negro hucksters with their wares. For there were always fine specimens of Indians, both men and women, young and old. I remember I nearly always on these occasions got a large cup of delicious coffee with a biscuit, for my breakfast, from the immense shining copper kettle of a great Creole mulatto woman (I believe she weigh'd 230 pounds.) I never have had such coffee since. (CP, 1201)

Despite Whitman's interest in blacks, Creoles, and American Indians, he continued to hold conventionally prejudiced views. In one article, "A Walk About Town," he recalled seeing a black man throw a large stone at the head of his mule because it would not pull an empty dray. In a line that recalls his plantation-owner fantasy in Franklin Evans, Whitman reflects: "Wished I owned the negro; wouldn't treat him as he treated the mule, but make him a present of a cow-skin, and make him whip himself" (UPP 1:223).

Whitman's personal attitudes toward blacks can best be measured in an extended portrait he wrote of a Creole woman who sold flowers. "Miss Dusky Grisette," published in the Crescent on March 16, 1848, was one of more than half a dozen sketches Whitman published that month of people he observed at a New Orleans hotel.[18] The article runs more than seven hundred words, making it the longest Whitman wrote about a black person since the Creole slave episode in Franklin Evans.[19] Not until his writing about black Civil War troops receiving their first pay in July 1863 would he again have so much to say about blacks. The essay demonstrates Whitman's primarily sexual understanding of—and perhaps desire for—African American women, a perspective that remains essentially unchanged from Franklin Evans.

The title signals Whitman's interpretation of the woman—or type— he is describing. "Grisettes" in France were salesgirls or factory workers who were also "kept women" of the upper classes. Many of these women were associated with the garment trade, in which gray cloth—"grisette"—was widely used.[20] Whitman appears to be striving for just such

18. Allen, The Solitary Singer, 96.

19. In one of the episodes of "Some Fact-Romances," a work of fiction by Whitman first published in December 1845, "an aged black widow-woman" begs for charitable contributions on behalf of a poor deaf mute girl, the daughter of "a wretched intemperate couple" (EPF, 322). Without minimizing the story's significance as a Whitman text about a black person, it is worth noting that after the initial description of the woman as black, her race is never again mentioned.

20. Francine de Plessix Gray, "Splendor and Miseries," The New York Review of Books 39, no. 13 (16 July 1992): 31–35.

an image of a woman who is sexually free, but not a prostitute, in his portrait of the Creole woman. He later told Horace Traubel his impressions of such mixed-race women:

> The Octoroon was not a whore, a prostitute, as we call a certain class of women here—and yet *was* too: a hard class to comprehend: women with splendid bodies—no bustles, no corsets, no enormities of any sort: large, luminous, rich eyes: face a rich olive: habits indolent, yet not lazy as we define laziness North: fascinating, magnetic, sexual, ignorant, illiterate: always more than pretty—"pretty" is too weak a word to apply to them.[21]

This class of women whom he saw in New Orleans—typified by "Mademoiselle Grisette," as he calls her—bears many of the same traits as the "Creole slave" Margaret in *Franklin Evans:* sexual magnetism, inscrutability, a voluptuous body, light complexion, and rich eyes. Like Margaret, Miss Grisette is respectable, if only superficially in this case. In the portrait, Whitman describes a hard-working flower girl who capitalizes on her sexual allure as a selling strategy:

> Miss Dusky Grisette is the young "lady" who takes her stand of evenings upon the pavement opposite of St. Charles Hotel, for the praiseworthy purpose of selling a few flowers by retail, showing off her own charms meanwhile, in a wholesale manner. She drives a thriving trade when the evenings are pleasant. Her neat basket of choice bouquets sits by her side, and she has a smile and a wink for every one of the passers-by who have a wink and a smile for her. (*UPP* 1:202–3)

Later he adds: "She sells her flowers, and barters off sweet looks for sweeter money" (*UPP* 1:204). Throughout the piece Whitman weaves the basic narrative of Miss Grisette's respectable daily forms of labor, first as a *marchande des fleurs* (florist), then as a coffee seller on the street, then as a washer-woman, through a second, parallel narrative hinting at the young woman's sexuality. The sexual subtext betrays Whitman's own, perhaps frustrated, desire for this woman (or these women). He is obsessed with her physical features—her "pretty eyes and pretty chin," her "beautiful teeth," vermilion cheeks, and "nearly straight . . . long glossy hair." He fantasizes: "What becomes of the flower-girl in the day time would be hard to tell: perhaps it would be in

---

21. Traubel, *With Walt Whitman in Camden*, 2:283.

bad taste to attempt to find out." Even the drudgery of her work Whitman transforms into moments of sexual possibility. As she washes clothes at the washtub, "they do say that her cousin Marie and herself have rare fun whilst splashing among the suds, in detailing the numerous conquests they (poor things!) supposed [themselves] to have made in the flower market the evening before" (*UPP* 1:205).

Like Franklin's Margaret, Whitman's Mademoiselle Grisette simultaneously baffles and attracts him. It is not in the scope of this study to define Whitman's sexual tendencies and attachments. But it is worth noting that two of Whitman's longest writings about African Americans before the 1855 edition of *Leaves of Grass* involve sexual or pseudosexual fantasies about mixed-race women. While both are described as seductive and changeable in nature, there are important differences between them. Margaret is a powerless slave whom Whitman's narrator Franklin marries, presumably sexually conquers, then immediately renounces, leading to her sickness and suicide. Mademoiselle Grisette, on the other hand, is an independent, capable, and powerful woman in her own right whose manipulations of men and markets draws a certain respect from Whitman, who remains at a distance and can only fantasize. Taken together, however, these portraits demonstrate that even as Whitman began writing poetry about blacks as dignified and equal people, his primary biographical—and biological—impulses were to consider blacks, especially black women, in purely physical ways.[22] These portraits might also suggest how Whitman's attitudes were constructed by social and generic expectations: how, for example, Whitman's description of these women rehearses a conventional sexual desire of mid-nineteenth-century white men, when in fact, as we know from Whitman's later poetry about homosexual desire, he may never have been sexually interested in these women at all.

Two months after writing this portrait, Whitman left New Orleans and returned home, not out of regret or disappointment but because his brother Jeff was homesick and both of them had grown tired of the dirt and the heat of New Orleans. In addition, Walt Whitman Sr. could not find work back in New York and the family was financially strapped.

22. At one point the theory existed that Whitman had shared a romantic relationship with what Gay Wilson Allen calls a "wealthy Creole of a proud family into which Whitman could not marry and which out of pride would always keep secret the paternity of the woman's children." This story has never been substantiated with "one concrete fact," Allen says, and is not taken seriously by contemporary scholars. (See Allen, *The Solitary Singer*, 97.) What no scholarship has pointed out, however, is that these two portraits of mixed-race women tell us more about Whitman than the rumor of a relationship that never existed.

The influence of the New Orleans experience on Whitman's development is difficult to measure. On one hand, New Orleans seemed to have little influence on his development as a writer. Whitman's writing experiments had already begun and the journey to New Orleans, according to biographer Paul Zweig, "did not supply either the form or the vision [for his poetry], which took several more years to emerge."[23] Moreover, the trip was not essentially a break from the past: he continued in his vocation as a journalist both in New Orleans and when he returned home.

But the influence of New Orleans on Whitman's consciousness and writing about African Americans is perhaps more significant, if not immediately apparent. He saw firsthand how blacks were treated by the public, the press, and local officials. In all probability he witnessed slave auctions. He had frequent, if superficial, encounters with people of color on the street. Deprived of a venue for his sentiments on slavery, he wrote about the black and mixed-race people he met, and these writings suggest the continuity of conventional racial attitudes on his part. Yet even in this, New Orleans gave Whitman the firsthand experiences that would provide the material for some of his most celebratory poetry about any human beings in the passages on African Americans in the 1855 *Leaves of Grass,* as we shall see.

In the two years that passed since Whitman first assumed editorship of the Brooklyn *Eagle,* a variety of influences began to affect the way he would ultimately portray blacks in *Leaves of Grass.* His passion for Free Soil, his early poetic response to the call of Emerson, and his brief immersion in Southern culture seem disparate and unrelated experiences. But under the twin pressures of the Union's fragmentation over slavery and Whitman's eagerness to assert an individual voice, these experiences would produce a vision of blacks and slavery that he could not fully anticipate, and for which his readership would not for some time be ready.

23. Zweig, *Walt Whitman,* 78.

4

THE 1850 COMPROMISE
AND AN EARLY POETICS OF
SLAVERY

Even before Whitman arrived home from New Orleans in June 1848, events on the national political scene were determining the direction of his future. The national conventions of both parties—the Democrats' in late May in Baltimore and the Whigs' in early June in Philadelphia—led to further intraparty fragmentation over the slavery question. New York Hunkers and Barnburners each sent a separate delegation to Baltimore, and when the convention voted to seat both delegations, the Barnburners walked out. The Democrats then nominated Cass, an arch-opponent of the Wilmot Proviso, to head their ticket. The Whig convention nominated the Mexican War hero Zachary "Rough and Ready" Taylor with the assumption that his ownership of more than one hundred slaves on Louisiana and Mississippi plantations would assure his "safety" on the slavery issue. Soon thereafter a faction known as "Conscience Whigs," opposed to the extension of slavery supported by "Cotton Whigs," bolted the party with the express purpose of realigning the political spectrum and forming what Charles Sumner called "one grand Northern party of Freedom."[1]

1. Sumner to Salmon P. Chase, 7 February 1848, Chase Papers, Library of Congress. Quoted in McPherson, *Battle Cry,* 60. For a discussion of the politics of slavery in the election of 1848, see McPherson, *Battle Cry,* 58–64.

These events signaled yet one more stage in a continuing crisis that threatened not only to destroy the major political parties but even to sever the Union. The slavery crisis of the late 1840s "paralyzed government and threatened the republic," and the push westward after the discovery of gold in California in 1848 only heightened the conflict.[2] Whitman responded eagerly to the slavery debate in these years, heading a Brooklyn Free Soil newspaper and serving as a delegate to the first national Free Soil convention. But the results of the Free Soilers' efforts were mixed: on one hand, they succeeded in placing the extension of slavery at the forefront of the national agenda, but on the other, the cause of Free Soil was consistently defeated in local and national elections. Moreover, the resolution to the slavery crisis in these years turned out to be the most significant defeat for Whitman and Free Soilers: the 1850 Compromise. Consisting of five separate bills highlighted by the extension of slavery into new territories and the enactment of a fugitive slave law, the 1850 Compromise marked a vital turning point in the life of the United States and in the evolution of Walt Whitman. Though, as one commentator points out, the Compromise was more "armistice" than "compromise," with neither North nor South agreeing to the terms of the other side on any single issue, most Americans welcomed it as a settlement of the intersectional struggle, however temporary and unsatisfying.[3] Whitman, however, as a radical Free Soiler, was incensed by what he saw as the final surrender of a weak-willed North to Southern demands on slavery. The Compromise represented for him the irrevocable turn of America away from the principle of freedom and toward a future in which the white laborer would be discouraged by the presence of black slaves in the new territories, and, in addition, federal authorities would interfere in the sovereignty of Northern cities and states by enforcing the return of fugitive slaves to the South.

The 1850 Compromise seems to have sapped the life out of Whitman. After its passage in September, he wrote several "letters" for the Free Soil newspaper *The National Era,* but he was essentially not heard from again until the publication of *Leaves of Grass* five years later. Meanwhile, however, Whitman continued to contemplate his future as a poet, inspired not only by Emerson but now also by essays on poetry he was reading in British journals. At the same time that his conventional prose failed to effect any change on slavery, he was more and more pulled toward the vision of himself as poet. And while his only poems during

2. Ibid., 75.
3. David Potter, *The Impending Crisis, 1848–1861* (New York: Harper and Row, 1976), 113.

this time—a series of hastily written verses advocating Free Soil—show him generally mired in conventional imagery and language, the twinning of poetry and slavery in these poems reveals the first glimmerings of more radical sentiments and the first poetic witness of a concern for slavery that would mark the 1855 *Leaves of Grass*.

When Whitman arrived in New York from New Orleans in June 1848, he immediately set to work for the Barnburner cause. A rival newspaper noted his return—"large as life, but quite as vain, and more radical than ever"—and predicted, in florid, though perhaps accurate, terms, that Whitman would begin a daily newspaper in Brooklyn:

> No bulldog ever clutched determinedly on cattle's nasal membrane (that tender spot)—no grimalkin ever worried horror-stricken mice—more than our amiable locofoco friend will be likely to clutch and worry old Hunkerism in King's County.[4]

New York Barnburners held their own convention in Utica in late June, choosing Martin Van Buren as their Presidential nominee and adopting a Wilmot platform. About fifty newspapers from throughout the state pledged their support to the ticket. Meanwhile, exchange papers from elsewhere brought evidence that throughout the nation members of the abolitionist Liberty party and Conscience Whigs were planning on joining the Barnburners in a Free Soil convocation at Buffalo. The focus of this meeting would be the assumption that the question of slavery extension ought to override all others.[5]

On August 5, one hundred Barnburners met in Brooklyn to elect delegates to represent Kings County at the Buffalo convention, and among the fifteen chosen was Walt Whitman, one of the evening's speakers. William Cullen Bryant's *Evening Post* reported:

> Mr. W. Whitman made some remarks introducing a resolution instructing the delegates from King's County to go unconditionally for the nomination of Martin Van Buren. At the particular desire, however, of some of the members of the meeting, he accepted an amendment preserving the spirit of the resolution [which simply condemned Cass for his anti-Wilmot stand and

4. Quoted without citation from *The Advertiser* in Rubin, *The Historic Whitman*, 206.
5. For an excellent discussion of the Barnburners and of the Free Soil convention in Buffalo, see Foner, *Politics and Ideology in the Age of the Civil War*, especially chapter 5, "Racial Attitudes of the New York Free Soilers," 77–93. See also Rubin, *The Historic Whitman*, 206–10; Allen, *The Solitary Singer*, 100–103; and McPherson, *Battle Cry*, 60–64.

Taylor for not taking any stand], but leaving out the positive instructions, which was adopted—though many preferred it in its first form.[6]

The Free Soil convention that Whitman attended later that month in Buffalo resembled a religious revival, with more than fifteen thousand people filling a park and listening to orators such as Frederick Douglass speak out against the extension of slavery and condemn the major parties. A 465-member executive committee met at a local church and hammered out a broad platform that successfully overcame Liberty, Whig, and Democratic differences on such issues as banking and tariffs by focusing on the single issue that brought them together. As one of the keynoters explained, "If we are wrong on the Tariff, it can be righted in twelve hours. If we are wrong on Banks, it can be righted by legislation. But if we are wrong on the subject of slavery, it can never be righted. It will reach down to posterity, inflicting curses and misery upon generations yet to come."[7]

Negotiations over the summer had laid the groundwork for the major agreements. Martin Van Buren, already the Barnburner nominee, was nominated for President, though Conscience Whigs and Liberty members who questioned the former doughface Democrat's commitment to the cause urged Barnburner support for a strong anti-slavery platform. Rallied by a common hope that it could change the course of American politics over the slavery question and choosing as its slogan "Free Soil, Free Speech, Free Labor, and Free Men," the Free Soil party was born. Frederick Douglass declared: "Anti-slavery thus far had only been sheet lightning; the Buffalo convention sought to make it a thunderbolt."[8] And indeed, the birth of the Free Soil party upset the Whig and Democratic strategy of trying to keep the slavery issue out of the campaign. Both major parties responded by manipulating their position on the issue, preaching anti-extension in the North while appealing to the preservation of slavery in the South.

Yet, as Eric Foner has pointed out, the Free Soil party was not without essential differences over basic rights for blacks.[9] The Barnburners were the major force behind the convention, but other factions were sharply critical of the racial prejudice that drove the Barnburners' passion for free soil. Even before the convention the *National Era* editorialized:

6. The *New York Evening Post*, 7 August 1848. Quoted in Allen, *The Solitary Singer*, 102.
7. Quoted in Rubin, *The Historic Whitman*, 209, without attribution.
8. Quoted in ibid., 210, without citation.
9. See Foner, *Politics and Ideology*, 85–91.

Studiously placing their opposition to the extension of slavery on the ground of abhorrence of "black slaves," rather than the despotism that imbrutes them, [Barnburners are] apparently fearful of having their Anti-Slavery position attributed to generous convictions of the brotherhood of the Human Race. . . . We distrust these men.[10]

At the convention the Liberty party had pushed hard for a plank endorsing suffrage for blacks, but in the end it surrendered this ideal. Gerrit Smith, a leader of the radical wing of the Liberty party, was outraged. Writing in an African American newspaper in New York City, the *Ram's Horn*, Smith condemned the choice of Van Buren, saying it was obvious that Van Buren was not making any efforts either to fight slavery or to combat racial prejudice. Van Buren, Smith said, differed little from the vast majority of Americans in his "views and treatment of the colored race." Since blacks could not expect any better treatment from a Free Soil government than from a Democratic or Whig administration, they should vote for him (Smith) rather than for Free Soilers, who "acquiesce, and even take part, in the proscription and crushing of your race."[11] Others were equally angered that an anti-slavery party disregarded the issue of black suffrage in its national platform. "The old negro-hating colonizationist of '33 would almost have accepted the Free Soil platform," the *Pennsylvania Freeman* complained, referring to colonizationist schemes that were fairly popular in the 1820s and 1830s but languished under attacks by abolitionists and the schemes' general failure to succeed.[12]

Among African Americans who attended the convention, there was sharp disagreement about whether the Free Soil party even deserved black support. Samuel R. Ward, an eloquent African American abolitionist, agreed with Smith. He stated that the absence of an equal-suffrage plank was deliberately designed to assuage the Barnburners. The Free Soilers of New York, Ward wrote in an African American newspaper, were "as ready to rob black men of their rights now as they ever were."[13] Frederick Douglass, on the other hand, urged friends of the slave to support Van Buren. He insisted that many Free Soilers had changed their attitude toward blacks and that bias in the party might be combated

10. *National Era*, 15 June 1848. Quoted in ibid., 91–92.
11. Quoted in ibid., 87.
12. *Pennsylvania Freeman*, 1 February 1848. Quoted in Foner, *Politics and Ideology*, 92.
13. *North Star*, 1 September 1848. Quoted in ibid., 88.

by blacks working within the new organization. For the most part, free blacks adopted Douglass's line of thinking.[14]

In the end, the party's platform was so broad that it could gain support from both those morally opposed to the institution of slavery and those opposed to the presence of blacks—slave *or* free—in the new territories. As the main organizational impulse behind the convention, the Barnburners had "changed the anti-slavery movement's course decisively," according to Foner. Once the commitment to equal suffrage had been removed from an anti-slavery party platform, it would "never again be reinstated."[15]

What Whitman thought of equal rights for blacks is difficult to ascertain. As a mainstream New York Free Soiler, he may well have shared in the historic prejudice of his local faction, though much of the racial prejudice came from upstate New York Barnburners. In addition, Barnburners were far less prejudiced than their Hunker opponents, who would not even have considered participating in a convention with black delegates.

Yet the Free Soil newspaper Whitman was to edit shortly after his return to Brooklyn indicated more strongly than ever that his radical opposition to the extension of slavery had little, if anything, to do with the rights of blacks. Financially supported by a local anti-slavery judge and organized by the Free Soil General Committee for Brooklyn (of which Whitman was a member), Whitman's *Brooklyn Freeman* made its boisterous debut on September 9.

> Free Soilers! Radicals! Liberty Men! all whose throats are not quite tough enough to swallow Taylor or Cass! come up and subscribe for the *"Daily Freeman!"* It will be chock full of the right sort of matter. Let us see whether we can't make both Whig and Democratic Old Hunkerism reel in Kings County.[16]

In the initial paragraph Whitman makes his program clear. The *Freeman* would advocate the "doctrine laid down in the Buffalo Convention," support the election of Van Buren, and "oppose, under all

14. Outside of New York, where Free Soil leaders were mostly former Liberty party members or Whigs who had traditionally supported black rights, African Americans overwhelmingly supported the new party. But in New York, Whitman's home state, many African Americans followed the advice of Ward to vote for Smith and the Equal Rights plank.
15. Ibid., 93.
16. Reproduced in *Catalogue of the Whitman Collection . . . Being a Part of the Trent Collection,* compiled by Ellen Francis Frey (Durham: Duke University Library, 1945).

circumstances, the addition in the Union, in future, of a single inch of *slave land,* whether in the form of state or territory."[17] The bulk of the paper consists of a reprint of Van Buren's lengthy acceptance letter to the Buffalo convention and an article by Whitman entitled "Jefferson on the Non-Extension and Abolition of Slavery." Whitman's piece rehearses the arguments about Jefferson—the "faithful, ever visible, generally acknowledged" light of the Democratic party—first made in the 1847 congressional debates, with slightly more radical claims. Whitman contends that Jefferson "was in the literal sense of the word an *abolitionist,*" as were "a large and influential body of Southerners at that time." Whitman quotes Jefferson several times at length, concluding with Jefferson's well-known passage from *Notes on the State of Virginia* that centers its opposition to slavery upon the well-being of whites:

> There must doubtless be an unhappy influence on the manners of our people produced by the existence of slavery among us. The whole commerce between master and slave is a perpetual exercise of the most boisterous passions, the most unremitting despotism on the one part, and degrading submissions on the other. Our children see this, and learn to imitate it; for man is an imitative animal. . . . With the morals of the people, their industry also is destroyed. For in a warm climate, no man will labour for himself who can make another labour for him.[18]

Despite Whitman's abolitionist-like sympathy for the slave in his recent poetry experiments, his invocation of Jefferson as an abolitionist here is not, however, a direct appeal for support of abolitionism, but rather a rhetorical strategy to include abolitionists within the Free Soil fold and to underscore Jefferson's unyielding opposition to the extension of slavery. Elsewhere Whitman makes clear that his primary concern is not the well-being or freedom of slaves. In condemning Cass's characterization of the extension of slavery as merely a "diffusion" of slavery, Whitman acknowledges that extension "rivets the fetters of the slave," but his more important point is that slaves carry with them "that degradation of free labor and the stagnation of enterprise, which weigh so heavily upon the prosperity of the South."

As with the later editorials of 1847, several of Whitman's arguments in this first issue of the *Freeman* are formulated in terms of a democratic

17. Ibid.
18. Thomas Jefferson, *Notes on the State of Virginia* (Chapel Hill: University of North Carolina Press, 1955), 162–63.

revolutionary struggle, or a class conflict, between the mass of laborers and an aristocratic elite. He asserts that the Kings County Democrats have been taken over by "a small clique" of Hunkers who have reduced the democratic process to "a mere game of cunning." He argues, as he did a year earlier, that the true South is not the "aristocratic few" slaveholders who dominate Southern politics, but rather the "masses of white citizens . . . averse to slavery." And he characterizes the Free Soil cause in David-versus-Goliath terms: "Our size will be small," he says, but "enthusiastic belief in the truth of what one is uttering . . . may overcome all that." He has faith that if his readers are fully informed of the "Great Truth," they cannot fail to be moved.

Whitman would not, unfortunately, ever know whether his faith in his readers would be rewarded. The night after the first issue of the *Freeman* was published, a fire broke out in a store on Fulton Street, destroying twenty acres of the lower section of Brooklyn, including the *Freeman* office. Whitman lost everything and was not able to resume publication for two months. Meanwhile, a hostile New York press taunted Free Soilers as "broken-down politicians and disappointed office seekers" who supported an "infamous coalition" with blacks at Buffalo, and youth gangs drove Free Soilers from assembly halls with firecrackers and threats of violence.[19] By the time Whitman restarted his newspaper on November 1, it may have been too late to have had any effect. Whigs won the November election at every level, sending Zachary Taylor into office, and Free Soilers failed to carry a single state. Nonetheless, Free Soilers professed satisfaction with the results. Charles Sumner claimed that "the public mind has been stirred on the subject of slavery to depths never reached before."[20] And New York Senator William Seward boasted: "Anti-slavery is at length a respectable element in politics."[21]

Indeed, despite the absence of institutional power, Free Soilism filtered into American politics just as the slavery conflict was about to reach a new level of intensity brought about by a dramatic turn of events. The discovery of gold at John Sutter's mill near Sacramento in January 1848 enticed a flood of more than eighty thousand gold-seekers to California, and so required that California and New Mexico be organized into territories and ultimately into states, once again raising the question of whether slavery would be allowed. In December 1848, lame-duck Presi-

19. Quoted in Rubin, *The Historic Whitman*, 213–14, without attribution.

20. Sumner to Salmon P. Chase, 16 November 1848. Quoted in McPherson, *Battle Cry,* 63.

21. Quoted in Foner, *Politics and Ideology,* 93. Originally cited in Frederick W. Seward, *Seward at Washington as Senator and Secretary of State,* 2 vols. (New York: Derby and Miller, 1891), 1:71.

dent James K. Polk recommended that the Missouri Compromise line—
dividing free and slave territories at 36°30'—be extended to the Pacific,
thus ensuring the extension of slavery in a sizable area of the new territories. The ensuing debate in Congress in the first months of 1849 erupted
into violent and intense disagreement. "Fistfights flared in both Houses,
Southern members shouted threats of secession, and no territorial legislation could command a majority," writes James McPherson.[22] In the
House, Northern congressmen reaffirmed the Wilmot Proviso and
drafted a bill for California that excluded slavery, and by the end of
1849 every Northern legislature except Iowa's had endorsed the proviso.
In the Senate, enraged Southerners used their power to quash the bill.

Whitman's concerns in early 1849, however, were local, and his mood
optimistic. In the *Freeman* he continued to assault the local Hunkers,
claiming "the desire to prevent them from ever taking their seats in high
places again; and we would resuscitate the Democrats of Brooklyn from
their palsying influence."[23] Despite his temporary alienation from the
Democratic party, his faith remained unshaken that the party could be
reconciled along Free Soil lines. In May he began daily publication of
the *Freeman,* and in June he became the first editor in the nation to
nominate Senator Thomas Hart Benton, a Missouri Free Soiler, for President, though Taylor had assumed office only a few months earlier.[24]

But events that summer turned against Whitman. New York Barnburners began working toward what Whitman had not thought possible—a reconciliation with Hunkers that could be achieved only by
compromising their position on the Wilmot Proviso. Throughout the
summer of 1849, Democrats of both factions began to seek an end to
dissension. Many Barnburners felt their goals to have been completed
in the defeat of Cass and other Hunkers. Many had joined the Free Soil
party with the primary purpose of restoring the balance of power within
the Democratic party by demonstrating that Cass could not be elected
without the votes of Northern Democrats. Others desired to defeat Cass
solely to revenge the denial of the Democratic nomination to Van Buren
four years earlier. With Cass defeated, many Barnburners were now
ready to regard the Hunkers, as one Barnburner put it, as "enemies in
war—in peace, friends."[25] Moderates of both groups sought an accord,

22. McPherson, *Battle Cry,* 65.
23. Quoted in the *Williamsburgh Daily Times,* 30 April 1849. Reprinted in Rubin, *The
Historic Whitman,* 217.
24. For Whitman's political activities and writings in 1849, see Rubin, *The Historic
Whitman,* 217–22.
25. Henry B. Stanton, *Random Recollections* (New York: Harper and Brothers, 1887),
165. Quoted in Foner, *Politics and Ideology,* 89.

and Whitman appears to have been at the center of the discussion. Whitman's name was suggested as the head of this new union, but the Hunkers of Kings County indicated "they would not extend amnesty" to him. His former paper, the *Eagle,* castigated him as "slow, indolent, heavy, discourteous, [and with] no political principles, nor, for that matter, principles of any sort."[26] In any case, Whitman would not have accepted the terms of compromise, as events would soon show.

In August "Union and Harmony" delegates from each faction met, but without resolving the major disagreement over the extension of slavery. The following month Hunkers chose a full slate of anti-Wilmot candidates for the fall elections, but announced for the sake of unity they would allow Barnburners to replace four of these. Whitman was confident that Barnburners would remain steadfastly principled, but his judgment was badly mistaken. Whitman learned, to his outrage, that at their meeting at Utica on September 12 the Barnburners would accept the joint ticket.

The reconciliation of the New York Democratic party without a united opposition to the extension of slavery deeply disappointed Whitman. "Utica became his symbol for the betrayal of Free Soil ideals by ambitious ex-officeholders, a place to be linked with surrender," writes Joseph Rubin.[27] Whitman now felt the need to choose between his principles or his position. On September 11, even before the Barnburners' meeting, he published his resignation, warmly thanking his friends but not leaving without a parting shot: "My enemies—and old hunkers generally—I disdain and defy just the same as ever."[28]

The Brooklyn *Star* saluted Whitman's principled defiance with a reference to Milton: "One man among the Free Soilers rejects the alliance of the Hunkers and holds out—the Abdiel of his party. This man is Walt Whitman."[29] But such praise must have been small consolation as Whitman found himself politically isolated. With the New York Barnburners back in the Democratic fold, Whitman belonged to a Free Soil party whose power base had been substantially eroded by the exodus of his own faction. To add to his woes, the Brooklyn *Advertiser* derided him in a caustic portrait on October 4, calling him "full of egotism," "a civilized but not a polished Aborigine" who "apes in some degree the gravity of the student" and who proclaims "Liberty, equality, fraternity" only on his own terms.[30]

26. Quoted in Rubin, *The Historic Whitman,* 221, without citation.
27. Ibid., 222.
28. Brooklyn *Eagle,* 11 September 1849. Quoted in ibid.
29. Brooklyn *Star,* 19 September 1849. Quoted in ibid.
30. Brooklyn *Advertiser,* 4 October 1849. Quoted in ibid., 223–24.

Yet while Whitman was suffering such personal and political setbacks, he was at the same time furthering his interest in the aesthetics and practice of poetry. For just as he had been inspired by Emerson one year earlier, Whitman throughout 1848–49 embarked on a course of reading that would influence the way he thought of himself as a writer and, consequently, the way he would express himself about African Americans and slavery. But the source of this reading now was distinctively un-American. Beginning in late 1848 and lasting through 1849, Whitman became an avid reader of several British reviews, particularly the *North British Review,* the *Edinburgh Review,* and the *Westminster Review,* a liberal journal that was praised by the *Democratic Review,* the American journal to which Whitman occasionally contributed from 1841 to 1847.[31] These British magazines were so popular at the time in the United States that they were pirated in American editions. Whitman made numerous clippings from these American editions, though because he bought some magazines after the original publication date it cannot be said with certainty when he may have read them. Maurice Bucke, a friend and biographer of Whitman, said on Whitman's authority: "These years he used to watch the English quarterlies . . . and when he found an article that suited him he would buy the number, perhaps second-hand, for a few cents, tear it out, and take it with him on his next sea beach excursion to digest."[32]

Whitman's dramatic shift from American to British journals in 1848 has been documented by Floyd Stovall. From 1845 to 1847, Stovall points out, Whitman clipped thirty-five articles from his two favorite American periodicals—the *Democratic Review* and the *Whig Review*—but only one from a British journal. From 1848 to 1849, however, those figures were reversed: he clipped no articles from American journals but thirty-one from British journals. The completeness of this shift indicates Whitman's growing interest in poetry and the poet's vocation. Many of the articles from the American journals, Stovall writes, "would have been useful to a writer of fiction or to a journalist trying to enrich his mind and improve his style," including articles entitled "Words," "On Style," and "Thoughts on Reading."[33] The few articles on poetry Whitman did clip from the American journals seemed to interest him for reasons other than poetry—articles, for example, on a poet's theory of

31. For discussions of Whitman's reading of British journals from 1848 to 1849, see Allen, *The Solitary Singer,* 130–34, and Stovall, *Foreground,* 143–52. In the following discussion, I will cite specific references to each text only where needed for clarification.

32. Maurice Bucke, *Walt Whitman* [1883] (New York: Johnson Reprint Corporation, 1970), 21.

33. Stovall, *Foreground,* 146.

evil. Until 1848, Stovall suggests, Whitman had been reading American journals "to improve his education without much consideration of the end to which it might be put."[34]

But the clippings of British journals from 1848 and after reflect Whitman's growing interest in literary criticism and in the art of poetry. Unlike American magazines, which were largely devoted to entertainment, British journals often included discussions of literature and literary merit. These articles focused on the identity and character of the poet, suggested that the materials of poetry lie in the material universe and the poet's actual experience, and encouraged restraint in the use of metaphors, overused figures, and other conventions. Many of Whitman's annotations show that ideas which scholars thought he derived from Emerson or some other American source could actually have come from these British reviews, though as Gay Wilson Allen points out, "British and American literary theory around 1850 were far more alike than is generally realized."[35] At the very least, what Whitman read in the British journals seemed to confirm and elaborate what he had been reading of Emerson a year earlier.

One of the most important of these articles was a long review essay, "R. M. Milnes' Life of Keats," in the *North British Review* of November 1848. In one of Whitman's annotations to a Keats quotation, he affirms his growing sense that the identity of the poet is unique. Keats had written: "A poet is the most unpoetical of anything in existence, because he has no identity; he is continually in for and filling some other body." To Whitman, who had "filled" the body of conventional poetry, fiction, and journalism with ideas and expressions not truly his own and who was now working to realize an Emersonian self-reliance, the statement called for a response. In a marginal note, he acknowledged that "the great poet" absorbs the identity and experiences of others. But he added that the poet "p[erceives] them all through the powerful press of *himself*" [my emphasis].[36]

Elsewhere Whitman demonstrated his confidence that the individual could not only survive the constraints of convention but even use them to develop as a writer. In a long review of [Sir Henry] "Taylor's Eve of the Conquest" in the April 1849 *Edinburgh Review,* Whitman headed one of the columns "Character." He drew a finger pointing to the re-

---

34. Ibid., 148.

35. Allen, *The Solitary Singer,* 130.

36. Clipped from the *North British Review,* American edition, 10 (November 1848): 39–52. Manuscript 167 of the Trent Collection in the Duke University Library. See *Catalogue of the Whitman Collection . . . Being a Part of the Trent Collection,* 77. Also quoted in Allen, *The Solitary Singer,* 131.

viewer's main arguments for the decline of character, such as, what Allen calls, "standardization, increasing self-consciousness, and the stagnating effect of conventionality."[37] Whitman did not object to this diagnosis, Allen notes, but he wrote in the lower margin that he would "take all these things that produce this condition and make them produce as great characters as any." Whitman affirms, then, that the very soil in which he might decay—the "stagnating effect of conventionality"—might also become the fertile ground for his own growth. He would take the stuff of everyday experience and make it into poetry, but without conventional trappings. Whitman's own experience in New Orleans, for example, had been enriched by his encounters with blacks, some of which would serve as the basis for his models of African Americans in the 1855 *Leaves of Grass*. In a clipping from the April 1849 *Edinburgh Review,* Whitman had emphatically marked a passage that would describe well the composing—or, more accurately, composting—process that produced *Leaves of Grass* six years later:[38]

> In this way minute portions of the past are constantly entering by new combinations into fresh forms of life, and out of these old materials, continually decomposed but continually recombined, scope is afforded for an everlasting succession of imaginative literature.[39]

In late 1849 or early 1850 he may also have read an essay in the October 1849 issue of the British journal *Blackwood's Edinburgh Magazine* that would have encouraged him to think and speak on a grander scale than the concerns of local politics. The essay, "Modern Poetry and Poets," stated concisely what would emerge as Whitman's own sense of poetic vocation: the poet as uniter and reconciler of the disparate factions of the American polis. Whitman underscored the following:

> As a thousand rivulets are blended in one broad river, so the countless instincts, energies, and faculties, as well as associations, traditions, and other social influences which constitute national

37. Clipped from the *Edinburgh Review,* American edition, 89 (April 1849): 183–96. Manuscript 170 of the Trent Collection. See *Catalogue of the Whitman Collection . . . Being a Part of the Trent Collection,* 78. Also quoted in Allen, *The Solitary Singer,* 131.

38. I am indebted to Professor Ed Folsom for the image of composting as a way of understanding Whitman's writing process.

39. Clipped from the *Edinburgh Review,* American edition, 89 (April 1849), 159. Manuscript 175 of the Trent Collection. See *Catalogue of the Whitman Collection . . . Being a Part of the Trent Collection,* 80. Also quoted in Allen, *The Solitary Singer,* 134.

life, are reconciled in him whom future ages are to recognize as the poet of the nation.[40]

Whether Whitman at this point had dreams of being "the poet of the nation," he increasingly felt that he had to find and express his own voice. He underscored from the same article this Emersonian statement: "True genius will soon cast aside whatever is alien to its individual nature."

That the nation needed some sort of reconciliation was no longer in doubt. When President Taylor in his January 1850 message to Congress urged the admission of California immediately and New Mexico soon thereafter, a faction of Southerners threatened disunion. Though disunionists were still in a minority, slave-state delegates had already scheduled their own convention for June. "There is a bad state of things here," said one Illinois congressman. "I fear this Union is in danger."[41]

In an attempt to avert crisis, Henry Clay of Kentucky offered a series of eight compromise resolutions to the Senate on January 29. The ensuing debates on Clay's proposals over the next eight months would, according to James McPherson, become "the most famous in the history of Congress."[42] Clay grouped the eight resolutions in pairs. The first three of these pairs offered a concession to each side. One pair would admit California as a free state yet organize the rest of the territory gained from Mexico without restrictions on slavery. Another would abolish the slave trade in the District of Columbia while guaranteeing the existence of slavery there. Another would settle the border dispute between Texas and New Mexico in a way that would generally satisfy both Northern and Southern interests. The final pair of resolutions, however, seemed to tip the entire package in favor of the South: it would deny congressional power over the interstate slave trade and enact a stringent fugitive slave bill, allowing slaveholders to recover their "property" when slaves fled to free states.

When Whitman learned of Clay's proposals, he judged this latter pair "repugnant," as was the resolution guaranteeing slavery in Washington.[43] Whitman's candidate Thomas Hart Benton labeled the entire bill a capitulation to those who threatened secession. The compromise gained widespread support, however, due to prevailing unionist sentiment in

40. Clipped from the *Edinburgh Review,* American edition, 90 (October 1849): 203–28. Manuscript 159 of the Trent Collection. See *Catalogue of the Whitman Collection . . . Being a Part of the Trent Collection,* 74. Also quoted in Allen, *The Solitary Singer,* 132.
41. Quoted in Potter, *The Impending Crisis,* 89.
42. McPherson, *Battle Cry,* 70.
43. Rubin, *The Historic Whitman,* 246.

the North and South, and Free Soilers, who were largely opposed to the
compromise, soon became the target of those adamant about the bill's
passage. Whitman witnessed a raid on a Free Soil assembly in which the
speakers' platform was deluged with garbage. Another time Reverend
Henry Ward Beecher and Frederick Douglass were heckled until the
persuasive oratory of Samuel Ward restored order. Whitman himself
experienced the wrath of those for compromise. At a meeting in Brooklyn, local Hunkers charged Whitman and eight others with attempting
to create a rebellion against the Democratic party and drove them from
the hall with shouts of "Down with the traitors!"[44]

No longer having access to an editorial venue with which to respond
to Clay's proposals, Whitman turned to satirical verse. "Song for Certain
Congressmen," published in the March 2 *New York Evening Post*,
seeks to build congressional and popular opposition to compromise by
mocking the weakness and opportunism of Northern "dough-faces"—
Congressmen who had supported Wilmot but now supported the compromise. As Whitman and other Free Soilers saw it, these men had simply
surrendered their anti-slavery principles in the face of disunionist threats.
The poem ironically assumes the voice of the congressmen targeted by
Whitman's attack.

> We are all docile dough-faces,
>   They knead us with the fist,
> They, the dashing southern lords,
>   We labor as they list;
> For them we speak—or hold our tongues,
>   For them we turn and twist.
>
>   (*EPF*, 44)

Throughout the poem Whitman apes what he takes to be dough-face
thinking: the desire to "put down [the] 'agitation'" of "'northern fa-
natics'" and "'traitors'"—that is, Free Soilers and abolitionists—and to
"pacify slave-breeding wrath / By yielding all the matter; / For otherwise,
as sure as guns, / The Union it will shatter." The poem bears none of
the marks of the experimental verse Whitman's notebooks suggested
might be imminent. Instead, it is an immediate, visceral response to what
Whitman considers a grave situation, and it draws expediently on the
very poetic conventions he had sought to eschew, employing a simple
iambic meter and rhyming format to express Whitman's rage. The publication of the poem in a daily newspaper rather than, say, a literary

---

44. Ibid., 246–47.

magazine, suggests the broader audience he is hoping to reach and so affects Whitman's rhetorical strategy.

In the poem's penultimate stanza, Whitman exhorts those Northern congressmen whom he fears will come out in support of the compromise.

> Take heart, then, sweet companions,
>   Be steady, Scripture Dick!
> Webster, Cooper, Walker,
>   To your allegiance stick!
> With Brooks, and Briggs and Phoenix,
>   Stand up through thin and thick!
>   (*EPF,* 45)

Joseph Jay Rubin writes that these were men whom Whitman, "based on first-hand knowledge of [their] political maneuvering since 1846," particularly believed to be "docile doughfaces."[45] At the time of the poem, however, only one of them appears to have been clearly in the "dough-face" camp. "Scripture Dick"—New York Senator Daniel Dickinson, a Democrat—had come out against Wilmot at the same time Whitman was fired from the *Eagle* in January 1848 and had firmly been a Hunker ever since.[46] Neither "Cooper" (Pennsylvania Senator James Cooper) nor "Brooks" (New York Representative James Brooks) had spoken in Congress about the slavery issue over the last two years, according to the 1848 to 1850 volumes of the *Congressional Globe.* "Walker" (Wisconsin Senator Isaac Walker) and Daniel Webster would make their views clearly known within a week. Walker did "stand up," arguing on March 6 and 7 against Jefferson Davis's claim about the "natural or divine foundation for slavery" and opposing the extension of slavery into any part of California.[47] Webster took a different stand.

In a March 7 speech before the Senate—later known simply as his "Seventh of March" address—Webster shocked and angered his former anti-slavery admirers and strongly influenced the course of the compromise debates. Speaking "not as a Massachusetts man, nor as a Northern man, but as an American," Webster urged "preservation of the Union" by arguing against legislation that would exclude slavery from the new territories and in favor of a fugitive slave law.[48] Though Webster's speech won him praise from conservatives in the North and South, Free Soilers

45. Rubin, *The Historic Whitman,* 247.
46. Ibid., 179, 222.
47. CG, 31st Cong., 1st sess., appendix, 277–90.
48. CG, 31st Cong., 1st sess., 474–84. Webster's speech may also be found in CG, 31st Cong., 1st sess., appendix, 269–76.

and abolitionists were outraged by what they took to be an act of betrayal. John Greenleaf Whittier captured the sense of a corrupted Webster in his poem "Ichabod":[49]

> So fallen! so lost! the light withdrawn
>   Which once he wore!
> The glory from his gray hairs gone
>   Forevermore!
>
> . . . . . .
>
> All else is gone; from those great eyes
>   The soul has fled;
> When faith is lost, when honor dies,
>   The man is dead![50]

Whitman, too, would choose a biblical theme and the genre of poetry
to excoriate Webster and others like him.[51] In "Blood-Money," published on March 22 in the *New York Tribune Supplement*, Whitman
opens with the image of Jesus betrayed by Judas and suggests the similarity of such betrayal to the 1850 Compromise.

> Of olden time, when it came to pass
> That the beautiful god, Jesus, should finish his work on earth,
> Then went Judas, and sold the divine youth,
> And took pay for his body.
>
> . . . .
>
> The cycles, with their long shadows, have stalk'd silently forward,
> Since those ancient days—many a pouch enwrapping meanwhile

49. The title is from 1 Samuel 4:21, where an Israelite mother, shamed at the birth of
her son during a time of national calamity, names him "Ichabod," meaning "no glory"
or "alas for the glory!" (*The New Oxford Annotated Bible,* 336).
50. John Greenleaf Whittier, "Ichabod," *The Complete Poetical Works of John
Greenleaf Whittier* (Boston: Houghton Mifflin, 1894), 504–5.
51. That Whitman, himself not an orthodox or practicing Christian, should choose a
biblical theme is not altogether surprising. Throughout the slavery debates in Congress,
each side attempted to buttress its position with references to the Bible. Southerners cited
the story of Sarah's maid Hagar, who fled from harsh treatment but was ordered by an
angel to return to her mistress, as evidence of divine authority for the fugitive slave law
(*CG,* 31st Cong., 1st sess., 241). Jefferson Davis engaged in a running battle with several
Northerners when he cited the curse of Canaan to be a slave to Shem as evidence "that
slavery was sanctioned in the Bible, authorized, regulated, and recognized from Genesis
to Revelation" (ibid., 287). Horace Mann of Massachusetts expressed his "most energetic
dissent from those who would justify modern slavery from the Levitical law" (ibid., appendix 219).

Its fee, like that paid for the son of Mary.
And still goes one, saying,
"What will ye give me, and I will deliver this man unto you?"
And they make the covenant, and pay the pieces of silver.

(EPF, 47–48)

"Blood-Money" has received slightly more critical attention than the largely ignored "Song for Certain Congressmen." Yet no commentators seem to have interpreted, much less recognized, the central, compelling image. Who—or what—is meant by Whitman's image of the betrayed Christ, and what are the implications of that image? On one hand, Christ stands in a broadly generalized way for a principled, Free Soil America sold out to Southern interests. Joseph Jay Rubin suggests this when he states, "To the poet who equated democracy with Christianity, the proposed legislation ensured another Calvary."[52] Christ is in some ways like Whitman's *Leaves of Grass* vision of an idealized democratic America: a "beautiful god," a "divine youth," an innocent "deliverer" from the dark past of feudalism and tyranny. Christ's death would presumably translate into the spiritual death of America, bereft of its democratic values. Whitman would even speak of the "ossification" of the American spirit within a few years.

But this interpretation alone is not satisfying. In the poem's second and concluding stanza, Christ is directly addressed as the "brother of slaves" who now bears witness to his own betrayal again, this time as an American slave:

Look forth, deliverer,
Look forth, first-born of the dead,
Over the tree-tops of Paradise;
See thyself in yet-continued bonds,
Toilsome and poor, thou bear'st man's form again,
Thou art reviled, scourged, put into prison,
Hunted from the arrogant equality of the rest;
With staves and swords through the willing servants of authority,
Again they surround thee, mad with devilish spite;
Toward thee stretch the hands of a multitude, like vultures' talons,
The meanest spit in thy face, they smite thee with their palms;
Bruised, bloody, and pinion'd is thy body,
More sorrowful than death is thy soul.

---

52. Rubin, *The Historic Whitman*, 249.

Witness of anguish, brother of slaves,
Not with thy price closed the price of thine image:
And still Iscariot plies his trade.

(*EPF*, 48)

The direct analogy of the suffering of Jesus to the suffering of slaves, especially fugitive slaves ("Thou art reviled, scourged, put into prison, / Hunted from the arrogant equality of the rest") signals a radically new rhetorical strategy for Whitman. Here, for the first time, Whitman not only publicly expresses sympathy for the fugitive slave, but even portrays that slave as a second Christ, captured and tormented by Southerners with "devilish spite."

Nothing he has published so far—with the exception of an 1846 editorial on the slave trade—suggests that his passions about slavery are fueled by concern for blacks. Could this be the first expression of Whitman the poet's egalitarian empathy? Perhaps. It is also likely, however, that Whitman was so outraged by Webster's speech that he was now moved to employ a particular rhetoric on behalf of a broader agenda: in depicting the dehumanization of *fugitive* slaves, Whitman appeals to a coalition of abolitionist and Free Soil forces opposed to the highly contested fugitive slave bill included in Clay's proposals. And yet he does so without calling for the larger abolitionists' agenda, such as emancipation or equality for blacks.

Moreover, despite the vivid and emotional depiction of the suffering of a second Christ, the language of the poem carefully avoids too close of an analogy. Nowhere does Whitman use such terms as "runaway slave," "negro," "hounded slave," or other terms specifically depicting fugitive slaves, as he will later in his poetry. The images here refer only to the suffering of Jesus: "staves and swords through the willing servants of authority," "The meanest spit in thy face, they smite thee with their palms" and so forth. Thus the poem's vagueness, like its symbolism, appeals to two different audiences: Free Soilers angered by Webster's appeal to compromise and abolitionists upset about the capture of a fugitive slave.

Despite the passionate rhetoric of his verse, Whitman and other Free Soilers saw no need to despair about the compromise as late as mid-April. New York Senator William Seward's "higher law" speech in Congress on March 11 had rallied anti-extension forces and served as a strong counterbalance to the appeals of Webster and Calhoun.[53] Seward

53. Calhoun, near the point of death, had his final speech read to the Senate on March 4. In it he condemned what he considered discriminatory legislation favoring the North and warned that if Southern equal rights in the territories and the intersectional balance

declared that emancipation was inevitable and morally right. Not only did the Constitution sanction the power of Congress to exclude slavery from the territories, but also "there is a higher law than the Constitution," the law of God in whose sight all persons are equal. All measures that fortify or extend slavery bring about violence, Seward contended, and all that check it result in peace. Clay's compromise was therefore "radically wrong and essentially vicious."[54] Southern congressmen were outraged by Seward's speech. Clay called it "wild, reckless, and abominable."[55] But a large segment of Northerners felt bolstered by it, as well as by President Taylor's unwavering stand on exclusion of slavery from the new territories.

Then on April 19, over Benton's objection, the Senate authorized a select committee of thirteen members—including six Northerners (Webster, Cass, and Dickinson among them)—to combine all resolutions into an omnibus bill. The idea that Northerners would assist in the passage of this legislation prompted Whitman to write a third editorial verse. In "The House of Friends," which appeared in the June 14, 1850, *New York Tribune*, Whitman again turns to the biblical theme of betrayal for his epigraph and controlling image:

> And one shall say unto him, "What are those wounds in thy hands?" Then he shall answer, "Those with which I was wounded in the house of my friends." (Zechariah 13:6)[56]

Whitman's essential message, delivered in a blistering tone, is that the "death stab" of freedom has come not from its "manlier foes"—Southerners like Calhoun—but from "the house of thy friends" in the North. Whitman spares no invective in describing the Northern betrayers: they are "Doughfaces, Crawlers, Lice of Humanity." His primary rhetorical

---

of power were not restored, disunion was imminent (*CG*, 31st Cong., 1st sess., 451–55). Calhoun died on March 31.

54. *CG*, 31st Cong., 1st sess., appendix, 260–69.

55. Allan Nevins, *Ordeal of the Union* (New York: Scribner, 1947), 1:301–2.

56. Whitman either did not understand the biblical verse within its larger context or assumed his audience would not. Zechariah 13:2–6 describes the oracle of the Lord against professional prophets within the house of Israel. A ritualistic practice of Judaic prophets was self-mutilation: "And they cried aloud, and cut themselves after their custom with swords and lances, until the blood gushed out upon them" (1 Kings 18:28). Here, the oracle of the Lord instructs the professional prophet not to claim credibility through self-mutilation, but rather to admit one's injuries are due to punishment by one's own community. To be "wounded in the house of friends," then, is to be shamed, not betrayed. The nuances apparently were not important to Whitman.

device is to compare these "slaves" of the North with slaves of the South
and to find the former less free.

> Vaunters of the Free,
> Why do you strain your lungs off southward?
> Why be going to Alabama?
> Sweep first before your own door;
> Stop this squalling and this scorn
> Over the mote there in the distance;
> Look well to your own eye, Massachusetts—
> Yours, New-York and Pennsylvania;
> —I would say yours too, Michigan,
> But all the salve, all the surgery
> Of the great wide world were powerless there.
>   (*EPF*, 36)

As in some of his earlier editorials, Whitman transmutes slavery here
from a horrible reality for blacks into a metaphor describing the behavior and condition of whites. Whitman's use of this image supports the
notion that his sympathy for slaves in the previous poem was perhaps
more rhetorical convention than deeply held belief. Moreover, although
the poem also employs the image of the betrayed Jesus as in "Blood
Money," here that betrayal refers not to the selling of slaves but to
America's betrayal by "doughface" congressmen: "Muck-worms, creep-
ing flat to the ground, / A dollar dearer to them than Christ's blessing"
(*EPF*, 36–37). "The House of Friends" concludes with an exhortation
to the "young North"—the "Faithful and few" who are "braver than
warriors"—to "arise," "fight on," and reclaim "Our elder blood [which
now] flows in the veins of cowards." Whitman sees himself, therefore,
as he did in the first issue of the *Freeman*: the spokesman for the vastly
outnumbered vanguard of those seeking to preserve America's founding
principle of freedom.

Whitman's poem did not go unnoticed. The Brooklyn *Advertiser*,
which had published a number of Whitman's short sketches that spring,
quoted part of the poem and noted:

> Here, now, is a specimen of the way one of the young democracy,
> Master Walter Whitman, lays it on to the members of "the party"
> whom he has had the pleasure of knowing—Master Whitman
> has evidently a very poor opinion of his old cronies; but who can
> wonder at that, after he was editor of the Brooklyn *Eagle* so long,
> and saw the operations of the Brooklyn "democracy"? . . . See

how he talks to 'em. (Brooklyn *Advertiser*, 22 June 1850. Quoted in *UPP* 1:26.)

Despite Whitman's increasing anger, he had not altogether lost hope. The fourth and final poem written during the compromise debates demonstrates his continuing faith that the cause of freedom—a universal, and not merely American, phenomenon—will ultimately triumph. "Resurgemus," published June 21, 1850, in the *New York Tribune,* pays tribute to the European martyrs of 1848 to 1849 who set off the revolutionary uprisings in France, Austria, Hungary, Germany, and Italy. Though the poem bitterly acknowledges the defeat of these revolutions, it proclaims one of Whitman's central beliefs:

> Not a grave of those slaughtered ones,
> But is growing its seed of freedom,
> In its turn to bear seed,
> Which the winds shall carry afar and resow,
> And the rain nourish.
> . . . .
> Liberty, let others despair of thee,
> But I will never despair of thee:
> Is the house shut? Is the master away?
> Nevertheless, be ready, be not weary of watching,
> He will surely return; his messengers come again.
>
> (*EPF,* 39–40)

The belief that the corpses of the martyred dead bear the seeds of a future freedom would later translate into Whitman's redemptive interpretation of the Civil War. Here that belief also implicitly expresses Whitman's faith that despite the impending setback of a compromise measure on slavery, liberty cannot ultimately be defeated. "Resurgemus" is the first of Whitman's poems to be included among the twelve untitled poems of the 1855 *Leaves of Grass,* though its specifically political content and sometimes conventionally "poetic" diction make it more similar to its predecessor poems in 1850 than to *Leaves of Grass.*

Taken together, then, Whitman's four 1850 poems grow out of a complex set of factors: the tension between his increasing anger at the turn of events toward compromise and his persistent faith in the triumph of freedom and Free Soil; his swift reaction to specific events regarding the slavery issue; his lack of another writing venue; and the influence of various texts with which he was familiar—editorials, congressional speeches, and the Bible. Yet for all these influences, and especially taking into account that Whitman had three years earlier begun his new experiments in poetry, the poems of 1850 are hardly less conventional than either *Franklin Evans* or his free soil editorials. Some critics have suggested that "Blood Money" and "The House of Friends" demonstrate Whitman's gradual evolution toward the style of *Leaves of Grass*. Paul Zweig, for example, feels that "Blood Money" has begun to "mutate" toward a "new tone and a new precision of diction," and he finds the language of "The House of Friends" as "the very dividing line" between "inflated editorial" and Whitman's 1855 verse.[57] But even Zweig admits that the voice of these poems "is still a voice from the press."[58] These poems are heavily dependent on biblical allusion and ponderous language that recollect Whitman's early fiction ("Curs'd was the deed, even before the sweat of the clutching hand grew dry," Whitman writes in "Blood Money"). What *is* striking, however, is that despite the conventional tone and diction, Whitman has at least worked the slavery issue into the shape of poetry. And in at least one case that has produced something new: sympathy for the slaves. This slight transformation alone might not seem significant, except that it is the very joining of this radically new sympathy for the slave and the genre of poetry that marks the 1855 *Leaves of Grass* as unique in terms of Whitman's racial rhetoric.

Why Whitman would not write poetry—or much else, for that matter—for another five years can best be understood in the context of national events that summer. After the omnibus bill stalled in Congress and was defeated on July 31, Illinois Senator Stephen A. Douglas took over management of the bill from a beleaguered Clay. By breaking the bill down into component parts that could each gain a majority, Douglas rather quickly won passage of the 1850 Compromise. From mid-August to mid-September Congress passed five separate bills: the admission of California, the adjustment of the Texas border, the organization of the New Mexico and Utah territories without restrictions on slavery, the enactment of a stringent fugitive slave law, and the prohibition of slave trade in Washington, D.C. On every issue, divisions occurred along sectional rather than party lines, signaling the impending demise of the existing two-party system. The compromise was achieved only because a bloc of Northern Democrats and upper-South Whigs supported each bill, and many Northerners abstained on the bills pertaining to Utah, New Mexico, and fugitive slaves. The fugitive slave bill, the least-

57. Zweig, *Walt Whitman*, 119–20. See also Erkkila, *The Political Poet*, 53–59.
58. Zweig, *Walt Whitman*, 120.

debated part of the Compromise, would turn out to be the most divisive issue of the settlement.[59]

Meanwhile President Zachary Taylor died suddenly on July 9, and the new President, Millard Fillmore, a New Yorker, worked for the passage of the Compromise and pronounced it "a final settlement" of all sectional problems.[60] Most Americans supported the Compromise, though Southerners more than Northerners regarded it as a victory. Only the political "extremes"—Calhounites in the South and abolitionists and Free Soilers in the North—challenged its finality. Among New York Free Soilers, however, many of the leaders accepted the Compromise and, according to Eric Foner, "expressed the hope that agitation of the slavery question was at an end."[61] In New York City, a pro-Union meeting was called by prominent merchants and ten thousand names were signed to a resolution approving the Compromise measures.[62] With anti-slavery hopes at a nadir, the Free Soil party of Kings County—Whitman's home—disbanded.[63]

Whitman clearly did not share in the enthusiasm for the Compromise. After spending the summer at his sister's home in Greenport, Whitman returned to Brooklyn in the fall and wrote three letters for the Free Soil journal *National Era,* including one in which he vented that "the cause of Hunkerism and slavery must go down. It may be years yet; but it *must* go."[64] But that was the last to be heard from Whitman on political issues until the mid-1850s. Whitman's sudden leave-taking of the arenas of politics and journalism shortly after passage of the 1850 Compromise lead one to believe that the compromise was a central, if not overriding, cause of his disenchantment and change of direction. The series of battles that he and other ardent Free Soilers had been waging since 1846 now had ended. While previous defeats had been temporary setbacks, the Compromise rang with a finality that even the eternally optimistic Whitman could not ignore.

59. See James M. McPherson, *Battle Cry,* 75–76.
60. Nevins, 1:345–46.
61. Foner, *Politics and Ideology,* 89.
62. See Stanley W. Campbell, *The Slave Catchers: Enforcement of the Fugitive Slave Law, 1850–1860* (Chapel Hill: University of North Carolina Press, 1970), 56.
63. Rubin, *The Historic Whitman,* 254.
64. Rollo G. Silver, "Whitman in 1850: Three Uncollected Articles," *American Literature* 19 (1948): 303.

5

AN AUDIENCE AT LAST

The five years leading up to the publication of *Leaves of Grass* in 1855 are among the most important, and least understood, in Whitman scholarship. Little is known about Whitman because so few texts by him or records about him exist. He published no poetry during this time and only a few journalistic pieces in 1851. Whitman himself provides few clues to this period of his life. In the autobiographical *Specimen Days* he notes merely: "'51, '53 occupied in house-building in Brooklyn" (*CP*, 705).

Yet during this time a peculiar coalescing of forces and events centered upon the nation's divided response to slavery would inspire Whitman to develop the radical new poetry about African Americans he had first begun in 1847. Little that he did or wrote in these years would seem to have much bearing on either his racial attitudes or his poetry. But when the nation erupted in 1854 over the Kansas-Nebraska Act and the case of the fugitive slave Anthony Burns, the long foreground of Whitman's deep interest in slavery well prepared him for a poetic response that would, at long last, find an audience. For having failed earlier to move his newspaper readers on slavery, Whitman was now encouraged, even compelled, by the changing national mood to express in his poetry a radical egalitarianism and sympathy for blacks. Thus liberated, Whitman could feel free to publish ideas about blacks and slavery that only a few years earlier would seem like abolitionist extremism. Whitman's own rhetorical emancipation on slavery may well have opened the doors to the wider range of ideas and language experiments he had been working on for eight years. When *Leaves of Grass* emerged in 1855, much of Whitman's new poetry would seem strange. But the ideas about blacks and slavery, more central than contemporary readers have imagined, would strike a responsive chord in many. To understand how these transformations in Whitman and his readers took place, we must examine carefully this little understood time in Whitman's life.

Following the disappointment of the 1850 Compromise, Whitman did not altogether forego politics, as might be supposed, but rather converted his political passions into an increasing interest in art. Whitman's involvement in the visual arts is an important, though often overlooked, influence on the form and content of *Leaves of Grass*.[1] Beginning already in 1849, at about the time he took a strong interest in questions of aesthetic and literary values in British journals, Whitman discussed the visual arts with increasing knowledge and sophistication in his journalistic writings. Whitman himself attached great importance in this shift toward the arts, telling Horace Traubel a few years before his death that he preferred the company of artists to writers as he composed the first edition of *Leaves of Grass*.[2] Like Whitman, many artists at mid-century were deeply involved in the social and political issues of the day. And like Whitman, they grappled with the problems of direction and self-definition, asking themselves what it meant to be an American artist and how one could integrate art effectively into the fabric of a democratic and heterogeneous society.

Whitman's friendship with the photographer Gabriel Harrison and his affiliation with the Brooklyn Art Union in the early 1850s illuminate the importance of his turn toward the visual arts. Harrison was a painter, poet, short story writer, and actor. And, like Whitman, he was also a liberal democrat who had been active in the Free Soil campaign of 1848–49, serving as president of Manhattan's fourteenth ward Free Soil League, but who had turned toward the arts following the defeat of the Free Soil party. In the early 1850s Harrison vigorously promoted various art causes in Brooklyn, working diligently to foster a democratic basis for the arts by supporting local art initiatives (including the short-lived Brooklyn Art Union), staging dramatic performances, and generally attempting to open the arts to a wider audience. According to Ruth Bohan, Harrison represented for Whitman "the successful merger of art

1. For an excellent discussion of the development and influence of Whitman's interest in the arts, see Ruth Bohan, "'The Gathering of the Forces': Walt Whitman and the Visual Arts, 1845–55," *The Mickle Street Review* 12 (1990): 10–30.

2. Traubel, *With Walt Whitman*, 2:502.

and politics and a model of the democratic spirit which motivated all his later writing."[3] In addition, Harrison's commitment to the promotion of photography as a fine art both provided Whitman with a photographic approach to poetry (as in his experimental poem "Pictures," discussed below) and suggested to Whitman the necessity of pushing his own art beyond conventional boundaries.

Without abandoning his commitment to pressing social and political issues, such as slavery, Whitman followed Harrison in the early 1850s by shifting his focus toward the arts, and particularly toward involvement in the newly formed Brooklyn Art Union. The Brooklyn Art Union, like others at the time, was modeled after the highly successful American Art Union, a New York gallery opened in 1838 that strove to stimulate interest in a national art expression through changing exhibitions of works devoted to American subjects produced by American artists. Whitman was highly supportive of the Brooklyn Art Union following its opening in late 1849, publishing three lengthy articles on art over a ten-month period in 1850–51. These articles constitute his initial efforts at formulating a comprehensive theory of the arts that for the first time in Whitman's career "placed the artist above the politician as society's moral and spiritual leader."[4] Artists were distinguished by the "life-giving quality" of their work, Whitman felt. In an article on painting he wrote that no matter the genre, "landscape, historical composition, portrait, comic group, even still life, it is the *spiritual* part of it you want above all the rest. That is its soul, its animose, and makes live art" (my emphasis).[5]

Several times in the past Whitman had stressed the social significance of the arts and had urged support of local arts groups. But not until this time did his comments demonstrate a clear sense that his own calling was shifting from politics to the arts. On the strength of Whitman's three published articles, the Brooklyn Art Union invited him to present the keynote address at its annual distribution of prizes on March 31, 1851. In his opening remarks, Whitman made clear the connection between his disgust with the drift of American society and his own desire to create something lasting and beautiful.

> Among such people as the Americans, viewing most things with
> an eye to pecuniary profit—more for acquiring than for enjoying

3. Bohan, "'The Gathering of the Forces,'" 13.

4. Ibid., 16.

5. Walt Whitman, "Brooklyn Art Union—Walter Libbey—A Hint or Two on the Philosophy of Painting," *Brooklyn Daily Advertiser,* 21 December 1850. Quoted in Bohan, 17.

. . .—ambitious of the physical rather than the intellectual; a race to whom matter of fact is everything, and the ideal nothing—a nation of whom the steam engine is no bad symbol—he does a good work who, pausing in the way, calls to the feverish crowd that in the life we live upon this beautiful earth, there may, after all, be something vaster and better than dress and the table, and business and politics. (*UPP* 1:241)

That artistic calling, something "vaster and better than . . . business and politics," would require of Whitman a willingness to stand apart from the conventions of a society that he felt had become spiritually moribund. In an earlier article he had praised his artist friends as "warm, impulsive souls, instinctively generous and genial," contrasting them with "the orthodox sons and daughters of the world." He hoped that it would not be "an absolute miracle, if a man differ from the present dead uniformity of 'society' in appearance and opinion, and still retain his grace and morals."[6] Whitman's passionate democratic yearnings, then, were not dead but rather were transferred to the artistic forum where the creator or poet might stand outside of political disappointments. For Whitman dreamed of an organization of young artists—"a close phalanx, ardent, radical and progressive"—who would "foster the growth of a grand and true art here, fresh and youthful, worthy this republic."[7]

Perhaps Whitman already hoped for himself the heroic role of the great artist. Later that year Whitman's notations of passages in journals suggest he was gaining artistic confidence and narrowing his focus. In an *American Whig Review* article on John Keats, he underlined the sentence, "If his genius is epical, but one theme will occur to him in the entire course of his life."[8] And from an article in the *Democratic Review*, Whitman underlined the following:

To continue striving at numerous kinds of composition, only proves continued immaturity, or a prurient vanity, which baffles concentration, and, though it may provoke the passing wonder of contemporaries, will scarcely ever be able to command the lasting honours of posterity.[9]

6. Walt Whitman, "Something About Art and Brooklyn Artists," *New York Evening Post*, 1 February 1851, *UPP* 1:237.

7. Ibid.

8. Clipped from the *American Whig Review*, n.s., 8 (October 1851): 317–22. See *Catalogue of the Whitman Collection*, 72–73. Quoted in Allen, *The Solitary Singer*, 133.

9. Ibid. Quoted in Allen, *The Solitary Singer*, 134.

Whitman took this advice seriously: from this time on he would not "continue striving at numerous kinds of composition" but would focus almost exclusively on poetry, writing only an occasional piece of journalism until the 1855 publication of *Leaves of Grass.*

Meanwhile, Whitman continued to remain an adamant supporter of Free Soil, despite the relative success and popularity of the 1850 Compromise. A series of highly publicized fugitive slave cases rallied some Northern anger, but by midsummer 1851 most of the agitation over the Fugitive Slave Law had subsided and the political landscape for the first time in five years remained calm.[10] The *Boston Courier* reported that despite efforts by radical Northerners to arouse opposition, public opinion had "settled into general and hearty acquiescence" of the Compromise, now regarded as a "final settlement."[11] In the fall, New York Democrats who pledged their support for the Compromise were victorious in local elections, and by the end of the year the Free Soil party was all but dead except in New England, Ohio, and Wisconsin. Across the nation, Union sentiment prevailed.

Nevertheless, a number of Northerners continued to resent the Fugitive Slave Law. They were outraged that federal troops could enter local communities and take a black person living freely on Northern soil back to the South. In August 1852 the "Free Democrats"—an amalgamation of remaining Free Soilers and abolitionists still fighting compromise—held their national convention in Pittsburgh. They denounced the two major parties and called for the repeal of the Fugitive Slave Law, deriding it as "repugnant" to the Constitution, common law, and the spirit of Christianity.[12] The angry radicalism of the convention was typified by Frederick Douglass, who told the delegates that the only way to make the Fugitive Slave Law a dead letter was "to make a half dozen or more dead kidnappers carried down South."[13]

Whitman remained in Brooklyn but followed the proceedings through detailed telegrams in the New York press. When Senator John Parker Hale of New Hampshire, an ardent Free Soiler, declined the nomination for President, Whitman wrote to him on August 14, urging him to reverse his decision. Whitman's letter demonstrates that though he was quiet during this time, his political convictions—and idealistic hopes—remained as passionate as ever. Whitman tells Hale that the Pittsburgh

10. See McPherson, *Battle Cry,* 81–88, and Campbell, *The Slave Catchers,* 63.

11. Quoted in Campbell, *The Slave Catchers,* 63.

12. For a description of the convention of Free Democrats and Whitman's response to it, see Rubin, *The Historic Whitman,* 273.

13. Philip S. Foner, *The Life and Writings of Frederick Douglass* (New York: International Publishers, 1950–55), 2:207.

platform may produce "a real live Democratic party," which, from small beginnings "like Jeffersonian democracy fifty years ago," will bring forth "an American Democracy with thews and sinews worthy this sublime age." Whitman asserts: "It is from the young men of our land—the ardent, and generous hearts—that these things are to come." He urges Hale to "look to the young men," and claims his own special knowledge of them:

> You are at Washington, and have for years moved among the great men. I have never been at Washington, and know none of the great men. But I know the people. I know well, (for I am practically in New York,) the real heart of this mighty city—the tens of thousands of young men, the mechanics, the writers, &c, &c. In all these, under and behind the bosh of regular politicians, there burns, almost with fierceness, the divine fire which more or less, during all ages, has only waited a chance to leap forth and confound the calculations of tyrants, hunkers, and all their tribe. At this moment, New York is the most radical city in America. It would be the most anti-slavery city, if that cause hadn't been made ridiculous by the freaks of the local leaders here.[14]

In this brief paragraph Whitman summarizes the essential ingredients of his continuing political ideology. Driven by his love of the working classes and confident of the "divine fire" of their passion for revolutionary democracy, Whitman hopefully asserts the "radical" nature of New York City politics. This labor-oriented focus leads Whitman also to surmise that New York "would be the most anti-slavery city" if not for "the freaks of the local leaders." In other words, New York would be a "free soil" city if not for Hunker and pro-Compromise politicians. Though it does not explicitly refer to "free soil," Whitman's appeal to Hale is implicitly rooted in the Free Soil position of the 1847 Wilmot editorials.

The persistent hopefulness of Whitman's vision is striking, as is his boldness in assuming that a letter from an ex-journalist turned journeyman carpenter would have some effect. And yet his words had a convincing ring. One historian notes that Whitman's letter "may have had an effect, for on September 6, 1852, Hale wrote the convention president Henry Wilson, formally accepting the Free Democratic nomination."[15]

14. Walt Whitman, *The Correspondence,* ed. Edwin Haviland Miller (New York: New York University Press, 1961), 39–40.

15. Richard Sewall, "Walt Whitman, John Parker Hale, and Free Democracy," *New England Quarterly* 34 (1961): 241.

Hale garnered only 156,000 votes that fall, but the significance of Whitman's letter goes well beyond Hale's candidacy. It demonstrates, at the very least, that Whitman was politically alive and well, and that his passion for free soil was as sure as ever.

Whitman's continuing commitment to free soil and his growing interest in the development of his art would seem to have little in common. Yet it is the very coalescing of these seemingly unrelated elements that will prepare him to respond to the passions that will shortly erupt over slavery. For beneath the seeming calm about slavery in the early 1850s there existed a volatile and unsettled public mood. On one hand, conventionally racist attitudes against blacks were bolstered by so-called "scientific" findings about race, and by the acts of several state legislatures to entirely exclude blacks—slave or free. On the other hand, an entirely different set of attitudes moved many Northerners to accept the sympathetic images of beleaguered and suffering slaves in *Uncle Tom's Cabin.* Published in the spring of 1852, Harriet Beecher Stowe's work sold more than three hundred thousand copies in the United States in the first year alone. As Eric Sundquist states, Stowe "may have captured the welling emotions of a guilty nation poised for cathartic release."[16] In the North, the story of the brutal Simon Legree and the long-suffering Tom served to "crystallize antislavery feeling" more than any other published work in the 1850s, according to George Fredrickson.[17] In the South, reaction to the book was equally strong. Whitman's former employer, the *New Orleans Crescent,* declared that "never before was anything so detestable or so monstrous among women as this."[18]

Stowe's work not only elicited the divided passions of North and South but indicated as well the persistence of an ambivalent Northern response to the race "problem" that defined part of the broader spectrum of racial attitudes in the early 1850s. George Fredrickson calls *Uncle Tom's Cabin* "the classic expression of romantic racialism," the idea that blacks were essentially different from whites, though supposedly not inferior.[19] The book demonstrates the "hard and dominant" characteristics of the Anglo-Saxon race and, in Stowe's words, the "confessedly

16. Eric Sundquist, "Slavery, Revolution, and the American Rennaisance," *The American Renaissance Reconsidered,* ed. Walter Benn Michaels and Donald E. Pease (Baltimore: Johns Hopkins University Press, 1985), 18. Sundquist goes on to point out, however, that though the novel "strengthened political resolve in some quarters," its more immediate effect was to produce a flood of sentimental items—"melodrama, graveyard poetry, popular songs, dioramas, engravings, gift books, card games, etc. . . . Sentiment, not antislavery, made the book popular" (18).

17. Fredrickson, *The Black Image in the White Mind,* 110.

18. Quoted in McPherson, *Battle Cry,* 90.

19. Fredrickson, *The Black Image in the White Mind,* 110.

more simple, docile, child-like and affectionate" characteristics of "the Negro."[20] Uncle Tom, for example, though not a typical slave, manifests such qualities as "gentleness" and the "facility of forgiveness."

Stowe's response to the evil of slavery articulated the sentiments of a growing portion of Northern humanitarians struggling yet to resolve the paradox of slaves on American soil. Particularly appealing was her call for black emancipation and colonization. Such thinking was fairly common in the early 1850s, which saw a general resurgence of an interest in colonizationist schemes popularized in the 1820s and 1830s. At the end of her work Stowe advocates the romantic racialist notion that blacks could return to Africa, morally and intellectually developed with the help of the church:

> To fill up Liberia with an ignorant, inexperienced, half-barbarized race, just escaped from the chains of slavery, would be only to prolong, for ages, the period of struggle and conflict which attends the inception of new enterprises. Let the Church of the north receive these poor sufferers in the spirit of Christ; receive them to the educating advantages of Christian republican society and schools, until they have attained to somewhat of a moral and intellectual maturity, and then assist them in their passage to those shores, where they may put in practice the lessons they have learned in America.[21]

Uncle Tom's Cabin was only one of several anti-slavery novels of the period that advocated the process of emancipation, education, and colonization as a long-range solution. Some Free Soilers supported colonization but for reasons different than Stowe's. In an 1853 *New York Tribune* editorial Horace Greeley defended colonization on the ground that African Americans must prove themselves abroad before aspiring to American citizenship. Others in the Free Soil press chided free blacks for their lack of realism in insisting on their full rights as American citizens instead of accepting voluntary emigration.[22] William Cullen Bryant, though opposed to compulsory colonization, praised the Colonization Society and the Anti-Slavery Society in his newspaper, the *New York Evening Post,* for "contemplating, in different ways, the good of

20. Harriet Beecher Stowe, *A Key to Uncle Tom's Cabin* (Boston: J. P. Jewett, Cleveland: Jewett, Proctor, and Worthington, 1853), 25. Quoted in Fredrickson, *The Black Image in the White Mind,* 111.

21. Harriet Beecher Stowe, *Uncle Tom's Cabin* (New York: New American Library, 1981), 473–74.

22. See Fredrickson, *The Black Image in the White Mind,* 147.

the African race."[23] Bryant and other Northern humanitarians believed that the separation of the races could be more likely achieved through the gradual migration of blacks southward. Belief in "natural" migration had long been an article of faith among political abolitionists and Free Soilers, according to George Fredrickson.[24] Gamaliel Bailey, editor of the Free Soil *National Era,* wrote that African Americans would naturally migrate to the tropics, leaving whites to occupy "the more temperate regions."[25] Free Soiler Salmon Chase wrote Frederick Douglass in 1850 that he was opposed to discrimination against blacks but "looked forward to the separation of the races" on the newly emerging theory that blacks and whites were adapted to different latitudes.[26]

Such race theories, though often benevolent in impulse, were but one small step removed from—and, in some cases, grew out of—a "scientific" racism then gaining popularity both North and South. The primary advocate of this new thinking was the pro-slavery apologist Dr. Josiah Nott, who in 1850 presented his "findings" in what he unapologetically called "niggerology" to the Southern Rights Association in Mobile.[27] Extending the theory of "polygenesis" advanced twenty years earlier by Dr. Charles Caldwell, Nott contended that blacks were innately inferior because of their separate origin from whites. He described Caucasians as having "in all ages been the rulers" and other, "inferior" races as due for gradual extinction.[28] As Fredrickson notes, "Nott was arguing less from the supposed facts of craniology or Egyptology than from a domestic white-racialist view of history, of the kind then coming into fashion all over the world as a justification not only for slavery but for imperial expansion."[29]

This new ethnology soon gained a popular following in the North as well as in the South. Many Northern whites welcomed the biological theory of a separate and inferior Negro species, both for psychological reasons and because it reinforced their sense of a Herrenvolk democracy.

23. *New York Evening Post,* 23 May and 30 July 1851. Quoted in Foner, *Politics and Ideology,* 90.

24. Fredrickson, *The Black Image in the White Mind,* 153.

25. *National Era,* 22 March 1849. Quoted in ibid.

26. Quoted in Hans L. Trefousse, *The Radical Republicans: Lincoln's Vanguard for Racial Justice* (New York: Alfred A. Knopf, 1969), 29.

27. For an excellent discussion of mid-century "scientific" approaches to race, see Fredrickson, *The Black Image in the White Mind,* chapter 3, "Science, Polygenesis, and the Proslavery Argument," 70–96.

28. J. C. Nott and George R. Gliddon, eds. *Types of Mankind: Or Ethnological Researches . . .* (Philadelphia: J. B. Lippincott, Grambo and Co., 1854), 79. Quoted in ibid., 79.

29. Fredrickson, *The Black Image in the White Mind,* 79.

The leading Northern proponent of "scientific" racism, Dr. John H. Van Evrie, linked slavery to a radical conception of white democracy in his 1853 work, *Negroes and Negro "Slavery."* Like Whitman in at least these ways, Van Evrie attacked all class distinctions among whites, predicted the triumph of democracy in Europe, and denounced the oppression of the working classes. Moreover, he appealed to part of the same audience that Whitman was always hoping to reach: socially insecure whites in search of a sense of identity that could help make the existing social and economic systems more tolerable.[30]

The new scientific racism was readily received in the Northern press. Bryant's *New York Evening Post,* for example, bluntly asserted that the white race was superior to blacks. In 1853 it published a series of articles on a "scientific" study of the Negro race—perhaps Nott's or Van Evrie's—which concluded that the Negro was by nature "indolent, mentally inferior, and 'hardly capable of elevating himself to the height of civilization.'" (Nonetheless, the *Post* concluded, the Negro was a man, and slavery was an abuse of his humanity.)[31] Moreover, this newly acceptable racism perhaps played a role in the passage of new, racially exclusivist legislation as state legislatures in the Midwest attempted to solve the "Negro problem." In 1851 Indiana prohibited all blacks— slave or free—from entering the state, and Illinois followed suit in 1853.

Whitman's own attitudes about blacks at this time mirrored those of a large segment of the Northern population. Like many others, Whitman subscribed to the stereotypically racist images of blacks then being purveyed in contemporary art and theater. In an 1851 writing on Brooklyn artists, Whitman admired a portrait of "a Long Island negro, the winner of a goose at a raffle." But given the choice between this portrait and that of a white boy with his flute, Whitman would choose the latter because it "has a character of Americanism about it." Though he acknowledged that the "negro" in the portrait "may be said to have a character of Americanism, too," Whitman "never could, and never will, admire the exemplifying of our national attributes with Ethiopian minstrelsy . . . as the best and highest we can do in that way."[32]

Whitman had long been a fan of "negro minstrelsy" on the New York stage. In the 1840s and early 1850s he often watched Dan Rice, whom he later recalled as "the original 'Jim Crow' at the old Park Theatre filling up the gap in some short bill." Whitman felt that "the wild chants and dances were admirable—probably ahead of anything since" (*CP,*

30. Ibid., 92–93.
31. Quoted in Foner, *Politics and Ideology,* 91.
32. Walt Whitman, "Something About Art and Brooklyn Artists," *New York Evening Post,* 1 February 1851, *UPP* 1:238.

1290). Such shows were enormously popular at this time as white Americans reveled in the racist, exotic depiction of blacks by white actors. Not one theater owner "in six . . . could fill his house unless he infused a dash of darkness in the drama," according to the *Literary World*.[33] But by the turn of the decade such shows had been so successful that a flood of "crude burlesques" and cheap imitations were thought by Whitman to have ruined the "quality" of African minstrelsy. Whitman asked in a January 1852 review: "How can such an intellectual people as the Americans really are, countenance before them the nigger monstrosities . . . who appear before us from time to time?"[34]

Yet at the same time that Whitman accepted a certain conventional image of blacks, he was struggling in his poetry experiments to develop images that would break free from perceptions and attitudes about blacks he had held his entire life. Two poetic experiments from his notebooks of this period demonstrate this tension as he attempts more sympathetically to represent black character and experience. The dating of these two texts—the unpublished poem "Pictures" and the poetic fragment of "the hunted slave," which would appear in "Song of Myself"—is, at best, problematic.[35] Yet through a careful examination of these texts it is possible to suggest a likely scenario of Whitman's developing poetic response to blacks and slavery prior to the important events of 1854, events that would transform the racial thinking of both Whitman and his readers.

"Pictures," an experimental poem from late 1853 or early 1854, suggests both the conflicting voices of the antebellum North in response to blacks as well as the tension in Whitman himself between conventionally racist perceptions and an attempt to transcend those perceptions.[36] "Pictures" is the first work that closely anticipates the long-line, catalogue style and the fluid, associative movement of the poems in *Leaves of Grass*. It consists of more than one hundred fifty randomly ordered "pictures" held together structurally only by the notion that all of these images hang suspended in the "picture house" of the poet's imagination:

33. Quoted in Rubin, *The Historic Whitman*, 278.
34. *The Brooklyn Star*, 23 January 1852. Quoted in ibid.
35. *Notebooks* editor Edward F. Grier repeatedly emphasizes the speculative nature of dating Whitman's notebooks, saying, for example, "I am not dogmatic about my conjectural dates" (1:xix).
36. Grier dates "Pictures" in "1855 at the earliest" (4:295). Paul Zweig cites "Pictures" as the beginning of Whitman's serious work on his book of poems which began in "1853 or 1854" (202–3). Allen dates "Pictures" as "not more than two or three years before the first *Leaves of Grass*" (144). For reasons that will become apparent—most important, the evidence of Whitman's development in his depictions of blacks in the early 1850s—I subscribe to an 1853 or early 1854 date.

> In a little house pictures I keep, many pictures
> hanging suspended—It is not a fixed house,
> It is round—it is but a few inches from one side
> of it to the other side,
> But behold! it has room enough—in it, hundreds
> and thousands,—all the varieties. . . .
> (*NUPM* 4:1296)

The scenes described throughout the poem approximate the range and types commonly found in large nineteenth-century exhibitions like those sponsored by the Brooklyn Art Union: historical scenes, portraits of famous and unknown personages, still lifes, bucolic landscapes, and urban and rural genre scenes. With little space separating one from another, "the painted images physically surrounded the spectator to create a cacophony of visual and intellectual stimuli."[37] More important for our purposes, "Pictures" includes four conflicting, highly charged "pictures" of African Americans. The four portraits largely reinforce dominant antebellum stereotypes and cultural attitudes toward blacks. But at the same time, the variety of these images suggests Whitman is thinking of African Americans in a broader, and perhaps more humane, way than he had in his journalistic writing, which tended to all but ignore blacks.

Since the poem is an accumulation of randomly ordered images, Whitman's four passages about blacks may be examined in isolation from their immediate context. Two of these passages are conventional antebellum perceptions of blacks drawn more from popular stereotypes than from an understanding of African Americans' human condition. In one, Whitman draws the brief picture of a scene that might have been familiar to him on the streets of Brooklyn:

> And here an old black man, stone-blind, with a placard on his hat, sits low at the corner, of a street, begging, humming hymn-tunes nasally all day to himself and receiving small gifts. . . .
> (*NUPM* 4:1304)

The speaker's attitude here is neutral, somewhere between sympathy and derision, though the visual details suggest a certain stereotype. While this portrait seems unimportant, its later connection to *Leaves of Grass* will demonstrate emphatically just how far Whitman will come in identifying with the black person's experience.

---

37. Bohan, "'The Gathering of the Forces,'" 24–25.

A second portrait from "Pictures" shows how inextricably embedded Whitman was in the racism of his culture even as he may have been seeking to liberate himself from it. The brief portrait of a slave work-gang stereotypically rehearses the worst of a black person's supposed traits:

> And here are my slave-gangs, South, at work upon the roads, the women indifferently with the men—see, how clumsy, hideous, black, pouting, grinning, sly, besotted, sensual, shameless. . . (*NUPM* 4:1302)

Whitman may have been slightly revising a scene he remembered from his 1848 trip to New Orleans. "Long monotonous stretch of the Mississippi," he writes in a notebook. "Planter's dwelling surrounded with their hamlets of negro huts—groves of negro men women and children in the fields, hoeing the young cotton" (*Notebooks* 1:85). But it is also likely that he was drawing upon images of blacks he had gleaned from the popular press, just as he had done earlier in *Franklin Evans*. Whitman's description echoes Thomas Jefferson's accounting of black traits in *Notes on the State of Virginia* and so demonstrates the historical consistency of racial stereotypes in American culture. Whitman's "clumsy, hideous, black" language corresponds to Jefferson's notion that white features were preferable to the "eternal monotony" of the "immoveable veil of black." Whitman's sense that blacks are "sensual, shameless" essentially repeats Jefferson's idea that the affection of black men toward women seems to be "more an eager desire, than a tender delicate mixture of sentiment and sensation."[38] Whitman's passage also suggests a proprietary, plantation-owner attitude toward blacks: they are "*my* slave-gangs" (my emphasis).

Yet two other passages from "Pictures," looked at in conjunction with the later "hunted slave" fragment, show Whitman expressing a more humane and sympathetic response in his portrayal of blacks. The first of these passages from "Pictures" depicts a black person as a "Lucifer" or "denied God," an image that will be repeated in *Leaves of Grass:*

> And this black portrait—this head, huge, frowning, sorrowful,—
>   is Lucifer's portrait—the denied God's portrait.
> But I do not deny him—though cast out and rebellious,
>   he is my God as much as any.)
>
> (*NUPM* 4:1300)

---

38. Jefferson, *Notes on the State of Virginia*, 138.

How Whitman came to equate a black person with "Lucifer" cannot be easily explained. "Lucifer," meaning "light giver," is the name tradition-ally given to the beautiful and proud archangel who, after seeking equal-ity with God, was cast down from heaven to earth.[39] Perhaps "Lucifer" was a recognizable trope among abolitionists and others for black slaves, but the image did not survive in texts from this period. Whitman likely knew of "Lucifer" from the depiction of the vengeful Satan in Milton's *Paradise Lost.*[40]

Whitman's Lucifer, a figure he later included in "The Sleepers," evokes a central contradiction in the white response to slaves and slavery. On one hand, Lucifer is a vengeful rebel, one whose very existence threatens the stability of the social order. Throughout the nineteenth century white Americans, especially Southerners, feared the possibility of a race war. Alexis de Tocqueville noted that "the danger of a conflict between the white and the black inhabitants of the Southern states of the Union (a danger which, however remote it may be, is inevitable) perpetually haunts the imagination of the Americans, like a painful dream."[41] Whit-man himself played on that fear with the character of the murderous Margaret in *Franklin Evans.* Yet on the other hand, Lucifer's revolt here is justified. He is a "denied God," one cast out from his rightful place in the community, according to the speaker. "I do not deny him—though cast out and rebellious, he is my God as much as any." Moreover, this Lucifer looks more like an iconographic image of Christ than Milton's Satan: "this head, huge, frowning, sorrowful."

The extremity of this division—the black "Lucifer" as both Satan and God (or a god)—stresses the severity of the divisions over images and attitudes about blacks in antebellum America. Lucifer is fallen, sinful, morally corrupt, one whose sin of pride was so great that for him hell was created. And yet Whitman's use of "Lucifer" also suggests for the first time what he will more fully articulate later—that black persons, far from being inferior to whites as contemporary "science" and society would suggest, are, or have the potential to be, divine. Their expulsion from the human race by means of slavery is not merely an infliction of

39. See *Mythology: An Illustrated Encyclopedia*, 163–64. Actually, Lucifer has consis-tently been erroneously equated with the fallen angel (Satan) due to a misreading of Isaiah 14:12—"How art thou fallen from heaven, O Lucifer, son of the morning"—a verse that applied to Nebuchadnezzar, king of Babylon. The name Lucifer was first applied to Satan by St. Jerome and other church "fathers."

40. ". . . what time his Pride / Had cast him out from Heav'n, with all his Host / Of Rebel Angels, by whose aid aspiring / To set himself in Glory above his Peers, / He trusted to have equall'd the most High" (Book I, lines 36–40). John Milton, *Complete Poems and Major Prose*, ed. Merritt Y. Hughes (New York: The Odyssey Press, 1957), 212.

41. Tocqueville, *Democracy in America* (New York: Vintage Books, 1972), 2:376.

human pain, but a denial of part of humanity's essential divinity. Moreover, "Lucifer" is a God to whom the poet claims a stubborn allegiance: "he is *my* God as much as any" (my emphasis).

Aside from these sharp divisions, however, the poet's depiction of Lucifer in essentially theological terms detracts from the slave's humanity. Lucifer is little more than the portrait of a head, detached from a body of history and experience. Whitman seeks to expand and incarnate that portrait in another image of the rebellious slave, offered some thirty lines later:

> And there, in the midst of the group, a quell'd revolted slave, cowering, / See you, the hand-cuffs, the hopple, and the blood-stain'd cowhide. . . . (*NUPM* 4:1303)

The image of the "cowering" slave surrounded by capturers makes concrete the abstract suffering of the rebellious "Lucifer," and so more readily evokes sympathy. And yet here, too, the slave is not rendered as fully human. The elements of oppression—"the hand-cuffs, the hopple, and the blood-stain'd cowhide"—are more visible than the slave himself.

It is useful to compare these two images to a later portrayal of Lucifer in Whitman's first version of the "hunted slave" fragment. That Whitman intended this fragment to be a fuller depiction of Lucifer is clear from a deleted verse, cited by Grier in the notes: "Deleted verse: 'What Lucifer [del.] felt, [ins.] cursed [ins.] when [on a line above] tumbling from Heaven'" (*NUPM* 1:110n97). The fragment appears within a larger passage reciting "All the beautiful disdain and calmness of martyrs," and is preceded by one-line descriptions of women burned as witches and of executed queens. Grier dates this fragment January 1854, at the earliest. Whitman's original, unedited text, which includes a number of "false starts" and unfinished lines, reads as follows:[42]

> The slave that stood could run no longer, and then stood
> by the fence, blowing panting and covered with sweat,
> And his eye that burns defiance and desperation hatred
> And the buck shot, were
> And how the twinges that sting like needles his breast and neck
> The murderous buck-shot planted like terrible
> This he not only sees but

42. This text is reconstructed both from an examination of a copy of Whitman's notebook No. 85 in the Thomas B. Harned Papers of the Library of Congress and from Grier's notes.

He is the hunted slave
Damnation and despair are close upon him
He clutches the rail of the fence
His blood presently oozes from and becomes thinned
    with the plentiful sweat
See how it
And trickles down the black skin
He slowly falls on the grass and stones,
And the hunters haul up close with their unwilling horses,
And the taunt and curse dark dim and dizzy in his ears
                                          (*NUPM* 1:109–10)

This passage combines the earlier portrait of the outcast Lucifer and that of the "revolted slave" into a much richer image that specifically details the nature of the slave's suffering: the chase of the slave hunt, the buck shot, the mingled blood and sweat, and so forth. The "fall" of Lucifer is here a literal fall to the "grass and stones," and the "curse" a literal curse of voices taunting his ears. This slave is neither "frowning" and "sorrowful" as in the first portrait nor "quell'd" or "cowering" as in the second, but enraged at his own suffering and injustice with an "eye that burns defiance and desperation hatred." Clearly Whitman has matured in his understanding of the slave's experience. Moreover, just as Whitman's first recorded poetic fragment in 1847 focused on slavery, so, too, does this passage break out from the prose-style paragraphs Whitman has been writing into long-line free verse. It is almost as if the radically sympathetic depiction of blacks compels Whitman toward an equally radical and new poetic form.

What accounts for these new forms? It is worth noting that Whitman's depiction is of a *fugitive* slave, as opposed to the slaves of the earlier portraits who could be plantation slaves. Whitman is narrowing his poetic focus along the lines of his political interests, and, in doing so, his poetic voice is gaining power. Thus, as Whitman's attention turns from slaves in general to fugitive slaves, his verse becomes more passionate, realistically detailed, and sympathetic. The passion of his poetry about slaves, first begun in 1847 ("I am the poet of slaves"), now combines with his passion about the Fugitive Slave Law to produce a poetry that surpasses his previous efforts, a poetry that is but one step—a small but crucial step—from the representations of blacks in *Leaves of Grass*.

Regardless of Whitman's growth, his potential audience in early 1854 (with the exception of ardent abolitionists) would hardly be prepared to respond to these more sympathetic images. Something would have to happen to his readers if Whitman believed they would be in any way receptive. And yet, remarkably—almost as if Whitman had personally willed it—something did happen. In January 1854 Senator Stephen Douglas of Illinois reported a bill to Congress over the settlement of the Kansas-Nebraska territory, and that bill proved immediately explosive. Kansas-Nebraska was a territory that attracted settlers because of its fertile soil and its potential to be a key link in a transcontinental railroad. Within the last few years, Kansas-Nebraska had become a hotly contested region in the heretofore quieted slavery debate. Southerners were not especially eager to have the territory organized since it lay north of the 36°30' line where slavery was excluded by the 1820 Compromise. The original bill reported in 1853 by Douglas, the architect of the 1850 legislation and himself an investor in real estate who had a stake in the building of the railroad from Chicago, organized the territory along the terms of the 1820 Compromise. Needing the support of at least half a dozen Southern senators for its passage, however, Douglas revised the bill in January 1854 to include what most Northerners considered unthinkable: an explicit repeal of the 1820 Missouri Compromise ban on slavery north of 36°30'. Moreover, the bill's division of the land into two territories—Nebraska west of Iowa and Kansas west of Missouri—looked like a device to reserve Nebraska for freedom and Kansas for slavery.[43]

Douglas's bill immediately provoked what James McPherson calls "a hell of a storm that made the debates of 1850 look like a gentle shower."[44] As in 1850, but more widespread, public meetings were held in every Northern state. The *New York Tribune* noted sixty-four such meetings between January 17 and February 24. In New York City, a mass gathering opposed to the overthrow of the Missouri Compromise met in the Tabernacle and included a large number of Union Safety Committee members who had "labored long and hard in support of the [1850] compromise but now felt as though they had been sold out."[45] Emerson also spoke at the Tabernacle, perhaps at the close of these hostile sessions. In Whitman's home of Brooklyn, after the largest demonstration in the city's history, more than three thousand citizens signed a petition and sent it to Senator William Seward to bolster his stand against the measure. "The tremendous storm sweeping the North seemed to gather new force every week," writes historian Allan Nevins. Northern clergy, lawyers, physicians, lecturers, and authors united in their vocal denunciation of Douglas's bill. And the Free Soil press "spoke with

43. For a discussion of the Kansas-Nebraska Act and its consequences, see McPherson, *Battle Cry*, 121–23, and Nevins, *Ordeal of the Union*, 2:93–154.
44. McPherson, *Battle Cry*, 123.
45. Campbell, *The Slave Catchers*, 84.

an energy for which the history of American journalism had no parallel."[46]

President Pierce, despite opposition to the repeal clause from almost his entire cabinet, surrendered to Southern pressure and made support of the bill a test of party orthodoxy. But throughout the North the tide of opinion was turning against the extension of slavery. Free Soilers and their allies published an "Appeal of the Independent Democrats" in the *National Era,* denouncing the bill as a "criminal betrayal of precious rights" and a plot to exclude American laborers and European immigrants from the new territory.[47] This appeal further inspired an outpouring of angry speeches, sermons, and editorials across the North. Richard Henry Dana said of an anti-Nebraska meeting in Boston's Faneuil Hall that "all attempts to get up applause for the measures and men of 1850 failed, and even great Webster's name fell dead, while every sentiment hostile to the Compromise measures of 1850, and everything of a Free Soil character, went off with rapturous applause . . . The Compromise men feel themselves sold."[48] The *New York Times* predicted that the Northern response could "create a deep-seated, intense, and ineradicable hatred of the institution [slavery] which will crush its political power, at all hazards, and at any cost."[49] One senator who had supported the 1850 Compromise said that Douglas's bill "needs but little to make me an out & out abolitionist."[50]

Despite fervent and widespread Northern opposition to the bill, Democratic party discipline and Douglas's legislative brilliance pushed the bill through the Senate 41–17 in March and through the House 115–104 on May 22. "For once," says Allan Nevins, "public opinion had singularly little direct effect upon Washington."[51]

Yet passage of the Kansas-Nebraska Act had a powerfully direct effect on the nation's political landscape. The passage of Douglas's bill effectively destroyed the Whig party and thus the intersectional two-party system. Every Northern Whig in Congress voted against the bill, while twenty-five of thirty-four Southern Whigs voted for it. (Democrats of both sections voted for the bill: Southern Democrats by 72 to 3 and

46. Nevins, *Ordeal,* 2:125.

47. Quoted in Rubin, *The Historic Whitman,* 292.

48. Charles Francis Adams, *Richard Henry Dana: A Biography* (Boston: Houghton, Mifflin and Company, 1891), 1:257–58. Quoted in Campbell, *The Slave Catchers,* 86.

49. *New York Times,* 24 January 1854. Quoted in McPherson, *Battle Cry,* 124.

50. William P. Fessenden to Ellen Fessenden, 26 February 1854, quoted in Richard H. Sewell, *Ballots for Freedom: Antislavery Politics in the United States, 1837–1860* (New York: Oxford University Press, 1976), 259.

51. Nevins, *Ordeal,* 2:136.

Northern Democrats 59 to 49.) "The Whig party has been killed off effectually by that miserable Nebraska business," wrote one Whig senator.[52] Filling the void left by the Whigs' demise would be a number of anti-slavery coalitions that formed throughout the North to contest the 1854 elections. Among these the Republican party emerged most prominently. Though the rise of the Republicans would revive the two-party system, the nation was now bitterly divided along sectional lines, and the idea of intersectional unity was shattered.

Equally important, though less measurable, the repeal of the Missouri Compromise signaled for Northern radicals and conservatives alike a Southern breach of trust in the agreed-upon terms of union. In New York, Horace Greeley summed up local reaction in the *Tribune:* "It now appears that the slave power keeps no truce, no plighted faith with Freedom, and that the Compromise, on which some people leaned, was only an audacious juggle."[53] The tide of Northern opinion had turned dramatically toward Whitman's Free Soil position. "What had been radical opinion in the North," says historian Allan Nevins, "now became general opinion; Douglas had converted more men to intransigent free soil doctrine in two months than Garrison and Phillips had converted to abolitionism in twenty years."[54]

In this atmosphere abolitionists and Free Soilers were finally able to exploit their deep-seated hatred of the expansion of slavery. At an anti-slavery meeting in New York in May, Wendell Phillips and William Lloyd Garrison attacked slavery so vehemently that just a few months earlier they "would have met with derision and possible violence." But now sympathetic audiences crowded the city's churches and halls and "their boldest utterances, recently so shocking, were heard without visible dissent."[55] Under these circumstances, Whitman could not have been but encouraged, perhaps even compelled, to develop and revise his poetry about blacks in such a way that would have been in line with the changing national mood.

As if Whitman needed further encouragement, just two days after Senate passage of the Kansas-Nebraska bill a second event further galvanized Northern opposition to the 1850 Compromise, and especially to the Fugitive Slave Law. On May 24 Anthony Burns, an escaped slave from Virginia, was arrested in Boston and placed under heavy guard in

---

52. Quoted in McPherson, *Battle Cry,* 125.
53. *New York Weekly Tribune,* 29 July 1854. Quoted in Campbell, *The Slave Catchers,* 92.
54. Nevins, *Ordeal,* 2:153–54.
55. Ibid., 154.

the federal courthouse.[56] The Fugitive Slave Law had been enforced generally without incident since 1851, but the anger fomented by passage of the Kansas-Nebraska bill gave rise to a newly emboldened citizen reaction. While Burns was in custody, a vigilance committee held a meeting at Faneuil Hall, resolving that "resistance to tyrants is obedience to God." Later that night, a biracial group led by Unitarian minister Thomas Wentworth Higginson attempted to rescue Burns in an attack on the courthouse with axes, stones, revolvers, and a battering ram. The attempt failed, and one of the guards was killed. Federal troops and a company of marines were called in. When the local marshal reported the situation to President Pierce, the President replied in a telegram: "Your conduct is approved; the law must be executed."

The trial of Anthony Burns lasted a week, during which crowds of up to several thousand anti-slavery demonstrators gathered in the courthouse square. The commissioner presiding over the case concluded that the Fugitive Slave Law was constitutional, and that his duty was merely to apply the law to the facts of the case. He found that the slave owner, Charles Suttle of Alexandria, Virginia, had established ownership of Anthony Burns.

The delivery of Anthony Burns was a spectacle unparalleled in the brief history of the Fugitive Slave Law. According to Stephen Malin, Burns was escorted from the courthouse to the wharf by "the entire Boston police force, two companies of light dragoons, eight of artillery, eleven of infantry, a corps of cadets, a detachment of lancers, and three corps of United States Marines."[57] A front-page headline in the *New York Times* announced there were no fewer than ten thousand troops under arms. A cannon was set up in the courthouse square before Burns emerged and was afterward drawn in the parade by a span of horses. Martial music accompanied the whole. More than twenty thousand people lined the streets, jeering the police with hisses and cries of "shame" and enthusiastically cheering Burns. Stores were closed and several buildings facing the square were draped in black.

National reaction to the Anthony Burns affair was swift and furious. Similar episodes of crowds numbering into the thousands standing vigil to protect escaped slaves from arrest by federal marshals occurred in

56. My discussion of the Anthony Burns affair is drawn from these sources: Campbell, *The Slave Catchers*, 124–32; McPherson, *Battle Cry*, 119–20; Rubin, *The Historic Whitman*, 293–96; and Stephen Malin, "'A Boston Ballad' and the Boston Riot," *Walt Whitman Review* 9, no. 3 (1963): 51–57. Because the information in each text is essentially the same, I will cite references to specific texts only when I quote the text directly.

57. Malin, "'A Boston Ballad,'" 53.

Milwaukee, Chicago, and Syracuse, among other places.[58] Legislatures in Maine, Massachusetts, Michigan, and New York called for the "immediate and unconditional repeal" of both the Fugitive Slave Law and the Kansas-Nebraska Act.[59] Massachusetts Senator Edward Everett wrote to a colleague that however much "anti-slavery agitation" was to be deprecated, "it is no longer possible to resist it." He continued:

> A change has taken place in this community within three weeks such as the 30 preceding years had not produced. While the minds of conservative men were embittered by the passage of the Nebraska bill, the occurrence of a successful demand for the Surrender of a fugitive Slave was the last drop, which made the cup run over.[60]

Another Bostonian put it more succinctly: "We went to bed one night old fashioned, conservative Compromise Union Whigs & we waked up stark mad Abolitionists."[61] By June 1854, anti-slavery resentment had become so pervasive and impassioned that it created what one historian calls "a wholly altered Northern attitude."[62]

Whitman himself was so outraged by the Burns affair that he felt compelled to write "A Boston Ballad," his first poem in four years. (It is worth noting that Whitman's *only* published poems from 1850 to 1854 are about slavery.) The focus and style of the poem, not published until it was included in the 1855 *Leaves of Grass*, point to the persistently complicated nature of Whitman's response. Even as his notebooks reveal him to be trying out poetry that is more sympathetic to blacks,

58. See Nevins, *Ordeal*, 2:152–53.

59. Campbell, *The Slave Catchers*, 87.

60. Edward Everett to Joseph S. Cottman, 15 June 1854. Quoted in Jane H. and William H. Pease, *The Fugitive Slave Law and Anthony Burns: A Problem in Law Enforcement* (Philadelphia: J. B. Lippincott, 1975), 51.

61. Amos A. Lawrence to Giles Richards, 1 June 1854. Quoted in Pease and Pease, *The Fugitive Slave Law and Anthony Burns*, 43.

62. Nevins, *Ordeal*, 2:152. It must be noted that anti-slavery fervor grew mostly out of the Kansas-Nebraska Act and was only heightened by opposition to the Fugitive Slave Law. In states such as Pennsylvania, Ohio, Indiana, and Illinois, where the fugitive slave problem was the greatest, abolitionists picked up considerable support, but a majority of people even in those states still favored enforcement of the Fugitive Slave Law over the potential threat of disunion. In New York, abolitionists gained support upstate but not in New York City. Although merchants in the city were opposed to the Kansas-Nebraska Act, they were even more opposed to anti-slavery agitation that could further antagonize sectional conflict and result in disunion. Largely because of business interests, there was little difficulty in returning fugitive slaves from New York City. See Campbell, *The Slave Catchers*, 92–93.

"A Boston Ballad," like his Free Soil editorials and the political poems of 1850, focuses exclusively on issues of liberty as they affect the rights of whites and leaves out any concern for fugitive slaves. The differences between "A Boston Ballad" and his poetic experiments may be accounted for primarily by Whitman's particular objections to the Fugitive Slave Law as yet one more, and perhaps the worst, example of federal interference in areas of local and state sovereignty. In other words, his response to the Anthony Burns case was driven not so much by his view of slavery as by his view of the Union as a collection of states and communities whose right to self-government needed to be fiercely protected. "A Boston Ballad" also differs from his poetic experiments because Whitman likely desired to respond immediately to the event in a way he hoped would rouse his readers, and so he employed the simpler and more familiar form of journalistic satire rather than the new and more radical verse that, in the days just after Burns's capture, his audience may have been ready to receive, had he only known.

"A Boston Ballad" opens with a character named "Jonathan" being ordered to "clear the way" for the "President's marshal," the "government cannon," and "the federal foot and dragoons."[63] Whitman's readers would be familiar with Jonathan as the famous rustic of the American stage who first appeared in Royall Tyler's 1787 comedy, *The Contrast*, and was immensely popular up until the Civil War. As Stephen Malin notes, Jonathan was more than a "simple country dolt." Beneath his "tobacco-chewing, stick-whittling" appearance lay a shrewd New Englander who prided himself on being "'a trueborn son of liberty'" and was always eager to rhapsodize at length on the virtues of democracy and perhaps even swing into a chorus of "Yankee Doodle."[64] In short, he was the stage symbol of the triumph of American democracy, and, as such, he enjoyed his greatest popularity during Whitman's formative years, from about 1830 to 1855. His being ordered—presumably by the speaker—to "clear the way" for the "federal foot" would immediately have struck Whitman's readers as the suppression of local rights and liberties by an intrusive federal power.

The speaker is apparently one of the many Bostonians who come to

63. What exactly happens at the beginning of the poem may not be clear to contemporary readers since, despite the poem's historical subject, there are few historical markers. As Stephen Malin notes, only by the seventh paragraph is one clearly aware that "something is going on in the city, some sort of procession" (51). Whitman's reliance on his readers' shared knowledge of the Burns affair is not surprising given the exhaustive press coverage surrounding the event. The *New York Daily Times,* for example, featured the story for over two weeks, seven times as its leading front-page article (ibid., 52).

64. Malin, "'A Boston Ballad,'" 55–56.

see "the show" with little interest in its causes. His excitement about the federal troops "marching stiff through Boston town" is suddenly interrupted when he sees at the back of the march "bandaged and bloodless" phantoms, risen from the graveyards. It soon becomes apparent that these are the ghostly ancestors of those present, revolutionary war heroes called from the dead to protest the violation of the republican ideals for which they fought and died. When these ancient warriors level their crutches as they would muskets to show their descendants the course of action required, the speaker understands this as merely a senile gesture:

> What troubles you, Yankee phantoms? What is all this
>   chattering of bare gums?
> Does the ague convulse your limbs? Do you mistake your
>   crutches for firelocks, and level them?
> If you blind your eyes with tears you will not see the
>   President's marshal,
> If you groan such groans you might balk the
>   government cannon.
>
> (CP, 135)

The appropriate response to the government show of power, the speaker feels, is an orderly respect:

> For shame old maniacs! . . . Bring down those tossed arms,
>   and let your white hair be;
> Here gape your smart grandsons . . . their wives gaze
>   at them from the windows,
> See how well-dressed . . . see how orderly they
>   conduct themselves.
>
> (CP, 136)

Horrified at the citizens' indifference and recognizing their impotence to stop the crush of federal power, the revolutionaries retreat "pell-mell" to the hills with the speaker's blessing: "I do not think you belong here anyhow."

Once the revolutionaries have fled, the speaker realizes the "one thing that belongs here" to make the scene complete. He convinces the mayor to send a committee to England to exhume the corpse of King George, bring it back to America, and crown it in Boston.

> Look! all orderly citizens . . . look from the windows women.
> The committee open the box and set up the regal ribs

and glue those that will not stay,
And clap the skull on top of the ribs, and clap a crown on top
of the skull.

You have got your revenge old buster! . . . The crown is
come to its own and more than its own.

(CP, 136–37)

Whitman's ironic depiction of Bostonians too complacent to recognize their revolutionary ancestors and even willing to give obeisance to a dead king is, of course, meant to represent an America indifferent or unable to respond to challenges to liberty and self-sovereignty. But to make this point Whitman had to contradict what he probably knew to be the truth about Boston's response, given the exhaustive press coverage and the details in the poem that suggest his close knowledge of the event. Throughout the week between Burns's arrest and his departure, public meetings featuring speakers such as Wendell Phillips and Theodore Parker were held at Faneuil Hall. Crowds sometimes swelling into the thousands gathered off and on in Court Square to protest Burns's capture.

More striking than the misrepresentation of Boston's response, however, is the complete focus on liberty as it applies to the white majority and the absence from the poem of Anthony Burns himself. Betsy Erkkila says that the failure to name Burns as the subject of the poem adds an "*unintentional* dimension of irony, which reveals as it conceals the racial phobia of Whitman and his age" (my emphasis).[65] But the absence of Burns may not be so unintentional. By simply eliding the fugitive slave from the narrative, Whitman focuses on his central concern: the usurpation of local rights and powers by federal authority. For the Whitman of this poem, the Anthony Burns case was not about Anthony Burns. Enforcement of the Fugitive Slave Law was to be resisted not because it jeopardized the freedom of blacks, but because it jeopardized the freedom of Northern white communities, signaling a tyranny as heinous as the return of British monarchs. Two nearly identical prose text fragments by Whitman that cannot accurately be dated underscore Whitman's point that the Fugitive Slave Law was to be opposed not out of sympathy for slaves but because enforcement of the law invaded the rights of Northern communities. The first text, dated "1855 or 1856" by Edward Grier (*NUPM* 4:2192) but including details—such as a reference to the Kansas-Nebraska debate—that suggest parts of it may have been com-

---

65. Erkkila, *Whitman the Political Poet*, 63–64.

posed earlier, is a collection of notes for a lecture opposing the Fugitive
Slave Law that Whitman perhaps intended to give. Whitman writes:

> What do you want in my free city of the North? The question of
> respect for the rights of blacks I defer for the present.—This is
> purely a question of my own rights, immunities and dignities.—
> These streets are mine—there are my officers, my courts, my
> laws.—At the Capitol is my legislature.—The warrant you bring
> with you, we know it not; it is foreign to my usages as to my
> eyes and ears. (NUPM 4:2196)

Similarly, in a manuscript on slavery whose "date and circumstances of
composition are unclear" and may have been composed and revised
anywhere from 1846 to 1858 (NUPM 4:2171–72), Whitman writes:

> What fetches you here? . . . I do not discuss any nigger question
> with you now; this is a vital question of my own dignities and
> immunities, which I decide at once and without parley. (NUPM
> 4:2188)[66]

Yet despite the ideology that pervades "A Boston Ballad" and these
prose fragments, Whitman's notebooks show an increasing interest in
and concern for blacks as well as a continuing effort to render black
experience more sympathetically. That Whitman was more and more
focusing on blacks and slavery can be seen by the surprising frequency
of comments about blacks in notebooks which Grier dates in late 1854
or 1855, just prior to the publication of Leaves of Grass.[67] Whitman
recalls, perhaps with pride, the scene of his great-grandmother surrounded by appreciative slaves:

66. That Whitman's opposition to the Fugitive Slave Law was largely based on his
objection to direct federal intervention in the affairs of states and communities can also
be seen by the fact that only two years after the Anthony Burns case he was prepared to
urge states to return slaves voluntarily to the South. In "The Eighteenth Presidency," a
long, unpublished 1856 prose tract that, among other things, articulates Whitman's theory
of the Union, opposes the attempts of the slave-owning South to inflict slavery on the
nation, and excoriates weak-willed and ineffectual politicians, Whitman titles one section
"Must Runaway Slaves Be Turned Back?" and answers simply, "They must." Whitman
exhorts the states to carry out "in spirit and in letter" a section in the fourth article of
the federal Constitution in which the states "compact with each other" to return fugitive
slaves (CP, 1320).
    67. As stated earlier, Grier is careful to acknowledge the conjectural nature of these
dates, some of which he specifies only as "in the early 1850s." Yet he can also more
confidently assert that a number of these fragments were written in 1854 or early 1855.
See NUPM 1:xvi–xx, 53–55, 102.

> Sarah White, my great grandmother Whitman, lived to be 90 years old.—She was a large, strong woman, chewed tobacco, opium &c.—petted her slaves, and had always a crowd of little niggers about her. (*NUPM* 1:11)

This scene of gracious paternalism toward blacks is repeated in a memory of his great-aunt in the next notebook manuscript:

> This latter [Vashti Plant] must have been mistress of quite an estate, for grandmother related that she has seen fourteen little niggers, belonging to the family, eating their supper at evening, all at once in the kitchen. (*NUPM* 1:12)

These scenes of slaves crowding around his female ancestors nostalgically recall an earlier, ideal slave owner–slave relationship and so distance Whitman (and his family) from the slavery and prejudice he was now prepared to denounce. "I will have nothing which any man or any woman, anywhere on the face of the earth, or of any color or country cannot also have," he writes in early 1855 (*NUPM* 1:123).

Moreover, Whitman's notebooks show him increasingly focusing his attention on *fugitive* slaves. In a prose critique of those who would take advantage of their wealth and privilege to the exclusion of the working classes and the poor, Whitman judges as equally heinous "usurping the rule of an empire" and "thieving a negro and selling him" (*NUPM* 1:121). In the same fragment Whitman defines disadvantaged persons as "the vast retinues of the poor [?] the laboring, ignorant man, black men, sinners, and [?] so on" (*NUPM* 1:122). The grouping of "the laboring, ignorant man" with "black men" marks a radical break from his free soil thinking. Whereas he had earlier considered the rights of white laborers in *opposition* to the rights of blacks, he now views whites and blacks as equally oppressed and excluded. His class critique of 1847 has now become biracially inclusive.

The strongest indication of Whitman's changed and changing thinking about blacks and slavery, however, is the poetry about blacks he revises and creates in his notebooks. It is likely that these poetry fragments were also written in late 1854 or early 1855, giving Whitman several months to digest the profound ramifications of the changes that had taken place in the national mood and to gauge his poetry accordingly. Note, for example, the two versions of the following fragment, the latter composed sometime in 1854 or early 1855:

[Earlier version]

Where others see some dolt, a clown, rags the Poet
beholds what shall be one day a mate for the
greatest gods.[68]

[*NUPM* version]

Where others see a slave a pariah an emptier of
privies the Poet beholds what when the days of the
soul are accomplished shall be peer of god.
(*NUPM* 1:115)

Whitman has changed his focus from "some dolt, a clown, rags" to "a
slave a pariah an emptier of privies." This change is accompanied by
a stronger sense of an ideal future ("when the days of the soul are
accomplished") in which the slave shall be no less than "peer of god."
Such a statement goes far beyond abolitionist humanitarian concern
for blacks and hopefully suggests a re-vision, or new outcome, of the
Lucifer story.

But nowhere is Whitman's changing perspective on blacks and slavery
more evident than in his re-vision of the "hunted slave" fragment. For
the purpose of analysis it is useful to see the earlier and later versions
together:

[Earlier version]

The slave that stood could run no longer, and then stood
    by the fence, blowing panting and covered with sweat,
And his eye that burns defiance and desperation hatred
And the buck shot, were
And how the twinges that sting like needles his breast and neck
The murderous buck-shot planted like terrible
This he not only sees but
He is the hunted slave
Damnation and despair are close upon him
He clutches the rail of the fence
His blood presently oozes from and becomes thinned with the
    plentiful sweat
See how it
And trickles down the black skin

68. Reconstructed from notes provided by Grier, *NUPM* 1:115.

He slowly falls on the grass and stones,
And the hunters haul up close with their unwilling horses,
And the taunt and curse dark dim and dizzy in his ears

[Later version]

The hunted slave who flags in the race at last, and leans up
    by the fence, blowing and covered with sweat,
And the twinges that sting like needles his breast and neck
The murderous buck-shot and the bullets.
All this I not only feel and see but am.
I am the hunted slave
Damnation and despair are close upon me
I clutch the rail of the fence.
My gore presently trickles thinned with ooze of my skin
    as I fall on the reddened grass and stones,
And the hunters haul up close with their unwilling horses,
Till taunt and oath swim away from my dim dizzy ears
                                        (*NUPM* 1:109–10)

The most striking change, of course, is that of the personal pronoun, from "He is the hunted slave" to "I am the hunted slave." This radical reconception of perspective from the objective to the subjective marks the key breakthrough in Whitman's understanding of the slave's experience, from that of distanced observer to participant in the slave's suffering. When or how Whitman came to this understanding cannot be accurately ascertained, though the transformation of the national mood to where "we waked up stark mad Abolitionists" could not have left him unaffected. It is also worth noting that the poet's identification with the slave extends to all of human suffering: "I am the man; I suffered, I was there" (*NUPM* 1:109). Much more will be said about this signal transformation in the following chapter, but the move toward sympathetic identification manifests itself in other revisions as well. Whitman's deletion of the line "And his eye that burns defiance desperation hatred" effectively changes the slave from a threat to a victim. Yet another telling indication of Whitman's more sympathetic intent is the addition of the word "feel," from "This he not only sees" to "All this I not only *feel* and see but am" (my emphasis).[69]

But what cannot be overlooked is that this deeper sympathy also has a clear *political* intent. For the very first change Whitman makes is from

---

69. A reading of Whitman's highly edited manuscript could also yield the reading: "All this I not only feel and am but see."

"The slave" to "The hunted slave." This simple revision is more than a renewed focus on the Fugitive Slave Law. For with much of the North now driven by the Kansas-Nebraska Act and the Anthony Burns case toward a new anti-slavery fervor, Whitman finds that his idealistic notions of 1847 ("I am the poet of slaves") now actually work as a political statement that will be readily received. What years of free soil journalism could not accomplish, the sweep of events in six short months has done: guaranteed Whitman an audience receptive to his once idealistic views. It may even be said that the events of 1854 and his readers' response to those events pulled him in the direction he wanted to go. Eager to take advantage of this new dynamic, Whitman revises his poetry to combine an abolitionist's sympathy for the slave with a Free Soiler's opposition to all of the events since 1850 that have compromised their call for "free soil, free labor, free men."

That Whitman saw himself playing the role of a uniting voice on slavery is evident from a key fragment in a late 1854 notebook:

My final aim

To concentrate around me the leaders of all reforms—transcendentalists, spiritualists, free soilers (*NUPM* 1:147)

Whitman's "final aim" of uniting "free soilers" and those associated with abolitionism ("transcendentalists, spiritualists") could find no riper moment than now. He soon began working on new poetry about blacks, including fragments entitled "A Man at Auction" and "A Woman at Auction" that would appear in *Leaves of Grass.* Gay Wilson Allen speculates that "probably late in 1854 or early 1855" Whitman gave up his house-building and began to devote his whole attention to preparation of his book of poems.[70] To maintain his resolve, he hung at eye level the motto "Make the Work."[71] Slavery had always been a central concern for Whitman, from the 1842 publication of *Franklin Evans,* through the debates over the Wilmot Proviso leading to the 1850 Compromise and up to now in 1854, when the nation was once again charged with the issue. What has not been considered, but now becomes clear, is how pivotal the events of 1854 were toward compelling Whitman not only toward a new representation of blacks, but toward the very publication of *Leaves of Grass.*

70. Allen, *The Solitary Singer,* 147.
71. Rubin, *The Historic Whitman,* 300.

6

A SLAVE'S NARRATIVE

The representation of African Americans in *Leaves of Grass* is unlike anything Whitman—or anyone, for that matter—had ever written. Published in 1855 in the wake of public ferment over the Kansas-Nebraska Act and the Anthony Burns case, *Leaves of Grass* portrays African Americans as equal partners with whites in a democratic future and as beautiful and dignified people, the paradigms of a fully realized humanity. In addition, African Americans are seen as essential to the speaker's—and the readers'—own humanity; Whitman repeatedly shows his white readers that to be a whole and fully realized human being in mid-nineteenth-century America is to participate in the experience of, and even identify with, black people.

Moreover, African Americans play a crucial role in the major themes and turning points of what are generally considered the three most important poems of the 1855 edition—poems that were later titled, "Song of Myself," "I Sing the Body Electric," and "The Sleepers." Whitman himself emphasized the transforming influence of slavery on his work. In the "Preface" to the 1855 edition, as Whitman concludes a catalogue of what the American poet needs to absorb into his poetry his last entry makes clear the immediate impact of slavery on the poet's work:

> [To him enter the essences of real things] . . . slavery and the tremulous spreading of hands to protect it, and the stern opposition to it which shall never cease till it ceases or the speaking of tongues and the moving of lips cease. *For such the expression*

of the American poet is to be transcendent and new. (CP, 8; my emphasis)[1]

Thus, the very nature of Whitman's 1855 poems as "transcendent and new" was, in his own mind, compelled by, among other things, a need to express slavery and its persistent and "stern" opposition. Whitman says later in the "Preface" that the "attitude of great poets is to cheer up slaves and horrify despots" (17).

Whitman's representation of slaves and slavery must, however, be understood in light of the broader conceptions he arrived at concerning the role of the poet. The "Preface" sets forth ideas about poetry and "the poet" that Whitman had formulated over the previous eight years, ever since his reading of Emerson around the time of the first defeat of the Wilmot Proviso compelled him to seek new forms of expression. The "Preface" itself is a new form of expression. Developed from Whitman's notebook meditations, it combines Emersonian epigrammatic sentences with Whitman's own long poetic lines into a loose, flowing, unstructured, prose essay that does not readily fit into traditional categories of genre. In employing this unique, mixed-genre form, Whitman prepares his readers for the poems that are to follow by describing what he is attempting to do and by modeling a radical break from conventionality, a break that will be paralleled by his radical break from conventional racial attitudes.

The essential idea in the "Preface" is that America itself is the very stuff of poetry ("The United States themselves are essentially the greatest poem" [5]), and that the American poet's vocation is to represent the amplitude and diversity of the nation. The poet is not merely to express the greatness of the land and its people; he is to "incarnate" them, to "enclose" them, to "be commensurate" with them (6–7). As we shall see, the poet's incarnation of a slave persona is perhaps the single most telling example of this transformation.

The poet's vision is also directed toward a perfectible America of the future—not what is, but what can be. "The future is in me as a seed or nascent thought," Whitman had written in his notebooks (*NUPM* 1:145), and he develops this idea in the 1855 "Preface":

Let the age and wars of other nations be chanted and their eras and characters be illustrated and that finish the verse. Not so the

1. All quotations in this chapter from either the "Preface" or the poetry of the 1855 *Leaves of Grass* are cited from Whitman's *Complete Poetry and Collected Prose (CP)*, unless otherwise noted.

great psalm of the republic. *Here the theme is creative and has vista. Here comes one [who] . . . sees the solid and beautiful forms of the future where there are now no solid forms.* (8; my emphasis)

While the great poet is immersed in the present, flooded with the "immediate age as with vast oceanic tides," he is also a "seer" whose special "eyesight" beholds in the distance what is "marvellous," "unlikely," and "mocks . . . all reasoning" (10). He places himself "where the future becomes present," showing "what no man can tell" (13). He projects himself "centuries ahead and judges performer or performance after the changes of time" (24); he "becomes himself the age transfigured" (23).

To borrow the language of critic Houston A. Baker Jr., Whitman's America is not a place but an idea: "AMERICA as immanent idea of boundless, classless, raceless possibility in America . . . as egalitarian promise, trembling imminence in the New World . . . an AMERICA singing that has never been heard before."[2] This notion of a forward-looking poet is crucial for understanding Whitman's "transfigured" conception of African Americans in *Leaves of Grass.* For they are seen not according to the prejudice of the present, but in the full bloom of their potential. They, like all other human beings, are ultimately divine:

The messages of great poets to each man and woman are, Come to us on equal terms. . . . Did you suppose there could be only one Supreme? We affirm there can be unnumbered Supremes, and that one does not countervail another. (14)

Throughout *Leaves of Grass,* Whitman emphasizes not the present degradation, but a glorious future for America and of African Americans.

Finally, the poet expresses the perfect balance between "pride" and "sympathy."[3] Whitman had learned from Emerson a "measureless pride which consists in never acknowledging any lessons but its own" (13).

2. Houston A. Baker Jr., *Blues, Ideology, and Afro-American Literature* (Chicago: University of Chicago Press, 1984), 65–66.

3. The "Preface" also describes, in no discernible order, other characteristics of the poet. For example, the poet is to demonstrate the greatest faith in democracy (9), "indicate the path between reality and the soul" (10), reject "rhyme and uniformity" and let his poems develop organically—"loosely as lilacs or roses on a bush" (11), embrace science as the underlying structure "of every perfect poem" (15), be the "voice and exposition of liberty" (17), reject ornamentation and the distortion of "natural models" (19), and tell histories, not romances (19). Some of these traits bear on Whitman's representations of blacks, but none, I believe, as importantly as the ones I have discussed.

But that assertion of the self *against* the world is balanced by an engagement of self *with* the world: "[The soul] has sympathy as measureless as its pride and the one balances the other and neither can stretch too far while it stretches in company with the other" (13). Whitman's writing about African Americans repeatedly will demonstrate the development and growth of the speaker toward "measureless" sympathy.

The poetic persona Whitman here projects suggests that his representations of blacks will be substantially different from anything he had written until this time. How he arrived at this point has been shaped by the complex interaction between his search for a new mode of expression, his evolving views on race and slavery, and his response to the changing views of his readership, radicalized by the events of 1854. As early as 1847, his desire to break free from conventional modes of discourse led to an all-embracing, innovative poetry that demanded from him a new way of thinking about his world—of which slaves and slavery were an important part. At the same time, Whitman's vision of an egalitarian, democratic, and fully inclusive America—a vision that would not readily be received within the conventional avenues of public discourse (newspaper editorials, lectures, prose essays)—was integral to what compelled him to seek out a radically new mode of expression. Whatever the precise nature of the dynamic that produced it, this new poetry matured and was tested over time, but it would not emerge full-blown until Whitman felt there existed a readership ready to embrace it. In the "Preface" Whitman sets forth for his readers the bold, new idealism of the American poet, and nowhere in *Leaves of Grass* is that more strongly felt than in his representation of African Americans.

Readers of "Song of Myself" generally agree that section 5 is the key, transformative moment in which a sexual union between the historical "I" and the timeless, transcendent "soul" brings about a wholly new, unified self, at one with God, others, and the natural world. But equally important from this ecstatic union is the birth of a new expressiveness that allows the poet, almost immediately, to speak a radical new word about blacks. The very purpose of this sexual union is described by the "I" in its invitation to "the soul":

> Loafe with me on the grass . . . loose the stop
>   from your throat,
> Not words, not music or rhyme I want . . . not
>   custom or lecture, not even the best,
> Only the lull I like, the hum of your valvéd voice.
>   (30)

This rejection of "custom or lecture, not even the best" and desire for one's own "valvéd voice" frames the poem from its beginning lines.

> I celebrate myself
> And what I assume you shall assume,
> For every atom belonging to me as good belongs to you.
>
> (27)

Throughout the early sections, the speaker emphatically rejects the divisive and negative polemics of the age, and chooses instead a new way of communicating: "I have heard what the talkers were talking . . . the talk of the beginning and the end, / But I do not talk of the beginning or the end" (28).

This new way of talking emerges out of the sexual consummation, what Allen Grossman describes as the "inaugural moment of Whitman's candor" where "primal communication" is enacted by "the tongue to the heart."[4]

> I mind how we lay in June, such a transparent
>   summer morning;
> You settled your head athwart my hips and
>   gently turned over upon me,
> And parted the shirt from my bosom-bone, and
>   plunged your tongue to my barestript heart,
> And reached till you felt my beard, and
>   reached till you held my feet.
>
> (30)

This moment not only creates a cosmic, transcendent, and egalitarian self ("And I know that the hand of God is the elderhand of my own, . . . And that all the men ever born are also my brothers, etc."), but creates *within* the self a new way of speaking, a knowledge that passes "all the art and argument of the earth" (30).

The profound effect of this new rhetoric on how the poet writes about blacks is immediately apparent. When the regenerated speaker begins his song with a meditation on the child's question, "What is the grass?" one of his responses is that the grass is "a uniform hieroglyphic . . .

---

4. Allen Grossman, "The Poetics of Union in Whitman and Lincoln: An Inquiry Toward the Relationship of Art and Policy," *The American Renaissance Reconsidered*, ed. Walter Benn Michaels and Donald E. Pease (Baltimore: Johns Hopkins University Press, 1985), 195.

Growing among black folks as among white" (31). The grass here is broadly representative of an egalitarian democracy where all peoples— "Kanuck, Tuckahoe, Congressmen, Cuff" (the latter being a diminutive of "Cuffy" or "Cuffee," at the time a black man's name or referring to any black male)—receive equal treatment from the poet.[5] The radicality of the sentiment is only fully appreciated when one recalls that at this time even many abolitionists, such as Lydia Maria Child, did not wish to "do violence to the distinctions" between blacks and whites by "forcing the rude and illiterate into the presence of the learned and refined."[6]

Yet the speaker's new vision about blacks becomes even more profoundly felt in the long section that follows the grass episode. Once the meditation on the grass has led to the recognition that life is cyclical and regenerative ("The smallest sprout shows there is really no death"), the speaker celebrates his own timeless and limitless existence: "I pass death with the dying, and birth with the new-washed babe . . . and am not contained between my hat and boots" (32). His immortality and cosmic breadth make possible a communion with all people:

> I am not an earth nor an adjunct of an earth,
> *I am the mate and companion of people,* all just
>   as immortal and fathomless as myself;
> They do not know how immortal, but I know.
>   (33; my emphasis)

From this point on the poem focuses for almost one hundred lines on "Every kind" of people with whom the speaker is "mate and companion," and it is in this key, early section that Whitman's radical word about blacks is first spoken.

In this part of the poem, which spans seven sections (7–13) of the final version, the speaker asks his readers: "Who need be afraid of the merge?" The "merge" is a central concept in *Leaves of Grass*. It is the speaker's attempt to make profoundly real his assertion, "I am the mate and companion of people." Jimmie Killingsworth says that "thematically and poetically, the notion dominates the three major poems of 1855: 'I

---

5. "Cuffy" and its variations—"Cuff," "Cuffee," and "Cuffey"—derive from several possible sources: *Kofi,* the day name for a male born on Saturday; *Kufi,* Angolan for "shortness"; *nKufi,* a name from the Belgian Congo; or the Dutch *Kaffi,* in Guiana a common name for blacks, and by custom one that was applied to those born on Friday (*Dictionary of American Regional English,* Frederic G. Cassidy, chief editor [Cambridge: The Belknap Press of Harvard University, 1985], 1:876).

6. Lydia Maria Child, ed., *The Oasis* (Boston, 1834), ix. Quoted in Fredrickson, *The Black Image in the White Mind,* 37.

Sing the Body Electric,' 'The Sleepers,' and 'Song of Myself.'" Killingsworth describes Whitman's notion of the merge as "the tendency of the individual self to overcome moral, psychological, and political boundaries."[7] To that definition might be added "racial boundaries," for throughout *Leaves of Grass* Whitman is looking to break down barriers of race through "the merge." When later in the poem Whitman invites various marginalized peoples (the "keptwoman," "sponger," "thief," and "slave") to the "meal pleasantly set," and then immediately follows with a description of intimate human contact—"the touch of my lips to yours"—he describes these moments as "the thoughtful merge of myself and outlet again" (44).

The poem moves toward the merge of the speaker's identity with that of others, through which the speaker fully realizes his own humanity. The movement is simultaneously toward sympathy and pride, toward identification and identity. The first critical stage in this merging is the development of a fully sympathetic personality, one who identifies and deeply empathizes with the experience of others, especially those who suffer. Through a series of early vignettes the speaker develops this sympathetic response along three fronts: from being observer to participant, from portraying others abstractly toward describing them in vivid, realistic terms, and from identifying with only those like himself to those who are "other" by race, gender, or ethnicity. In the early vignettes, for example, the speaker is only an observer of human experience: "I lift the gauze and look" at a sleeping child, "I peeringly view" adolescents on a hillside, "I witnessed the corpse" of the suicide (33). Beginning with a description of the speaker in a country barn, however, he changes from observer to actively engaged participant: "I am there. . . . I help. . . . I came stretched atop of the load" (34).

At this point, however, the speaker's fellow human beings (the harvest workers and the "boatmen and clamdiggers") are abstract, ghostly presences, felt but unseen. In the next section, with the marriage of the trapper and the squaw "in the open air in the far-west," the speaker takes one step further toward developing a sympathetic response by seeing others not as abstractions but as vivid and palpable individuals. The trapper is "dressed mostly in skins . . . his luxuriant beard and curls protecting his neck," with one hand on his rifle and the other holding "the wrist of the red girl." The American Indian bride is likewise vividly described: "She had long eyelashes . . . her head was bare . . . her coarse straight locks descended upon her voluptuous limbs and reached to her

7. M. Jimmie Killingsworth, *Whitman's Poetry of the Body* (Chapel Hill: University of North Carolina Press, 1989), 1.

feet" (35). Moreover, with this scene the speaker also describes "the merge" in a double sense: the sexual "merge" of a man and woman through marriage as well as the "merge" of Americans of different race and origin.

In these seemingly unrelated vignettes, then, Whitman's speaker describes the development of the self through participation in human community, through sensual, tactile perception of others, and, like the trapper, through consummation of a relationship with an "other"—an American, yet one outside the speaker's race, gender, or ethnicity. None of these portraits, however, yet includes what Whitman defined in the "Preface" as the soul's primary virtue: "sympathy as measureless as its pride" (13). Significantly, it is in the story of the "runaway slave" that this sympathy is added to bring about the first critical stage in the "merge" of the speaker's humanity with others:

> The runaway slave came to my house and stopped outside,
> I heard his motions crackling the twigs of the woodpile,
> Through the swung half-door of the kitchen I saw him
>   limpsey and weak,
> And went where he sat on a log, and *let* him in and
>   assured him,
> And brought water and filled a tub for his sweated body
>   and bruised feet,
> And gave him a room that entered from my own, and gave him
>   some coarse clean clothes,
> And remember perfectly well his revolving eyes and
>   his awkwardness,
> And remember putting plasters on the galls of his
>   neck and ankles;
> He staid with me a week before he was recuperated
>   and passed north,
> I had him sit next me at table . . . my firelock
>   leaned in the corner.
>
>   (35–36)

This vignette, the longest so far of any in the poem, profoundly advances the speaker's growth toward full personhood. As in previous vignettes, the speaker moves from observer ("Through the swung half-door of the kitchen I saw him") to participant ("And went where he sat on a log, and led him in and assured him"). More specifically, the speaker discards the childlike egocentrism of previous episodes ("I jump from the crossbeams, and seize the clover and timothy" [34]), adopting instead a posture of selflessness and sacrifice: "And gave him a room that entered from my own, and gave him some coarse clean clothes." The speaker's actions on the slave's behalf are not just broadly humanitarian, but, in a way that might repulse many Northern readers, they are intimate, physical gestures, extended as if by a loving comrade. He leads the slave into the house, for example, "putting plasters on the galls of his neck and ankles" and sitting with him at the table.

The poet emphasizes the bond between speaker and slave through the repeated use of "And" at the beginning of the poetic line. The repeated "And" has occurred in only one other place to this point: the speaker's transcendent recognition of his union with all others—"And I know that the hand of God is the elderhand of my own, etc." (31). Moreover, the repeated "And" occurs only three other places in "Song of Myself," each time emphasizing the speaker's union with that which is universal.[8] "And," then, represents a sort of cosmic bonding.

Yet if the speaker has moved toward a sympathetic humanity and cosmic bonding with the slave, the passage also reveals tensions in Whitman's representation. The "picture" of the black in some ways rehearses the romantic racialist notion of blacks as helpless, docile children. The runaway slave is "limpsey and weak," with "revolving eyes" and "awkwardness." (The portrait only slightly revises the image from "Pictures" of a "quell'd revolted slave, cowering" [*NUPM* 4:1303].) Moreover, the slave's identity is elided: he is no longer an actor but rather a body acted upon, objectified and consumed by the speaker's passion to assert his own humanitarianism. One critic notes that the speaker "is altogether too conscious of his tolerance" and that "the benevolence of [his] liberalism . . . is suspect."[9] In this way the passage reminds one of Whitman's support of the Wilmot Proviso and opposition to the Fugitive Slave Law. In all of these instances, the slave benefits from the speaker's actions, but an equal and perhaps primarily intended beneficiary is Whitman himself and other whites for whom he stands. Note also that the object of his empathy is a "runaway" or fugitive slave: the speaker's humanitarianism usefully advances the political goal of opposing the Fugitive Slave

8. The three instances of the repeated "And" are: (1) a catalogue of animals the speaker "acknowledges" as "playing within me" (37–38); (2) a description of the interconnectedness of every object in the cosmos—"I believe a leaf of grass is no less than the journeywork of the stars, / And the pismire is equally perfect" (57); and (3) an assertion of the body's unity with the soul to form the universal self—"And I have said that the body is not more than the soul, / And nothing, not God, is greater to one than one's self" (84).

9. E. Fred Carlisle, *The Uncertain Self: Whitman's Drama of Identity* (Ann Arbor: University of Michigan Press, 1973), 40.

Law in the wake of the Anthony Burns case while not—or at least, not yet—challenging slavery itself.

If the "merge" that the speaker seeks is possible, then this slave's body must be not only succored but embraced. And to embrace this body, the speaker must first of all clearly see it, and even see it as beautiful. Only then can he close the physical distance that separates him from identification and merger with black persons. The next section moves the speaker toward this sort of visual embrace through the portrait—and celebration—of the black drayman.

This section actually starts with the well-known episode of the "twenty-ninth bather." The narrative of the "lonesome" twenty-eight-year-old woman hiding behind the blinds of her window and passing her "unseen hand" over the bodies of twenty-eight bathing men has received considerable commentary, much of it focusing on suppressed sexual desire. And yet to isolate the passage from those that follow it is to overlook important interpretive possibilities. For in framing the object of the woman's desire, the speaker focuses on the bodies of the men with a close, almost cinematographic attention to detail:

> The beards of the young men glistened with
> wet, it ran from their long hair,
> Little streams passed all over their bodies.
>
> . . . .
>
> The young men float on their backs, their
> white bellies swell to the sun.
>
> (36)

As Michael Moon points out, this close observation is an expression not only of the woman's desire but also of the speaker's: "The speaker passes through the window and across the space between into the water with the twenty-eight bathers *along with* the young woman."[10] After this section concludes with a pseudosexual climax ("They do not think whom they souse with spray"), the poem moves in yet another seemingly new direction with brief descriptions of laborers at work: the butcher-boy sharpening his knife and blacksmiths hammering their fiery sledges. But the important and perhaps overlooked connection is that the speaker takes delight in the beauty of these workers' bodies just as did the speaker/woman observing the swimmers, although that delight is now much less explicitly sexual. The speaker enjoys the butcher-boy's "shuffle

10. Michael Moon, *Disseminating Whitman* (Cambridge: Harvard University Press, 1991), 43.

and breakdown," notes the "grimed and hairy chests" around the black-smith's anvil, and follows their movements: "The lithe sheer of their waists plays even with their massive arms" (36–37).

Moving from swimmers to laborers, Whitman's speaker begins to define the perfect human form—now, however, within the context of daily work. That perfect human form is realized not, as one might suspect, in the image of a white laborer or farmer but in the description of an African American drayman:

> The negro holds firmly the reins of his four horses . . .
> the block swags underneath on its tied-over chain,
> The negro that drives the huge dray of the stoneyard . . . steady
> and tall he stands poised on one leg on the stringpiece,
> His blue shirt exposes his ample neck and breast and loosens
> over his hipband,
> His glance is calm and commanding . . . he tosses the slouch
> of his hat away from his forehead,
> The sun falls on his crispy hair and moustache . . . falls
> on the black of his polish'd and perfect limbs.
>
> (37)

Just as the "runaway slave" episode climaxed the first critical stage of the speaker's "merge" with others, so now does the "negro" drayman define the apex of human beauty. To understand how radical this description is, one need only recall the stereotypes of blacks accepted and perpetuated by Whitman himself: the wild emotionalism of the "tragic mulatto" Margaret in *Franklin Evans,* the sexual suggestiveness of "Dusky Grisette," and the "clumsy, hideous, black, pouting, grinning, sly, besotted, sensual, shameless" members of a slave work-gang in the experimental poem "Pictures." Whitman's speaker not only casts aside these culturally entrenched notions but demands that they be replaced by celebrations of every facet of a black person's body: the "ample neck and breast," "his crispy hair and moustache," and "the black of his polish'd and perfect limbs."

Yet it is not only the black man's body that the speaker celebrates. For the "negro," thought by the vast majority of white Americans to be emotional, lazy, and lacking in self-control, here "holds firmly the reins of his four horses." He has power over himself and his circumstances: "the block swags underneath," "steady and tall he stands poised on one leg," and "his glance is calm and commanding." These phrases reverse the control usually exercised over the black person by the master and overseer in the South and by legal and extralegal discriminations in the

North. The vignette here may be a description of something Whitman once saw, but it is also a hopeful vision of the future. For the "limpsey," "weak," and fearful fugitive slave of the earlier section has become his own master. Whitman has endowed the black person with what he considers the highest personal and political blessing, what blacks in America—slave or free—did not yet have: self-sovereignty.

Moreover, it seems especially telling that Whitman's description is of a black man at *labor*. Whitman's entire political philosophy, as we have seen, was based on a passionate concern for the opportunities of the laborer. But the artisans and yeomen he celebrated in his newspaper editorials were white. His concern for the degradation of black slave labor was confined to whatever rhetorical uses he might make of it for his Free Soil agenda. Furthermore, advocacy for the slave and for the white laborer were thought to be not only separate but *competing* political agendas. As we have seen, Free Soilers criticized abolitionists' attention to the plight of slaves as detracting from what they considered the more important issue of the plight of white laborers. Here Whitman seeks to achieve what he called his "final aim" of uniting these competing voices as he merges the dignity of labor with a tacit opposition to slavery in the person of the black drayman.

At the end, the speaker once again moves beyond observation to sympathetic participation:

> I behold the picturesque giant and love him
> . . . and I do not stop there,
> I go with the team also.
>
> (37)

"I do not stop there" may be Whitman's subtle criticism of Northern humanitarians who professed concern for "Negros" but did little to guarantee their freedom or advancement. Yet the speaker himself only accompanies the black person and does not fully identify with him—that is, "become" him—as he will later. As one critic points out, however, the description of the black man here matches the "dress and posture" of the drawing of Whitman *himself* that replaces his name on the title page of the 1855 *Leaves of Grass*.[11] Like Whitman in the picture, the drayman "stands poised," his blue shirt exposing "his ample neck and breast" as with a "calm and commanding" glance he "tosses the slouch of his hat away from his forehead" and the sun falls "on his crispy hair and

11. Karen Sanchez-Eppler, "To Stand Between: A Political Perspective on Whitman's Poetics of Merger and Embodiment," *ELH* 56 (Winter 1989): 926.

moustache" (37). The likeness of the black man to Whitman suggests that the ultimate merge of identities is possible, but not yet accomplished within the world of the poem.

At this point the poem is only about one-sixth of the way down the open road Whitman invites the reader to travel, and already it is clear how significant African Americans are to the poet's conceptions of human dignity and equality, to his vision of a fully inclusive, multiracial democracy, and to his own self-realization. The next one-third of the poem, while not focusing on African Americans so extensively, nonetheless continues to show how black persons are repeatedly figured into the poet's idea of an egalitarian American community. It also demonstrates that no matter how inclusive and idealistic Whitman's vision may be, culturally racist notions occasionally intrude.

In general, this portion of the poem continues to tell the story of the speaker's enormous and absorbing self. "What is commonest and cheapest and nearest and easiest is Me," he proclaims (38), and goes on to demonstrate his expansiveness with catalogues of human beings, all of whom "more or less I am" (42), with praise of the earth (48) and with a sexual embrace of the sea (49). The speaker stops momentarily to again offer a self-definition ("Walt Whitman, an American, one of the roughs, a kosmos" [50]), claims for himself the role of spokesperson of democracy ("I give the sign of democracy" [50]), and asserts a divinity that makes holy "whatever I touch or am touched from" (51). The speaker, who cannot be "proved" by "writing and talk" (53), explores and develops his magnificent senses by listening to all things (53–54) and by touching all things, experiencing in the touch of his flesh to another's an explosive sexuality that is "quivering me to a new identity" (55). The speaker finds he "incorporates" all things that only "in vain" can resist him (57–58).

Throughout this portion of the poem Whitman shows in subtle ways that African Americans are an integral part of the speaker's cosmos, and are in fact part of the very reason for the speaker's self-expression. In the first catalogue of more than sixty types of human beings whom the speaker feels he is part of (for example, the first three are "the pure contralto," "the carpenter," and "the married and unmarried children"), he includes three portraits of blacks: a "quadroon girl" being auctioned, "woollypates" hoeing in the sugarfield, and a "darkey" bearing a target for a military company's shooting excursion. As Betsy Erkkila notes, the very nature of these catalogues is to "collapse the distinctions of race, class, and gender." But as she goes on to point out, these descriptions also "bear the traces of an oppressive, hierarchic order" through the consistent depiction of blacks in subordinate positions.[12] Unlike the portrait of the drayman, the descriptions rehearse, rather than reject, conventional roles and perceptions of blacks.

Likewise, when the poet invites the slave to the "meal pleasantly set," the passage's magnanimous egalitarianism is undercut by racist stereotypes. The "meal" is the opportunity for all marginalized peoples to satisfy their "natural hunger" for justice and equality in the American republic. Unlike even Northern liberals at the time who were resurrecting colonizationist schemes, the poet "will not have a single person slighted or left away. . . . There shall be no difference between them and the rest" (44).

But when the poet invites the slave, he invites the "*heavy-lipped* slave" (44; my emphasis), an image that recalls the stereotypes reinforced by the new "scientific" racism and by stage minstrelsy. Moreover, the list of invitees to the "meal" works ambivalently with respect to blacks. While the poet reaches out to the most rejected and ostracized persons in society—the prostitute, the thief, the "venerealee"—the slave's place among them suggests, however subtly, that the character and status of the slave is the result of an illness or moral failing. This notion is underscored several pages later when the poet asserts his role as spokesperson for those people and things who traditionally have no public voice:

> Through me many long dumb voices,
> Voices of the interminable generations of slaves,
> Voices of prostitutes and of deformed persons,
> Voices of the diseased and despairing, and of
>   thieves and of dwarves,
> Voices of cycles of preparation and accretion,
> And of the threads that connect the stars—and
>   of wombs and of fatherstuff,
> And of the rights of them the others are down upon,
> Of the trivial and flat and foolish and despised,
> Of fog in the air and beetles rolling balls of dung.
>
>   (50)

Whitman is of course claiming a role to speak not only for those who are oppressed but for all of creation, from "the threads that connect the stars" to "beetles rolling balls of dung." He will especially speak for those who have been abused, degraded, and silenced. Yet the very indiscrimination that accepts and speaks for "the interminable generations

12. Erkkila, *Whitman the Political Poet*, 101.

of slaves" also puts them on the same level with "the diseased and despairing," and perhaps even with the "beetles rolling balls of dung." Throughout this part of the poem, the poet projects a radically inclusive voice that will "accept nothing which all cannot have . . . on the same terms." But that same voice flattens all distinctions, implicitly suggesting, perhaps, that African Americans were what the vast majority of white Americans thought them to be: physically different and inferior, perhaps not even fully human.

Yet if Whitman's treatment of blacks in these short passages reveals how culturally conditioned perceptions could not be excised from his idealistic vision, the final extended portrait of an African American dramatically completes the speaker's quest to merge with all others and so resolves for the speaker nothing less than what it ultimately means to be a human being.

The story of the "hounded slave" occurs toward the end of section 33, a major section that anchors the poem by virtue of its length (160 lines, or about one-eighth the poem's total) and its thematic content. The section continues to define the speaker's cosmic, boundless self, unlimited by space or time. That self now literally takes off and begins to traverse the globe:

> My ties and ballasts leave me . . . I travel . . . I sail . . .
>   my elbows rest in the sea-gaps,
> I skirt the sierras . . . my palms cover continents,
> I am afoot with my vision.
>
> (59)

An eighty-line catalogue details the many places where the speaker passes beyond boundaries to participate in every human and animal activity. In the first few lines alone he prospects for gold, hoes an onion patch, camps with lumbermen, and walks "where the panther walks."

As the section proceeds, the formal movement from single-line descriptions to longer vignettes signals a simultaneous movement in subject matter from relatively safe activity to scenes and events that are increasingly dangerous and violent:

> We are about approaching some great battlefield
>   in which we are soon to be engaged,
> We pass the colossal outposts of the encampments
>   . . . we pass with still feet and caution;
> Or are entering by the suburbs some vast and ruined city.
>
> (64)

This movement toward danger suggests that full humanity for the cosmic self entails the risk of entering into *all* experience, however painful. Throughout this section the speaker is still wholly "other," a presence who accompanies or replaces others but is separate from them.

Yet when the vignettes turn toward even more brutal and personal terror, the notion of a separate self begins to erode:

> My voice is the wife's voice, the screech by the rail of the stairs,
> They fetch my man's body up dripping and drowned.

>   (64)

The speaker's stance is not merely one of empathy or compassion, but a near identification, almost a becoming of the newly widowed woman. And yet it is not complete identification. For despite the perspective that wails "my man's body," the woman is still objectified and set apart: "My voice is *the wife's* voice" (my emphasis). Likewise, when the speaker describes how a brave ship's captain saved the company of people on a drifting shipwreck, the actors are consistently described in the third person until the final line: "I am the man . . . I suffered . . . I was there." But even here it is not clear who the speaker is—the captain? one of the saved?—or how he was "there." As the cosmic self develops and expands, he pushes toward fully becoming an "other," but he cannot complete the difficult metamorphosis.

It is not until—and only with—the description of the "hounded slave" that the speaker makes this critical transition:

> The hounded slave that flags in the race and leans
>   by the fence, blowing and covered with sweat,
> The twinges that sting like needles his legs and neck,
> The murderous buckshot and the bullets,
> All these I feel or am.

> I am the hounded slave . . . I wince at the bite of the dogs,
> Hell and despair are upon me . . . crack and again
>   crack the marksmen,
> I clutch the rails of the fence . . . my gore dribs thinned
>   with the ooze of my skin,
> I fall on the weeds and stones,
> The riders spur their unwilling horses and haul close,
> They taunt my dizzy ears . . . they beat me violently
>   over the head with their whip-stocks.
> Agonies are one of my changes of garments;

I do not ask the wounded person how he feels . . . I myself
    become the wounded person,
My hurt turns livid upon me as I lean on a cane and observe.

                                                 (65)

Here at last Whitman's speaker makes the final leap of the sympathetic
and imaginative self: not merely from observer to participant but from
wholly self to wholly other, from object to subject, from "he" to "I."
(As we saw in Chapter 5, Whitman editorially made this metamorphosis
by changing the pronoun in the wake of the Anthony Burns affair and
other well-known fugitive slave cases.) "All these I feel or am" marks
the last stage in the speaker's merging with the world, and his final, most
radical word in "Song" about African Americans and slavery: to truly
sympathize with the black experience, one must imaginatively, passionately, enter into it. As George Fredrickson points out, a distinguishing
characteristic of abolitionists was the way in which they "sought sympathy with the slave" by trying to "participate vicariously in his suffering."[13] Whitman pushes this notion of vicarious suffering to its farthest
extreme. "I do not ask the wounded person how he feels," the speaker
says in an implicit critique of tepid humanitarianism, "I myself become
the wounded person."

    D. H. Lawrence, in his famous work *Studies in Classic American
Literature* (1923), focuses on this passage as an example of how Whitman completely misunderstood the notion of "sympathy" that he so
emphatically proclaimed. Lawrence objected to the speaker's identification with the slave, arguing that it was not truly a sympathetic act.
"Sympathy means feeling *with*," Lawrence said, "not feeling for" (my
emphasis).[14] What Whitman claimed in identifying with the slave was
not sympathy, Lawrence said, but "merging and self-sacrifice."

    If Whitman had truly sympathized, he would have said: "That
    negro suffers from slavery. He wants to free himself. His soul
    wants to free him. . . . If I can help him I will: I will not take over
    his wounds and his slavery to myself. But I will help him fight
    the power that enslaves him when he wants to be free, if he wants
    my help, since I see in his face that he needs to be free."[15]

    13. Fredrickson, *The Black Image in the White Mind,* 33.
    14. D. H. Lawrence, *Studies in Classic American Literature* (New York: Penguin Books,
1986), 183.
    15. Ibid., 184.

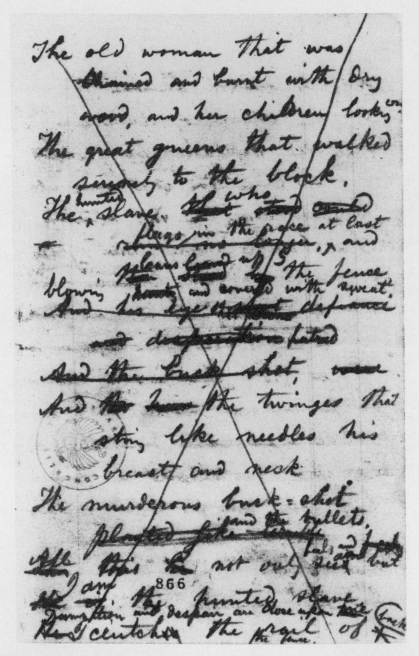

Figs. 1 and 2.   Whitman's revisions of the "hounded [hunted] slave" section from "Song of Myself." Courtesy of the Library of Congress.

my gore   trickles
blood presents

thinned with the
                salt ooze of my skin
And   the black
And the hunters haul up close

        with their unwilling horses,
Till   taunt and   oath
        and dizzy   ears.

What Lucifer   from
        heaven

What the rebel,   gaily
        adjusting his neck to the
        rope noose,

What the   savage lashed to
        the stump,   it till
yell and laughter   at every foe

What rage of hell   urged

Yet recent scholarship on slave narratives has shown that Whitman's imaginative entry into the runaway slave's life may well be the most compassionate response possible. In his provocative study of the slave narrative, William Andrews argues that the central rhetorical problem in early black autobiography was how it might "move its white reader in one direction, from an alien to a consubstantial relationship with the text and the black self presumably represented by the text."[16] In his attempts to represent black experience to a white audience, Whitman struggles with this same problem in "Song of Myself." Only when we understand the novel rhetorical strategies of the most well-known slave narrative of the time, the 1845 *Narrative of the Life of Frederick Douglass*, can we appreciate how radical—and how similar to Douglass's work—is Whitman's poem.

Andrews argues that for the first time in African American autobiography Douglass "declared a new and crucial role for the *imagination* as a mode of mediation . . . in black-white discourse" (my emphasis).[17] Toward the end of the *Narrative*, Douglass urges his reader to "place himself in my situation" as he seeks to describe his state of mind when he arrives in the North. Douglass writes:

> The motto which I adopted when I started from slavery was this—"Trust no man!" I saw in every white man an enemy, and in almost every colored man cause for distrust. It was a most painful situation; and, *to understand it, one must needs experience it, or imagine himself in similar circumstances.* Let him be a fugitive slave in a strange land—a land given up to be the hunting ground for slaveholders—whose inhabitants are legalized kidnappers—where he is every moment subjected to the terrible liability of being seized upon by his fellowmen, as the hideous crocodile seizes upon his prey!—*I say, let him place himself in my situation*—without home or friends—without money or credit—wanting shelter, and no one to give it—wanting bread, and no money to buy it,—and at the same time let him feel that he is pursued by merciless men-hunters, and in total darkness as to what to do, where to go, or where to stay. . . . *I say, let him be placed in this most trying situation,—the situation in which I was placed,—then, and not till then, will he fully appreciate the*

---

16. William Andrews, *To Tell a Free Story: The First Century of Afro-American Autobiography, 1760–1865* (Urbana: University of Illinois Press, 1986), 135.
    17. Ibid., 137.

hardships of, and know how to sympathize with, the toil-worn and whip-scarred fugitive slave. (my emphases)[18]

In this passage, Andrews says, Douglass points toward "an unprecedented answer to the central rhetorical problem of the slave narrative—how to build a bridge of sympathetic identification between the diametrical points of view of the northern white reader and the southern black fugitive." That answer, according to Andrews, is "imaginative self-projection of the reader into the text." Such imaginative entry must be "the basic preparatory condition for the kind of understanding that Douglass wanted whites to derive from his story, the understanding of the individual emotional significance of the facts of a fugitive's life. Thus Douglass repeatedly insisted of the white reader, " 'let him place himself in my situation.' " In declaring the centrality of the imagination in the reading of slave narrative, Douglass "helped to open up rhetorical options of black autobiographers as they had never been explored before," Andrews concludes.[19]

What Andrews says about Douglass's attempts to mediate between white readers and black experience can also be applied to Whitman's rhetorical strategies in his writing about blacks in "Song of Myself." Neither Douglass nor Whitman want readers to approach their texts from what Andrews calls "the standpoint of the distanced, uncommitted, merely curious." Neither want to "indulge his reader in a servile way."[20] (Recall that Whitman wrote: "You shall no longer take things at second or third hand . . . / You shall not look through my eyes either, nor take things from me" [28].) Both Douglass and Whitman show that real sympathy can be achieved only through "an imaginative leap into the total situation of the fugitive and the world of the text."[21]

It is not clear to what extent Whitman was familiar with Douglass's rhetorical strategy of inviting his readers or listeners to engage in an act of sympathetic imagination. Nowhere in Whitman's correspondence or notebooks does he mention Douglass's *Narrative,* though the work was so widely known among abolitionist circles in the North that it would be hard to imagine him not having come across it. We know that Whitman may have heard Douglass speak (such as at the 1848 Free Soil convention in Buffalo), and a number of Douglass's speeches include exactly this strategy. In an address delivered in May 1848 at the Convention Hall in New York City, Douglass asked his readers to "suppose you

18. Frederick Douglass, *Narrative of the Life of Frederick Douglass* (New York: New American Library, 1968), 111–12.
19. Andrews, *To Tell a Free Story,* 138.
20. Ibid., 137.
21. Ibid., 138.

yourselves were black, and that your sisters and brothers were in slavery, subject to the brutality and the lash of the atrocious tyrant who knew no mercy."[22]

The connection, then, between Douglass's message and Whitman's writing about African Americans in "Song of Myself" appears to be more than coincidental. Whitman's writing, in fact, seems rather like a direct and remarkable response to Douglass's urgent request to "let him place himself in my situation." On the narrative level Whitman's two extended passages about fugitive slaves directly recite some of the details and emotional intensity of Douglass's passage. But even beyond that, in placing himself in the situation of a fugitive slave, Whitman responds to Douglass's original request: he places the *reader* in that situation as well. Put another way, it might be said that merging is accomplished simultaneously on several levels. As the reader merges with the speaker throughout the course of the poem ("what I assume you shall assume"), and the speaker merges into the identity of the "hounded slave," so now does the reader feel the "murderous buckshot," "the bite of the dogs," and the feeling of "hell and despair" as one stumbles, bloody, on the "weeds and stones." Moreover, Whitman is perhaps in a position to evoke a sympathetic reaction more effectively than even Douglass himself. For Whitman's whiteness allows a sympathetic reaction to his *imagined* black experience that would not be possible with a white audience's response to an actual black experience.

For Whitman, as for Douglass, sympathy and imagination are necessarily linked: in the only writing previous to *Leaves of Grass* in which Whitman clearly showed sympathy for the African American's experience—an 1846 editorial on the "middle passage" of slaves from Africa—Whitman repeatedly asks his readers to "imagine" the suffering of more than three hundred slaves cramped in the hold of a ship (*GF* 1:189). Yet the appeals to imagination in Whitman's poetry serve an immediate political goal as well. By focusing two of his three extended passages about African Americans in "Song of Myself" on *fugitive* slaves, Whitman works to build opposition to the Fugitive Slave Law and so again to accomplish what he had defined as his "final aim" of concentrating around him both "transcendentalist" reformers and "free soilers" (*NUPM* 1:147). Moreover, since Whitman concentrates on the fugitive slave rather than on slavery itself, it might be said that one's attention is diverted from an outright opposition to slavery, or even that the focus

22. Frederick Douglass, *The Frederick Douglass Papers*, ed. John W. Blassingame (New Haven: Yale University Press, 1982), 2:129. At the time Whitman was just concluding his work in New Orleans, though he would have had access to Douglass's speech from New York newspapers that reprinted it in May and June (see ibid., 128).

on sympathy, while perhaps preparatory to political or social action, as Frederick Douglass hoped, may function in Whitman's poetry as a substitute for such action.

Even given these considerations, and contrary to Lawrence's implicit criticism that merging or identification comes too easily for Whitman, fully becoming the fugitive slave requires a complete, passionate, and risky commitment. For when the speaker becomes the hounded slave, the gates are opened for experiences of human tragedy and terror, increasing in length and intensity, that almost crush the speaker into speechless angst. The speaker undergoes a series of devastating metamorphoses: "I am the mashed fireman with breastbone broken" and "I am an old artillerist" who sees and hears the "fall of grenades," the "ambulanza slowly passing and trailing its red drip," and the "gurgles" in the mouth of "my dying general" (65–66).

These brief vignettes give way to longer narratives of inhumanity, terrible violence, and mass death. The speaker tells of "the murder in cold blood of four hundred and twelve young men" at the massacre by Mexican troops of a company of Texans after their surrender at Goliad in 1836.[23] Equally horrific is the "oldfashioned frigate fight" where the "formless stacks of bodies and bodies" eerily anticipate the carnage Whitman would witness during the Civil War:

> The hiss of the surgeon's knife and the gnawing teeth
>   of his saw,
> The wheeze, the cluck, the swash of the falling blood . . .
>   the short wild scream, the long dull tapering groan,
> These so . . . these irretrievable.
>
>   (69)

Finally, the pain of these accumulated experiences becomes too much. "O Christ! My fit is mastering me!" the speaker cries, overwhelmed by having become "any presence or truth of humanity here"—what in a later version he called the act of embodying "all presences outlaw'd or suffering." The speaker continues in shorter vignettes to take on the suffering of the convict, the captured young thief, and the cholera patient. But ultimately he is reduced to a quiet and beaten retreat from the world: "I project my hat and sit shamefaced and beg" (70). (How completely Whitman has by this point identified *himself* with the suffering of black Americans may be noted by comparing this line to Whit-

23. Walt Whitman, *Leaves of Grass*, ed. Sculley Bradley and Harold W. Blodgett, 168.

man's portrait of "an old black man" from the poem "Pictures," who, "with a placard on his hat, sits low at the corner, of a street, begging.")[24]

The cosmic "I" has been "stunned" by disease and terror, and now he needs a "little time" to discover himself "on a verge of the usual mistake." That mistake would be to let the suffering overtake life, rather than to absorb it into life's wholeness. The remedy, the *only* remedy, is a re-membering of all parts of human experience—the hopeful as well as the despairing, the ecstasy and the suffering:

> I remember . . . I resume the overstaid fraction,
> The grave of rock multiplies what has been confided
>   to it . . . or to any graves,
> The corpses rise . . . the gashes heal . . . the
>   fastenings roll away.
>
> (71)

Pulling together every "fraction" of human experience brings about the Christ-like resurrection of the speaker. But in his recovery he is not alone.

> I troop forth replenished with supreme power, one
>   of an average unending procession,
> We walk the roads of Ohio and Massachusetts and
>   Virginia [etc.] . . .
> Inland and by the seacoast and boundary lines
>   . . . and we pass the boundary lines.
>
> (71)

Having pulled the totality of human experience into himself, this complete and regenerated self now becomes part of the American republic, "one of an average unending procession" of all Americans who are similarly resurrected. Together, they walk the roads of every state, move past the final "boundary lines"—not of land only but of race and ideology— and discover that all people are divine: "they who have eyes are divine, and the blind and the lame are equally divine" (69).

This journey with the readers has just begun, but in another sense it is almost complete as the poem comes to a close. From here until the end of the poem the speaker addresses the reader, exhorting him or her to be bold and independent—that is, to become the proud and sympathetic self the "Preface" and this poem have helped create.

24. Whitman, *NUPM* 4:1304.

Whitman's own trope to describe the experience of reading "Song of Myself" is of a journey down an open road:

> Failing to fetch me at first keep encouraged,
> Missing me one place search another,
> I stop somewhere waiting for you
>
> (88)

Yet read with a focus on Whitman's writing about African Americans, the poem becomes something entirely different—a slave narrative.[25] It is interesting to note, for example, how "Song of Myself" replicates some of the formulaic elements of slave narrative, according to a list of conventions suggested by James Olney. The poem contains "a title page that includes the claim 'Written by Himself'" (Whitman's opening line: "I celebrate myself"); "an account of one very strong, hardworking slave who refuses to be whipped" (the black drayman); a "description of slave patrols, of failed attempts to escape, of pursuit by men and dogs" (the "hounded slave"); and a "description of successful attempts to escape, lying by during the day and travelling by night guided by the North Star, given generous reception in a free state by Quakers (or others on the Underground Railroad)" (the succor extended to the "runaway slave").[26] But even beyond these rather striking similarities, "Song of Myself" works as a slave narrative on more fundamental levels. First, the poem's narrative is often about slaves' and other oppressed persons' condition and their transformation to liberation. Second, several of the poem's themes as well as the overall structure depend decisively on passages about slaves. Third, the poem becomes a slave narrative in just the way that Douglass had asked—its writer and readers fully identifying with the fugitive slave. And finally, "Song of Myself" becomes Whitman's own escape from slavery.

It would be dishonest and reductive to suggest that "slavery" to the conventions and expectations of mid-nineteenth-century American culture was at all comparable to the oppressive and violent slavery that existed for millions of blacks. Whitman is careful here not to use slavery

25. I am indebted to Professor Ed Folsom for the idea of reading "Song of Myself" as a slave narrative, which I develop in my own way here. For Folsom's reading, see "Introduction: Recircuiting the American Past," *A Profile of Twentieth-Century American Poetry,* ed. Jack Myers and David Wojahn (Carbondale: Southern Illinois University Press, 1991), 20.

26. James Olney, "'I Was Born': Slave Narratives, Their Status as Autobiography and as Literature," in *The Slave's Narrative,* ed. Charles Davis and Henry Louis Gates Jr. (New York: Oxford University Press, 1985), 152–53.

as a convenient metaphor for other forms of oppression, as he did in his journalism or earlier poems such as "The House of Friends."[27] Yet "Song of Myself" is Whitman's slave narrative in the same way that the writing of autobiography by former slaves was not merely a record of their progress from bondage toward liberation, but "uniquely self-liberating," the final act in their quest for freedom, a way of declaring themselves free and of redefining their freedom.[28] The slave's struggle to "become" not only constitutes the story but culminates in its telling—and so for Whitman, too. "Song of Myself" is not only the story but the *act* of his own liberation from nineteenth-century conventions of discourse and racial thinking.

Whitman could not, of course, entirely escape racial prejudice, even within the transcendent expanse of his poetry. But, like Frederick Douglass, he was able to inscribe a self on its own terms—magnificently large and diverse, and capable of leaps of imagination into the experience of African Americans and other marginalized peoples that modeled what it meant to be fully human—or, what for Whitman meant essentially the same thing, to be fully American.

27. Whitman is not alone among mid-nineteenth-century writers who employ slavery as a useful metaphor for other problems. In the opening pages of *Walden,* Thoreau writes: "I sometimes wonder that we can be so frivolous, I may almost say, as to attend to the gross but somewhat foreign form of servitude called Negro Slavery, there are so many keen and subtle masters that enslave both North and South. It is hard to have a Southern overseer; it is worse to have a Northern one; but worst of all when you are the slave-driver of yourself." (Henry David Thoreau, *Walden and Civil Disobedience,* ed. Sherman Paul [Boston: Houghton Mifflin, 1960], 4.)
28. Andrews, *To Tell a Free Story,* 103.

SPEAKING A NEW WORD

Two other major poems in the 1855 *Leaves of Grass* extend the slave narrative begun in "Song of Myself," and they do so in ways that sharpen Whitman's radical notion that the slave's experience is at the heart of American identity. In "I Sing the Body Electric," the celebration of the human body as sacred becomes the basis for an egalitarian democracy where the slave and the immigrant belong "here or anywhere just as much as the welloff . . . just as much as you" (122). In "The Sleepers," the wrongs committed against the slave represent the farthest extreme of human alienation and urgently call for a reconciliation of the diverse elements of the national polis. Taken together, the three major poems of 1855 show that the lives and experiences of African Americans are not just interesting to Whitman but are intimately bound up with American character and destiny.

In "I Sing the Body Electric," the portraits of a male and female slave being sold at auction are the heart of the poem, not only modeling the divine human form but also representing the poet's ultimate vision of a multiracial American republic. The first two-thirds of the poem builds toward the notion that the sacredness of every body is the basis of democracy. The speaker celebrates the beauty and perfection of the human body with the sorts of catalogues, vignettes, and transitional statements employed in "Song of Myself." He describes how the "expression of a well-made man" appears not only in his face but in every movement of his body. After cataloguing those human types with whom he longs to be in contact ("[I] swim with the swimmer, and wrestle with wrestlers, and march in line with the firemen" [119]) and portraying the "wonder-ful vigor and calmness and beauty" of an eighty-year-old farmer (120), the speaker, as in "Song of Myself," enters into a highly charged sexual union. This time the partner is the "female form" and the procreative act ("Limitless limpid jets of love hot and enormous") leads to the "bath of birth," the ultimate "merge" of "small and large and the outlet again" (121). The cumulative effect of his repeated physical contact with others and of the sexual union leads to the poem's central, political message:

> The man's body is sacred and the woman's body
>   is sacred . . . it is no matter who,
> Is it a slave? Is it one of the dullfaced immigrants
>   just landed on the wharf?
>
> Each belongs here or anywhere just as much as the
>   welloff . . . just as much as you,
> Each has his or her place in the procession.
>
> All is a procession,
> The universe is a procession with measured and
>   beautiful motion.
>
> Do you know so much that you call the slave or
>   the dullfaced ignorant?
> Do you suppose you have a right to a good sight . . .
>   and he or she has no right to a sight?
> Do you think matter has cohered together from its diffused
>   float, and the soil is on the surface and water runs and
>   vegetation sprouts for you . . . and not for him or her?
>   (122)

Whitman's speaker locates the basis of a fully inclusive and egalitarian democracy in the universal "sacred"-ness of every human body, what Jimmie Killingsworth calls the "common denominator" that links "all classes, races, and divided groups."[1] Moreover, Whitman directly chal-lenges his readers ("Do you know so much") to include the very two groups of outcasts that were the focus of the nation's political debates: slaves and immigrants. He rejects notions of privilege and exclusivity, asserting that "Each belongs here or anywhere just as much as the well-off . . . just as much as you."

Whitman's emphasis on including the slave among the universe of

---

1. Killingsworth, *Whitman's Poetry of the Body*, 8.

"sacred" human bodies leads naturally to the narrative of a slave auction. In Whitman's longest poetic writing about African Americans, the value of the slave is shown to be beyond anyone's imagination:

> A slave at auction!
> I help the auctioneer . . . the sloven does not
>   half know his business.
>
> Gentlemen look on this curious creature,
> Whatever the bids of the bidders they cannot be
>   high enough for him,
> For him the globe lay preparing quintillions of
>   years without one animal or plant,
> For him the revolving cycles truly and steadily rolled.
>
> In that head the allbaffling brain,
> In it and below it the making of the attributes of heroes.
> Examine these limbs, red black or white . . .
>   they are very cunning in tendon and nerve;
> They shall be stript that you may see them.
>
> Exquisite senses, lifelit eyes, pluck, volition,
> Flakes of breastmuscle, pliant backbone and neck,
>   flesh not flabby, goodsized arms and legs,
> And wonders within there yet.
>
> Within there runs his blood . . . the same old
>   blood . . . the same red running blood,
> There swells and jets his heart . . . There all passions and
>   desires . . . all reachings and aspirations;
> Do you think they are not there because they are not
>   expressed in parlors and lecture rooms?
>
>   (123)

It may seem troubling that the speaker helps the auctioneer and objectifies the slave as a "curious creature" whom the speaker strips so that potential buyers may have a closer look at the slave's body. The speaker seems to be a collaborator in the very dehumanization that he decries. But in replacing the auctioneer Whitman criticizes his office, demonstrating how the auctioneer, like the bidders, cannot possibly fathom that the object of their financial interests is of a value paid for by all time and all creation: "For him the globe lay preparing quintillions of years without one animal or plant, / For him the revolving cycles truly and steadily rolled."

The speaker's "auction" becomes a corrective retelling of a scene Whitman observed—perhaps many times—while in New Orleans. As an editor at the *Crescent* he had read advertisements of auctions held at the Charles Street Banks' Arcade, where "merchandise" from Virginia or North Carolina would be put on the block:

> Jerry, aged 26, a superior cotton picker and
> leader in the field, fully guaranteed;
> Sarah Ann, 17 years, house girl, and her
> infant girl, fully guaranteed;
> Etty, 30 years, an excellent cook and washer,
> fully guaranteed excepting sometimes drinks.[2]

Since the Arcade was a gathering place for journalists, Whitman often would see the whole spectacle: the chattels who filled benches having to open their mouths so that buyers could inspect their gums and teeth; slave auctioneers sipping brandy and water while they conducted the sales; and planters lounging "at the huge bar that filled an entire side wall of the Arcade and, abolitionists charged, became drunk while their neighbors bought themselves rich in Negroes."[3]

In some respects Whitman's entire poem parallels a slave auction. As Karen Sanchez-Eppler notes, the business of the poet, like that of the auctioneer, is to stand between product and buyer and "to sing the value of the thing at hand."[4] Like the slave auction, Whitman's poem focuses on the value of the human body. But, as in "Song of Myself," the black person is praised not for his body only: in his head is "the allbaffling brain," in his heart "all passions and desires . . . all reachings and aspirations," and in his spirit "pluck, volition." Whitman provokes his genteel readers to consider the inherent similarities between their own characteristics and those of the slaves: "Do you think they are not there because they are not expressed in parlors and lecture rooms?"

Moreover, Whitman's auctioneer is not content merely to sing the praises of the African American as an isolated individual. When he asks the bidders to "Examine these limbs, red black or white," he invites them to see not a person but a nation. The clustering of the three colors, unseparated by comma or other marker, serves as a visual representation of what the poet hopes the United States can become: a complete, equal,

---

2. Quoted without attribution in Rubin, *The Historic Whitman*, 190.

3. Ibid. For another description of these New Orleans slave auctions, see Zweig, *Walt Whitman*, 72.

4. Sanchez-Eppler, "To Stand Between," 926.

and undifferentiated amalgamation of races. That these colors represent
the body politic is confirmed by a similar use of them in the following
poem, later titled "Faces." That poem's essential theme is that human
faces, like the human body, all show a divine origin despite their differences in character and quality: "their descent [is] from the Master himself" (127). No one is excluded from this truth, Whitman says: "red
white or black, all are deific." In "I Sing the Body Electric," Whitman
reaches out to include all bodies—red, white, and black—within the
physical and political landscape of nineteenth-century America. It is a
remarkable gesture, for in claiming space for all peoples Whitman rejects
every expression of racial exclusivism that formed the earlier contexts
of his racial thinking: New York Democrats' attempts to exclude blacks
from the electorate; Free Soilers of Whitman's own Barnburner faction
basing their opposition to the extension of slavery on the "abhorrence"
of blacks; and the increasingly separatist tenor of the 1850s, when states
were moving to ban blacks, colonizationist schemes appeared anew, and
pseudoscientists proclaimed the superiority of whites and the inferiority
of all others, especially African Americans.

Whitman sees the auctioned slave not only as representative of the
nation but as the progenitor of many nations, making the crime of slavery against him all the more destructive.

> This is not only one man . . . he is the father of
>   those who shall be fathers in their turns,
> In him the start of populous states and rich republics,
> Of him countless immortal lives with countless embodiments
>   and enjoyments.
>
>   (123)

A Northern reader might find in this line encouragement for colonization. After all, "the start of populous states and rich republics" need
not be in this land. But Whitman quickly dispels such thinking with a
challenge to his readers to consider their common origin with African
Americans:

> How do you know who shall come from the offspring
>   of his offspring through the centuries?
> Who might you find you have come from yourself if
>   you could trace back through the centuries?
>
>   (123)

These provocative questions scandalize Whitman's Northern readers
with the possibility that what was true in the South might be true in the

North as well: that *any* American may be of mixed-race origin. In rejecting the popular notion of polygenesis and asserting instead a single origin for the human family, Whitman insists that the very existence of slavery implicates the reader in the oppression, dehumanization, and commodification of a person related to him or her self.

Whitman continues this line of thinking in a portrait of "a woman at auction."

> She too is not only herself . . . She is the teeming
>   mother of mothers,
> She is the bearer of them that shall grow and be mates
>   to the mothers.
>
> Her daughter or their daughters' daughters . . . who knows
>   who shall mate with them?
> Who knows through the centuries what heroes may come
>   from them?
>
> In them and of them natal love . . . in them the divine mystery
>   . . . the same old beautiful mystery.

(124)

Whitman's words here would likely shock his readers—even the most liberal of them—as a form of racial heresy. Far from condemning miscegenation as he did thirteen years earlier in *Franklin Evans,* Whitman offers it as the very possibility of a multiracial future: "Who knows who shall mate with" the female progeny of the female slave? The boldness of this line is even more striking when one recalls that in the racial politics of mid-century America violent hostility against miscegenation had been steadily on the rise since 1830, largely because the South felt more and more compelled to justify slavery—and thus the separation of the races—in response to attacks by abolitionists.[5] As in the "Preface," Whitman was envisioning an American identity that perhaps could be imagined only by the transcendent "poet," one who could rise above the racial thinking of his day and look ahead into the future. That vision would be captured more than one hundred years later by another poet, Langston Hughes:

> You are white—
> yet a part of me, as I am a part of you.

5. Christian, "Shadows Uplifted," 190.

That's American.
Sometimes perhaps you don't want to be a part of me.
Nor do I often want to be a part of you.
But we are, that's true![6]

Moreover, the woman at auction, like her male counterpart, is seen as the matriarch of a race or nation, "the teeming mother of mothers." Whitman's description omits entirely his focus—perhaps "obsession" would be the better word—on the physical traits of women of color in earlier writings such as *Franklin Evans* and "Dusky Grisette." He views the African American woman here not as a prostitute or sexual object but as divine mother, one who, with her female progeny, exhibits "the divine mystery" of "natal love." The woman is still represented as an abstraction or type, but that representation takes on universal significance. On one level, Whitman, like Douglass and other ex-slave narrators, reminds his readers that African American mothers and their children experience the same loving relationship as do all mothers and children, and the universality of this experience makes all people equal. Indeed, that is the very point of the next lines.

Have you ever loved a woman?
Your mother . . . is she living? . . . Have you been much
    with her? and has she been much with you?
Do you not see that these are exactly the same to all in all
    nations and times all over the earth?

                                                                (124)

But on another level Whitman may be saying something even more radical and profound. For in calling the woman at auction "*the* teeming mother of mothers" (my emphasis) and the enfolder of "the divine mystery," Whitman points to her unique role in an ancient past. Likewise, his question—"Who might you find you have come from yourself if you could trace back through the centuries?"—suggests a similar role for the male slave. In short, Whitman is prodding his readers to do nothing less than consider the notion that this man and woman are their primal parents, are, in Judeo-Christian terms, Adam and Eve. A notebook draft entry from late 1854 makes this very point:

6. Langston Hughes, "Theme for English B," *The Langston Hughes Reader* (New York: Applebee, 1958), 109.

> Men and women at auction./
> I see Here is—Adam and Eve again
> I see the old myths
> (*NUPM* 1:153)

For a nineteenth-century reader, the implications of such a claim are enormous. Whitman is not only rejecting the increasingly popular hypothesis of polygenesis and the inherent inferiority of certain races. He is asserting that the common origin of all people might well be black persons not unlike those who were poked and prodded and sold like animals in America. In this way, the crime of slavery becomes a wrong against all humanity and all history. In bartering off this man and woman, those who do so are buying and selling the progenitors of the world, their own fathers and mothers.

The poem's closing lines sharply reiterate Whitman's condemnation of the degradation of the sacred human body by any means, but especially through slavery:

> Who degrades or defiles the living body is
>   cursed,
> Who degrades or defiles the body of the dead is
>   not more cursed.
> (124)

Whitman's use of "degrades" would call to his reader's mind at least two contemporary connotations of the word: (1) the way that white laborers were thought by free soilers and others to be "degraded" by working in the same territory or state as blacks; and (2) the way that abolitionists felt blacks were "degraded" by slavery—that is, made less than their natural state. In choosing the second of these meanings, Whitman suggests not only how far he has come in his thinking but also, and more significantly, how his insistence on the cosmic, historical significance of African Americans transcends the most radical and humanitarian of abolitionist claims.

While "I Sing the Body Electric" challenges its readers to appreciate the significance of African Americans both to America's past and to its democratic future, "The Sleepers" apocalyptically asserts that slavery so long as it exists can lead only to the nation's self-destruction. The third and final 1855 poem in which blacks play a vital role, "The Sleepers" is a complex psychic drama in which the cosmic self wanders through the night visiting various persons who are sleeping and then becomes them, entering their dreams. Sleep is figured as the great democratic equalizer, reconciler, and healer. Though the poem contains only one passage about a black person, that passage provides the poem's narrative turning point and moral center as the horror of slavery represents the nadir of human existence, the darkest descent into alienation and suffering.

Despite the variety of interpretations of "The Sleepers," modern readers have generally agreed on the cyclical structure of the poem—specifically, its movement from sexual ecstasy to violence and alienation and then to recovery and wholeness.[7] The early part of the poem describes the poet's wandering among a variety of sleepers. "I wander all night in my vision," the speaker says as he begins his remarkable journey. He visits sleepers who are alienated and suffering ("The gashed bodies on battlefields, the insane in their strong-doored rooms") and sleepers who are at peace ("The married couple sleep calmly in their bed, he with his palm on the hip of his wife"). As in "Song of Myself," the speaker's sympathetic imagination soon transforms him from observer to participant, from object to subject:

> I go from bedside to bedside . . . I sleep close
>   with the other sleepers, each in turn;
> I dream in my dream all the dreams of the other
>   dreamers,
> And I become the other dreamers.
>
>   (108)

After experiencing a series of metamorphoses into "the other dreamers" (he becomes actor, actress, voter, politician, emigrant, exile, criminal), the speaker emerges as a woman in bed at night with her lover.

---

7. A generation of earlier critics read "The Sleepers" in psychological terms, summarized perhaps best by Richard Chase's characterization of the poem as "the descent of the as yet unformed and unstable ego into the id, its confrontation there of the dark, human tragedy, its emergence in a new, more stable form" (Chase, *Walt Whitman Reconsidered* [New York: Sloane, 1955], 54). More recent critics have seen a connection between the psychological and political. Jimmie Killingsworth, for example, sees the poem as "a psychic drama metaphorically relating the cyclic stages of sexual development," with sexual awareness leading to an "unbounded sympathy" that constantly erodes "the boundaries society creates—race, class, gender, creed" (Killingsworth, *Whitman's Poetry of the Body*, 16, 26). Likewise, Betsy Erkkila notes that "the poet's anxiety about the nature of things is linked with anxiety about the democratic dream of America" (Erkkila, *Whitman the Political Poet*, 120). For a provocative reading based on Julia Kristeva's psychoanalytic definitions and emphasis on the interdependence of opposites, see Carol Zapata Whelan, "'Do I Contradict Myself?': Progression Through Contraries in Walt Whitman's 'The Sleepers,'" *Walt Whitman Quarterly Review* 10, no. 1 (1992): 25–39.

But the lover leaves, and night itself becomes the lover, representing "a generalized sexual energy that has been awakened in the speaker."[8]

> The cloth laps a first sweet eating and drinking,
> Laps life-swelling yokes . . . laps ear of rose-corn,
>   milky and just-ripened:
> The white teeth stay, and the boss-tooth advances in darkness,
> And liquor is spilled on lips and bosoms by touching glasses,
>   and the best liquor afterward.
>
> (110)

As in the previous two poems, the moment of sexual ecstasy leads to a dramatic turning point. But here the turning is not toward communion with the world ("Song of Myself") or the "bath of birth" ("I Sing the Body Electric"), but rather toward guilt, fear, and shame. Why this experience should do so has puzzled critics. Harold Aspiz offers perhaps the most satisfactory interpretation when he suggests that what the speaker experiences is masturbation—sexual ecstasy but without human communion. As Aspiz goes on to point out, the speaker's "hysterical and disconsolate" response illustrates the "textbook behavior of the hapless self-abuser," according to nineteenth-century scientific lore: gloomy and despondent feelings, thoughts of impending evil, and perhaps even an urge to commit suicide.[9]

Following the sexual moment, the speaker begins a long, nightmarish descent: "I descend my western course . . . my sinews are flaccid" (110). Giving in to the common nineteenth-century fear that sexuality drains one's vitality, he first imagines old age—becoming a "yellow and wrinkled" old woman—and then experiences death itself: "It is dark here underground . . . it is not evil or pain here . . . it is blank here, for reasons" (110). The speaker then drifts into visions of violent, deathly situations that reflect his own. Like the "twenty-ninth bather" of "Song of Myself," the speaker sees "a beautiful gigantic swimmer swimming naked through the eddies of the sea." But here the swimmer is dashed "headforemost on the rocks," his body "baffled and banged and bruised" and finally borne away "in the circling eddies." Likewise, the outcome of a shipwreck is tragically reversed from "Song of Myself." Where in the first poem the tenacious captain of another ship "saved the drifting company at last" (64), here "not one of the company is

8. Killingsworth, *Whitman's Poetry of the Body,* 19.
9. Harold Aspiz, *Walt Whitman and the Body Beautiful* (Urbana: University of Illinois, 1980), 207–8.

washed to us alive." The speaker is left to "help pick up the dead and lay them in rows in a barn" (111).

The poem continues on a downward spiral, but now the speaker's deathly descent represents the descent of the nation. Three vignettes increasingly show the pain of human alienation and suffering within the democratic, unitary, and multiracial United States. In the first, the poet recalls the revolutionary defeat at the battle of Brooklyn where a stoic George Washington could not hold back tears at the sight of "the slaughter of the southern braves confided to him by their parents" (112). As Betsy Erkkila points out, at a time when North and South were becoming two separate nations, the image of Washington weeping over the deaths of Southern soldiers would both remind Americans of their common struggle in the war for independence and warn them about the enormous human loss in a future civil conflict.[10] The tragedy of these deaths is redeemed, in part, by the love Washington bestows on the surviving soldiers after peace has been declared: "The chief encircles their necks with his arm and kisses them on the cheek, / He kisses lightly the wet cheeks one after another . . . he shakes hands and bids goodbye to the army" (112).

Likewise, the pain of separation in the second vignette is redeemed by at least the possibility of love and community within the American republic. A "red squaw" visits the home of the speaker's mother. The squaw's beautiful face, voice, movement, and character elicit a genuine and tender love from the mother:

> The more she looked upon her she loved her,
> Never before had she seen such wonderful beauty
>   and purity;
> She made her sit on a bench by the jamb of the
>   fireplace . . . she cooked food for her,
> She had no work to give her but she gave her
>   remembrance and fondness.
>
> (113)

Just as in "Song of Myself" where the speaker's experience of "the merge" first becomes multiracial through the marriage of the trapper and the "red girl," here the speaker's vision of American community becomes multiracial through the bond between a white person and an American Indian.

10. Erkkila, *Whitman the Political Poet*, 120.

But the union cannot last. In the afternoon the squaw goes away, leaving the mother longing to see her:

> All the week she thought of her . . . she watched
>   for her many a month,
> She remembered her many a winter and many a
>   summer,
> But the red squaw never came nor was heard of
>   there again.
>
> (113)

Whatever the reason for the woman's departure, the impermanence of this ideal, biracial relationship represents not only an individual's alienation from an "other" but also the nation's alienation from itself—that is, from the full possibility of democratic community.

Yet it is only in the third and final of these vignettes, that of the tormented slave, that the nadir of personal and national descent is fully realized. As in "Song of Myself," the poet sympathetically enters the experience of the slave, giving voice to the bitter frustration of the "heir" of "Lucifer":

> Now Lucifer was not dead . . . or if he was I
>   am his sorrowful terrible heir;
> I have been wronged . . . I am oppressed . . .
>   I hate him that oppresses me,
> I will either destroy him, or he shall release
>   me.
> Damn him! how he does defile me,
> How he informs against my brother and sister
>   and takes pay for their blood,
> How he laughs when I look down the bend after
>   the steamboat that carries away my woman.
>
> Now the vast dusk bulk that is the whale's
>   bulk . . . it seems mine,
> Warily, sportsman! though I lie so sleepy and
>   sluggish, my tap is death.
>
> (113)

Far different from the "hounded slave" of "Song of Myself," this slave is angry, not fearful, and he suffers not from violence against himself but from separation from those he loves: a brother and sister, fugitive slaves turned in by a paid informer, and a wife or lover sold and sent away by steamboat.[11] This portrait radically challenges the notion of the "liveliness and cheerful good-humor" of slaves that Whitman had himself perpetuated thirteen years earlier in *Franklin Evans*. Here the slave's experience represents what Jimmie Killingsworth aptly calls "the depths, the ultimate separation from God and his fellow human beings: hell."[12] Since the passage represents various forms of slave oppression, the slave's curse indicts not any particular oppressor but the entire system of slavery and society's indifferent response. Here, more than anywhere else, Whitman's challenge to slavery moves beyond the forced return of fugitive slaves.

Moreover, Whitman's use of the "Lucifer" figure achieves what other slave narratives, concerned about alienating their audience, could not. For it fully expresses the slave's violent rage—"I will either destroy him, or he shall release me"—and yet arouses sympathy as well. The slave-speaker's threat to "destroy" the oppressor becomes understandable to white readers in the specific context of the white informant who laughs in derision as the speaker's wife or lover is carried away. Whitman appears to long for and even invite a slave revolt as a purgation of national guilt, just as Thomas Jefferson realized that a slave uprising would manifest divine retributive justice.[13]

Whitman's final, curious image of the slave-speaker as "the whale's bulk" who looks to destroy the "sportsman" may at first seem an odd and incongruent trope to represent the slave's experience. Yet the image works in multiple ways that might not be possible with another metaphor. On one level, it demonstrates the slave's complete alienation from the human community. He has been degraded to the status of an animal,

11. The passage has not always been apparent to readers as focusing on the barely repressed rage of an enslaved black man. It has confused commentators perhaps because of its seeming unrelatedness to what has gone before, its vague allusions ("Who *is* Lucifer?" a first-time reader might ask), and the complex and surprising image of a "whale's bulk." An earlier generation of critics tended to read the passage in psychological terms. E. H. Miller characterized the speaker of the poem as "voicing his oedipal murderous tendencies" (*Walt Whitman's Poetry: A Psychological Journey* [Boston: Houghton Mifflin, 1968], 81). Ivan Marki saw the image of the "huge, threatening phallic bulk of the whale" as representing a "vengeful father" (*The Trial of the Poet* [New York: Columbia University Press, 1976], 239).

12. Killingsworth, *Whitman's Poetry of the Body*, 24.

13. Jefferson writes: "Indeed I tremble for my country when I reflect that God is just: that his justice cannot sleep for ever: that considering numbers, nature and natural means only, a revolution of the wheel of fortune, an exchange of situation, is among possible events: that it may become probable by supernatural interference! The Almighty has no attribute which can take side with us in such a contest" (*Notes on the State of Virginia*, 163).

outside the pale of humanity. Moreover, the speaker's self-descriptive adjectives seem to express the very prejudices about black people that Whitman's readers would likely have. African Americans, like the whale's bulk, are seen to be "sleepy and sluggish," an undifferentiated mass of black humanity that is huge, unknowable, and imminently violent.

But here Whitman undermines the reader's conventional expectations: the whale's bulk only *seems* "sleepy and sluggish." In reality it has amazing strength and will, and its violence may be justified: "my tap is death." Whitman's readers would be familiar with Old Testament images of behemoths as "natural avengers," principles of "retributive justice or the 'wrath of God.'"[14] Some might even have read *Moby-Dick*. Whitman's image, then, which at first appears to reduce, rather than enhance, the black man's humanity, ultimately captures the complexity and power of his experience. Just as Whitman seeks by the genre of poetry to express radical, new ways of thinking about African Americans, so, too, *within* his poetry he seeks to extend the possibilities of imagery in order to express a reality beyond his own.

With the slave's threat to "destroy" his oppressor, the poem's downward spiral is complete. The alienation of the slave points beyond itself to the anger of all other slaves and to a nation so alienated from its ideals that destruction is imminent. Yet just on the verge of this violence, the speaker is suddenly restored to wholeness through the healing effect of the speaker's contact with nature, and the downward spiral is reversed.

> A show of summer softness . . . a contact of something
>   unseen . . . an amour of the light and air;
> I am jealous and overwhelmed with friendliness,
> And will go gallivant with the light and air myself,
> And have an unseen something to be in contact with
>   them also.
>
> (113)

Readers have found this abrupt return to community and wholeness unsatisfactory and problematic. Betsy Erkkila, for example, says that "Whitman's declaration of faith is a declaration by fiat" and that his hopeful assertions here do not resolve "the personal and political tensions that have erupted in the poem."[15] Whatever the logical or aesthetic

14. Walt Whitman, *Leaves of Grass*, ed. Bradley and Blodgett, 628. For biblical texts, see, for example, Job 40:15–24.
15. Erkkila, *Whitman the Political Poet*, 124.

shortcomings of this reversal, it leads outward from the self as the speaker returns to witness the many sleepers he viewed at the beginning of the poem—especially those who were dispossessed or suffering—and to record his changed perceptions:

> I swear they are averaged now . . . one is no better than
>   the other,
> The night and sleep have likened and restored them.
>
> I swear they are all beautiful,
> Every one that sleeps is beautiful . . . every thing in the dim
>   night is beautiful,
> The wildest and bloodiest is over and all is peace.
>   (114–15)

A final vision pairs opposites of sleepers in an act of reconciliation. The male and female, the father and son, the learned and unlearned—all are at rest "hand in hand over the whole earth from east to west as they lie unclothed" (115). Moreover, "the call of the slave is one with the master's call . . . and the master salutes the slave" (116). How exactly the slave is united with the master—in fact, gains the *respect* of his master—is, again, not clear.

But if the poem seems less coherent than either "Song of Myself" or "I Sing the Body Electric," it shares with them the vital notion that selfhood and nationhood can only be completed through the full incorporation of African Americans. In "The Sleepers" the final image of joining hands across barriers of race, class, and gender may not fully resolve social divisions, as community can be achieved only in a dreamlike sleep. But the poem hauntingly prophesies discord and violence when the dream-vision of a multiracial, egalitarian nation is obstructed or simply not achieved. The continuation of slavery, Whitman is saying, can only mean death—for the heir of Lucifer and for us.

Although there are nine other poems in the 1855 *Leaves of Grass,* the three poems I have discussed comprise more than three-fourths of the total poetic lines and have received the lion's share of critical attention.[16]

16. For example, Jeanetta Boswell in *Walt Whitman and the Critics: A Checklist of Criticism, 1900–1978* (Metuchen, N.J.: Scarecrow Press, 1980) lists 121 articles on the twelve poems that appear in the 1855 *Leaves of Grass.* Of these, 108 are about the three poems discussed here (eighty-eight on "Song of Myself" alone), and only thirteen are on the remaining nine poems. It must be added that it cannot be ascertained from such a list how many of these articles confine their discussion to the 1855 edition of the poems.

Even so, in the remaining poems Whitman continues to incorporate black persons, even when the subject matter would seem not to require it. In "Song of Occupations," for example, Whitman insists on the value of a human being apart from one's social background or financial achievement, and he sees beyond racial categories to affirm the inherent worth of all people: "I see not merely that you are polite or whitefaced [. . .] not merely the slave . . . not Mexican native, or Flatfoot, or negro from Africa" (90). In "Song of the Answerer" the poet's vocation is to see all people as equals: "He says indifferently and alike, How are you friend? to the President at his levee, / And he says Good day my brother, to Cudge that hoes in the sugarfield" (130). In "There Was a Child Went Forth," the child who becomes every object he looks upon also becomes "the barefoot negro boy or girl" (138). And, as we have seen, in "To Think of Time" and "Faces," African Americans are affirmed equally with all others as "deific" human beings (129) whose lives must be given "strict account" by the poet (104).

And what of "A Boston Ballad"? The poem that elides the African American who is ostensibly its subject seems at odds with the representation of blacks in the major poems of *Leaves of Grass*. But looked at another way the poem is perfectly fitting, for its true subject is America's wrongheaded response to slavery. Written in the immediate aftermath of the Anthony Burns affair, "A Boston Ballad" may well be the generative moment for all the images of blacks in *Leaves of Grass,* most of which Whitman would push to "radical" extremes as he recognized the potential receptiveness of his readers. Standing on its own, the poem does not suggest that Whitman transcended conventional, Free Soil responses to slavery, or that he felt a particular compassion or sympathy for slaves. But placed within the 1855 *Leaves of Grass,* "A Boston Ballad" functions as an organic part of the whole. For the fugitive slave who was absent from the poem is now fleshed out in the other poems as fully human: Anthony Burns is the "runaway slave" who seeks respite at the home of a sympathizer; he is the "hounded slave" who has "wince[d] at the bite of the dogs" (65); he is "Lucifer" in hellish despair and anger at his white tormentors; and he is the "exquisite" father of future nations (123). Moreover, the speaker of "A Boston Ballad," who had mocked the aged phantoms of the revolution for their desperate attempts to oppose the fugitive slave's capture by aiming their crutches as if they were "firelocks" (135), now *himself* keeps "my firelock" in the corner, ready to use it in defense of the slave's freedom (36). Finally, the difference between the fairly conventional satire of "A Boston Ballad" and the content and style of the other *Leaves of Grass* poems suggests that if America is to resolve the slavery crisis and bring all peoples "red black or white" into the national community, a radically new word must be spoken.

What may be as striking as Whitman's portrayal of African Americans in *Leaves of Grass* is his implicit portrayal of his *readers*—readers he believed would themselves speak a new word about slavery. "As he sees the farthest he has the most faith," Whitman wrote of the poet in the "Preface" (9), and Whitman's ability to look into the future and find the possibilities of a collectively humane response to slavery sets him apart from others seeking to resolve the crisis. What is required, Whitman stresses in *Leaves of Grass*, is a change of heart by *all* Americans to include blacks and other marginalized peoples in a diverse and united democracy, and he seeks to make it so.

Epilogue
"On the Extremest Verge"

As stunning as Whitman's representations of African Americans may be in *Leaves of Grass,* no less remarkable is his almost immediate retreat from these new and radical claims in the years following. For while the 1855 *Leaves of Grass* represents Whitman at the dramatic emergence of his commitment to writing sympathetically about African Americans, it marks as well a sort of endpoint—the pinnacle of his public concern for slaves and his representation of them as dignified human beings. Both his poetry and prose in the years immediately after the first edition make clear that just as suddenly as his writing about slavery rallied to the peculiar confluence of forces in 1854, it returned to a less idealistic rendering of his free soil concerns. The enigma of this reversal is not helped by Whitman himself, who, toward the end of his life, offered contradictory testimony as to the endurance of his anti-slavery views. "Well, when I was young I had an intense anti-slavery spirit, which was shown in my writings," Whitman told a newspaper reporter during a trip to Canada in 1880. "Since that time I have been down South, and found out that there was no more slavery there fifty years ago than there is to-day in the North."[1] But Whitman also told Horace Traubel: "I have been anti-slavery always—was then, and am now; and to all other slaveries, too, black or white, mental or physical."[2] Whitman's latter

1. Cyril Greenland and John Robert Colombo, *Walt Whitman's Canada* (Willowdale, Ontario: Hounslow Press, 1992), 15. The problem with Whitman's claim, however, is that his only real trip to the South—excluding an 1862 visit to his brother George on a Virginia battlefield—is his time in New Orleans (1848–49) before he had even developed an "intense anti-slavery spirit" from which to depart. Whitman's inconsistent statements about his anti-slavery views reflect not only the complexity of these views (and perhaps also the nature of memory) but also his tendency toward self-fashioning for different audiences in different contexts.

2. Traubel, *With Walt Whitman in Camden,* 3:76.

interpretation notwithstanding, it is clear from the available evidence that in fact Whitman's attitudes about African Americans and slavery did change in the years immediately after the publication of *Leaves of Grass*.

Beginning already in 1856, Whitman appears to retreat from his commitment to placing the experience of African Americans and slavery at the center of the poet's vision and concern. This change is suggested not so much by the total output of his writing about blacks—future editions of *Leaves of Grass* would include most of the important passages about African Americans from the 1855 edition—but by the diffusion of focus on blacks through the addition of new poems. In the 1855 edition, for example, nine of the twelve poems include at least one reference to African Americans, and the three poems I have examined include substantial passages on blacks or slavery. In the 1856 edition only seven of twenty new poems mention any reference to blacks or slavery, and only one includes a passage longer than two lines. Moreover, that passage—from "Salut Au Monde"—focuses not on African Americans' experience of slavery but on their place within the "evolutionary parade" as Whitman comes to accept popular notions of eugenic merit and the inherent inferiority of certain races. He encourages the "Hottentot," "Austral negro," and "Caffre," among others to realize that "You will come forward in due time to my side" (*CP*, 296).[3]

The pattern of Whitman's attenuation of writing about African Americans becomes even more pronounced throughout the remainder of his career. Only seven of 135 new poems in the 1860 edition have anything to say about African Americans, and none for more than two lines. Even more striking, Whitman remains essentially silent about blacks throughout the Civil War, mentioning black soldiers and nurses only briefly in *Specimen Days* and not including any poetry about blacks in *Drum-Taps*. Whitman only incorporates blacks into the Civil War experience later in 1867 with "Ethiopia Saluting the Colors," a curious fifteen-line vignette about a black woman watching the march of Sherman's troops toward the sea. That this woman is alien to Whitman and his vision of a post–Civil War America is evident not only from his representation of her—she is, after all, "Ethiopia," of whom the speaker asks, "Who are you dusky woman, so ancient hardly human"—but also from the syntactically awkward pattern of her speech and from the stilted rhythms and rhyming scheme so uncharacteristic of Whitman

---

3. For a discussion of Whitman's racial thinking in these years, see Harold Aspiz, *Walt Whitman and the Body Beautiful*, 190.

verse. Though the poem first appeared in the 1871 *Leaves of Grass,* it was not transferred to the *Drum-Taps* section until 1881, again suggesting Whitman's reluctance to include blacks as a significant presence in the Civil War experience.[4]

Whitman scholars are also familiar with his later prose writings and statements that appear, at times, to apologize for slavery and to disavow any humane commitment to slaves.[5] In a May 1857 editorial on an abolition convention in New York, Whitman writes that "the institution of slavery is not at all without its redeeming points," and two months later he avers that for some Southern states "the infusion of slaves and the prevalent use of their labor are not objectionable on politico-economic grounds," though he concludes that "America is not the land for slaves, on any grounds."[6] Perhaps Whitman's most surprising and widely noted journalistic writing about blacks is his 1858 editorial contemplating the new constitution of Oregon, which would prohibit blacks—slave or free—from entering the state. Whitman writes:

> Who believes that the Whites and Blacks can ever amalgamate in America? Or who wishes it to happen? Nature has set an impassable seal against it. Besides, is not America for the Whites? And is it not better so? As long as the Blacks remain here how can they become anything like an independent and heroic race? There is no chance for it.[7]

4. Another way to underscore Whitman's overall retrenchment is to note the rough total of new lines written about blacks in successive *Leaves of Grass* editions: 1855—110 lines; 1856—15; 1860—8; 1865 *Drum-Taps and Sequel*—2; all other post–Civil War poetry—15 lines ("Ethiopia Saluting the Colors"). Moreover, after 1855 Whitman begins to delete passages about blacks he had previously written, most notably the "Lucifer" section of "The Sleepers," taken out in 1876.

5. For Whitman's attitudes toward blacks in the post–Civil War years, see Erkkila, *Whitman the Political Poet,* chapter 10, and Kenneth Price, "Whitman's Solutions to 'The Problem of the Blacks,'" *Resources for American Literary Study* 15 (1985): 205–8.

6. Both editorials appeared in the *Brooklyn Daily Times.* The first was written May 14, 1857 (Walt Whitman, *I Sit and Look Out: Editorials from the Brooklyn Daily Times,* ed. Emory Holloway and Vernolian Schwarz [New York, 1932], 88), the second on July 17, 1857 (*UPP* 2:10).

7. The *Brooklyn Daily Times,* 6 May 1858 (Walt Whitman, *I Sit and Look Out,* 90). Even today Whitman's pronouncements in this editorial are recalled by those wishing to point out the disparity between America's ideals and its everyday attitudes and practices toward persons of color. A "Talk of the Town" piece in the *New Yorker* magazine begins: "Somewhere in the enormous space between the ideals of American democracy and the history of American race relations, the darkest part of the American character long ago formed. . . . Who remembers that Walt Whitman, the supreme poet of democracy, was at times a white supremacist? In 1858, writing in the *Brooklyn Daily Times,* Whitman ap-

Finally, Whitman's postwar vision for America's future, *Democratic Vistas* (1871), begins with the question of universal suffrage but then turns away from any consideration of blacks, an absence all the more remarkable in light of the recently passed Thirteenth, Fourteenth, and Fifteenth Amendments.[8] Whitman, in fact, feared that blacks would vote as a block, and, according to Traubel, "he took the ground that the Negro franchise would never truly be granted till the Negro vote was a divided, not a class one."[9] And in his very last years Whitman seemed increasingly to exclude African Americans from their place in American society and culture. "Of the negro race he had a poor opinion," reported Charles Eldridge of the firm Thayer and Eldridge, publisher of the 1860 *Leaves of Grass*. "He said that there was in the constitution of the negro's mind an irredeemable trifling or volatile element, and he would never amount to much in the scale of civilization."[10] Indeed, Whitman even speculated that "the Nigger, like the Injun, will be eliminated: it is the law of races, history, what-not . . . Someone proves that a superior grade of rats comes and then all the minor rats are cleared out."[11]

This catalogue of Whitman's later views suggests the limited duration of his passionate commitment to slaves in the 1855 *Leaves of Grass*, and urges, as I have argued throughout, that any real understanding of Whitman's writing about blacks and slavery must be understood in light of a close reading of the particular historical context at any given moment in Whitman's career. It is not within the scope of this writing to take up the project of accounting for Whitman's post-1855 writings and attitudes about slavery, though one critic provides a useful starting point for such a discussion. "The nightmare of slavery was for [Whitman] always inseparable from the dream of labor," Wynn Thomas argues, suggesting that Whitman's writing about slavery—and a good many other things, for that matter—was always subordinate to his concern for labor.[12] In the years between 1855 and the start of the Civil War, for example, Whitman practiced what Thomas calls "the rhetoric of

---

plauded the fact that the new state constitution of Oregon excluded blacks, and asked his readers, "'Who believes that the Whites and Blacks can ever amalgamate in America?, etc.'" ("The Talk of the Town: Notes and Comment," *The New Yorker*, 1 July 1991, 21.)

8. Whitman writes: "I will not gloss over the appalling dangers of universal suffrage in the United States. In fact, it is to admit and face these dangers I am writing" (*CP*, 930).

9. Traubel, *With Walt Whitman in Camden*, 7:158.

10. Charles W. Eldridge, "Walt Whitman as a Conservative," *New York Times*, 7 June 1902. Quoted in Florence Bernstein Freedman, *William Douglas O'Connor: Walt Whitman's Chosen Knight* (Athens: Ohio University Press, 1985), 148.

11. Traubel, *With Walt Whitman in Camden*, 2:283.

12. M. Wynn Thomas, "Whitman and the Dreams of Labor," in *Walt Whitman: The Centennial Essays*, ed. Ed Folsom (Iowa City: University of Iowa Press, 1994), 139.

conciliation."[13] Whitman's conservative-sounding prose and dilution of concern for slaves in his poetry may be explained by his desire to preserve not only the Union but also, more specifically, a free and democratic west for the masses of the wage-earning underclass. This he hoped to do, Thomas says, by conciliating Southern opinion without compromising his free soil principles. Whitman's "conciliatory discourse" is especially evident in "The Eighteenth Presidency," the unpublished tract written in 1856, in which, as before, he pits the interests of the "three hundred and fifty thousand masters" against the "true people, the millions of white citizens, mechanics, farmers, boatmen, manufactuers, and the like" (CP, 1311). Whitman asks his worker-readers: "Shall no one among you dare open his mouth to say he is opposed to slavery, as a man should be, on account of the whites, and wants it abolished for their sake?" (CP, 1321).

Given Whitman's central concerns for Union, for labor, and for the rights and opportunities of the white masses, how, then, do we account for his singularly bold proclamation of the humanity and worth of African Americans in the 1855 *Leaves of Grass?* In this study I have suggested one answer—namely, that Whitman's passionate rhetoric about African Americans developed from a unique and perhaps unrepeatable coalescing of historical and discursive forces at the very moment he was seeking to create a work transcendent and new. Whitman's writing about slaves and slavery suggests the fragile and transitory nature of genius— how dependent it is on history, circumstance, inspiration—and luck.

Yet despite my attempts to name and define what happened, I am only too aware that, as with much else in Whitman, the truth lies somewhere beyond our comprehension. Ultimately it is Whitman himself who best describes for us how for one moment, at least, he captured the transcendent possibilities of seeing and responding to African Americans in a way that might inspire white readers entrenched in a racism whose origins preceded those of the republic. The poet "exhibits the pinnacles that no man can tell what they are or what is beyond," Whitman writes in the "Preface." "He glows a moment on the extremest verge" (CP, 13).

13. Ibid.

Bibliography

Adams, Charles Francis. *Richard Henry Dana, A Biography.* 2 vols. Boston: Houghton, Mifflin, and Company, 1891.

Allen, Gay Wilson. *The Solitary Singer.* Chicago: University of Chicago Press, 1985.

Andrews, William. *To Tell a Free Story: The First Century of Afro-American Autobiography, 1760–1865.* Urbana: University of Illinois Press, 1986.

Arvin, Newton. *Whitman.* New York: Macmillan, 1938.

Ashworth, John. *"Agrarians" and "Aristocrats": Party Political Ideology in the United States, 1837–1846.* London: Royal Historical Society, 1983.

Aspiz, Harold. *Walt Whitman and the Body Beautiful.* Urbana: University of Illinois, 1980.

Asselineau, Roger. *The Evolution of Walt Whitman.* 2 vols. Cambridge: Harvard University Press, 1960–62.

Baker, Houston A., Jr. *Blues, Ideology, and Afro-American Literature.* Chicago: University of Chicago Press, 1984.

Benson, Lee. *The Concept of Jacksonian Democracy.* Princeton: Princeton University Press, 1961.

Bohan, Ruth. "'The Gathering of the Forces': Walt Whitman and the Visual Arts, 1845–55." *The Mickle Street Review* 12 (1990): 10–30.

Boswell, Jeanetta. *Walt Whitman and the Critics: A Checklist of Criticism, 1900–1978.* Metuchen, N.J.: Scarecrow Press, 1980.

Brasher, Thomas L. *Whitman as Editor of the Brooklyn Daily Eagle.* Detroit: Wayne State University Press, 1970.

Brodie, Fawn M. *Thomas Jefferson: An Intimate History.* New York: W. W. Norton, 1974.

Brown, Herbert. *The Sentimental Novel in America, 1789–1860.* Durham: Duke University Press, 1940.

Bucke, Maurice. *Walt Whitman* 1883. Reprint, New York: Johnson Reprint Corporation, 1970.

Campbell, Stanley W. *The Slave Catchers: Enforcement of the Fugitive Slave Law, 1850–1860.* Chapel Hill: University of North Carolina Press, 1970.

Carby, Hazel. *Reconstructing Womanhood.* New York: Oxford University Press, 1987.

Cargill, Oscar. "Walt Whitman and Civil Rights." *Essays in American Literature Presented to Bruce Robert McElderry.* Ed. Max. F. Schulz. Athens: University of Ohio Press, 1970. 48–58.

Carlisle, E. Fred. *The Uncertain Self: Whitman's Drama of Identity.* Ann Arbor: University of Michigan Press, 1973.

Catalogue of the Whitman Collection . . . Being a Part of the Trent Collection. Compiled by Ellen Francis Frey. Durham: Duke University Library, 1945.

Chase, Richard. *Walt Whitman Reconsidered.* New York: Sloane, 1955.

Christian, Barbara. "Shadows Uplifted." *Feminist Criticism and Social Change.* Ed. Judith Newton and Deborah Rosenfelt. New York: Methuen, 1985. 181–215.

Clinton, Catherine. *The Plantation Mistress: Woman's World in the Old South.* New York: Pantheon, 1982.

Congressional Globe. 29th Cong., 1st sess. 1846.

———. 29th Cong., 2nd sess. 1847.

———. 31st Cong., 1st sess. 1850.

Dalke, Anne. "'Whitman's Literary Intemperance': *Franklin Evans,* or The Power of Love." *Walt Whitman Review* 3 (Winter 1985): 17–22.

Dictionary of American Regional English. 3 vols. Ed. Frederic G. Cassidy. Cambridge: The Belknap Press of Harvard University, 1985.

Douglass, Frederick. *The Frederick Douglass Papers.* Vol. 2. Ed. John W. Blassingame. New Haven: Yale University Press, 1982.

———. *Narrative of the Life of Frederick Douglass.* New York: New American Library, 1968.

Downey, Jean. Introduction. *Franklin Evans, or The Inebriate.* New Haven: College and University Press, 1967.

DuBois, W. E. B. *The Souls of Black Folk.* New York: New American Library, 1982.

Du Plessix Gray, Francine. "Splendor and Miseries." *The New York Review of Books* 39, no. 13 (July 16, 1992): 31–35.

Emerson, Ralph Waldo. *Essays and Lectures.* Ed. Joel Porte. New York: Library of America, 1983.

Erkkila, Betsy. *Whitman the Political Poet.* New York: Oxford University Press, 1989.

Fiedler, Leslie. *Love and Death in the American Novel.* New York: Criterion Books, 1960.

Fishburn, Katherine. *Women in Popular Culture: A Reference Guide.* Westport, Conn.: Greenwood Press, 1982.

Folsom, Ed. "Introduction: Recircuiting the American Past." *A Profile of Twentieth-Century American Poetry.* Ed. Jack Meyers and David Wojahn. Carbondale: Southern Illinois University Press, 1991.

Foner, Eric. *Politics and Ideology in the Age of the Civil War.* New York: Oxford University Press, 1980.

Foner, Philip S. *The Life and Writings of Frederick Douglass.* 4 vols. New York: International Publishers, 1950–55.

Fredrickson, George. *The Black Image in the White Mind: The Debate on Afro-American Character and Destiny, 1817–1914.* New York: Harper and Row, 1971.

Freedman, Florence Bernstein. *William Douglas O'Connor: Walt Whitman's Chosen Knight.* Athens: Ohio University Press, 1985.

Genovese, Eugene D. *Roll, Jordan, Roll: The World the Slaves Made.* New York: Random House, 1976.

Graham, Mary-Emma. "Politics in Black and White: A View of Walt Whitman's

Career as a Political Journalist." *CLA Journal* 17 (December 1973): 263–70.

Greenland, Cyril, and John Robert Colombo. *Walt Whitman's Canada*. Willowdale, Ontario: Hounslow Press, 1992.

Greenspan, Ezra. *Walt Whitman and the American Reader*. Cambridge: Cambridge University Press, 1990.

Grossman, Allen. "The Poetics of Union in Whitman and Lincoln: An Inquiry Toward the Relationship of Art and Policy." *The American Renaissance Reconsidered*. Ed. Walter Benn Michaels and Donald E. Pease. Baltimore: Johns Hopkins University Press, 1985.

Gwin, Minrose C. "Green-Eyed Monsters of the Slavocracy: Jealous Mistresses in Two Slave Narratives." *Conjuring*. Ed. Marjorie Pryse and Hortense J. Spillers. Bloomington: Indiana University Press, 1985. 39–52.

Hughes, Langston. "Calls Whitman Negroes' First Great Poetic Friend, Lincoln of Letters." *Chicago Defender*, 4 July 1953, 11.

———. "An English Professor Disagrees on Whitman's Racial Attitudes." *Chicago Defender*, 18 July 1953, 11.

———. "Like Whitman, Great Artists Are Not Always Good People." *Chicago Defender*, 1 August 1953, 11.

———. "Theme for English B." *The Langston Hughes Reader*. New York: Applebee, 1958. 108–9.

Hutchinson, George B. "Whitman and the Black Poet: Kelly Miller's Speech to the Walt Whitman Fellowship." *American Literature* 61 (March 1989): 46–59.

Jefferson, Thomas. *Notes on the State of Virginia*. Chapel Hill: University of North Carolina Press, 1955.

Kaplan, Justin. "Nine Old Bones: *Walt Whitman's Blue Book*." *The Atlantic Monthly* 221, no. 5 (1968): 60–64.

———. *Walt Whitman: A Life*. New York: Simon and Schuster, 1980.

Killingsworth, M. Jimmie. *Whitman's Poetry of the Body*. Chapel Hill: University of North Carolina Press, 1989.

Kinney, James. *Amalgamation!: Race, Sex, and Rhetoric in the Nineteenth-Century American Novel*. Westport, Conn.: Greenwood Press, 1985.

Laurie, Bruce. *Artisans into Workers*. New York: Hill and Wang, 1989.

Lawrence, D. H. *Studies in Classic American Literature*. New York: Penguin Books, 1986.

Leggett, William. *Democratick Editorials: Essays in Jacksonian Political Economy*. Ed. Lawrence H. White. Indianapolis: Liberty Press, 1984.

Litwack, Leon F. *North of Slavery: The Negro in the Free States, 1790–1860*. Chicago: University of Chicago Press, 1961.

Loving, Jerome. *Emerson, Whitman, and the American Muse*. Chapel Hill: University of North Carolina Press, 1982.

———. *Walt Whitman's Champion: William Douglas O'Connor*. College Station: Texas A & M University Press, 1978.

Malin, Stephen. "'A Boston Ballad' and the Boston Riot." *Walt Whitman Review* 9, no. 3 (September 1963): 51–57.

Marki, Ivan. *The Trial of the Poet*. New York: Columbia University Press, 1976.

Martin, Reginald. "The Self-Contradiction Literatus: Walt Whitman and His Two Views of Blacks in America." *Calamus: Walt Whitman Quarterly: International* 27 (March 1986): 13–22.

McPherson, James M. *Battle Cry of Freedom: The Civil War Era.* New York: Oxford University Press, 1988.

————. *Ordeal by Fire: The Civil War and Reconstruction.* New York: Alfred A. Knopf, 1982.

Miller, Edwin H. *Walt Whitman's Poetry: A Psychological Journey.* Boston: Houghton Mifflin, 1968.

Milton, John. *Complete Poems and Major Prose.* Ed. Merritt Y. Hughes. New York: The Odyssey Press, 1957.

Moon, Michael. *Disseminating Whitman.* Cambridge: Harvard University Press, 1991.

Mythology: An Illustrated Encyclopedia. Ed. Richard Cavendish. New York: Rizzoli International Publications, 1980.

Nevins, Allan. *Ordeal of the Union.* 2 vols. New York: Scribner's, 1947.

The New Oxford Annotated Bible. Ed. Herbert G. May and Bruce M. Metzger. Oxford: Oxford University Press, 1973.

Olney, James. "'I Was Born': Slave Narratives, Their Status as Autobiography and as Literature." *The Slave's Narrative.* Ed. Charles T. Davis and Henry Louis Gates Jr. New York: Oxford University Press, 1985. 148–75.

Pease, Jane H., and William H. Pease. *The Fugitive Slave Law and Anthony Burns.* Philadelphia: J. B. Lippincott, 1975.

Peeples, Ken, Jr. "The Paradox of the 'Good Gray Poet' (Walt Whitman on Slavery and the Black Man)." *Phylon* 35 (March 1974): 22–32.

Potter, David. *The Impending Crisis, 1848–1861.* New York: Harper and Row, 1976.

Price, Kenneth. "Whitman's Solutions to 'The Problem of the Blacks.'" *Resources for American Literary Study* 15 (1985): 205–8.

Ratner, Lorman. *Powder Keg: Northern Opposition to the Antislavery Movement, 1831–1840.* New York: Basic Books, 1968.

Rubin, Joseph Jay. *The Historic Whitman.* University Park: The Pennsylvania State University Press, 1973.

St. Armand, Barton Levi. "*Franklin Evans:* A Sportive Temperance Novel." *Books at Brown* 24 (1971): 136–47.

Sanchez-Eppler, Karen. "To Stand Between: A Political Perspective on Whitman's Poetics of Merger and Embodiment." *ELH* 56 (Winter 1989): 923–49.

Sewell, Richard. *Ballots for Freedom: Antislavery Politics in the United States, 1837–1860.* New York: Oxford University Press, 1970.

————. "Walt Whitman, John Parker Hale, and Free Democracy." *New England Quarterly* 34 (1961): 239–41.

Silver, Rollo G. "Whitman in 1850: Three Uncollected Articles." *American Literature* 19 (1948): 301–17.

Sollors, Werner. "'Never Was Born': The Mulatto, An American Tragedy." *The Massachusetts Review* 27 (1986): 293–316.

Stanton, Henry B. *Random Recollections.* New York: Harper and Brothers, 1887.

Stovall, Floyd. *The Foreground of "Leaves of Grass."* Charlottesville: University of Virginia Press, 1974.

Stowe, Harriet Beecher. *Uncle Tom's Cabin.* New York: New American Library, 1981.

Sundquist, Eric. "Slavery, Revolution, and the American Renaissance." *The*

American Renaissance Reconsidered. Ed. Walter Benn Michaels and Donald E. Pease. Baltimore: Johns Hopkins University Press, 1985.

"The Talk of the Town: Notes and Comment." *The New Yorker,* 1 July 1991, 21.

Thomas, M. Wynn. *The Lunar Light of Whitman's Poetry.* Cambridge: Harvard University Press, 1987.

———. "Walt Whitman and the Dreams of Labor." *Walt Whitman: The Centennial Essays.* Ed. Ed Folsom. Iowa City: University of Iowa Press, 1994.

Thoreau, Henry David. *Walden and Civil Disobedience.* Ed. Sherman Paul. Boston: Houghton Mifflin, 1960.

Tocqueville, Alexis de. *Democracy in America.* Vol. 2. New York: Vintage Books, 1945.

Traubel, Horace. *With Walt Whitman in Camden.* 6 vols. Boston: Small, Maynard and Co., 1906.

Trefousse, Hans L. *The Radical Republicans: Lincoln's Vanguard for Racial Justice.* New York: Alfred A. Knopf, 1969.

Turner, Lorenzo Dow. *Anti-Slavery Sentiment in Literature.* Washington, D.C.: The Association for the Study of Negro Life and History, 1929.

Types of Mankind: Or Ethnological Researches . . . Ed. J. C. Nott and George R. Gliddon. Philadelphia: J. B. Lippincott, Grambo and Company, 1854.

Van den Berghe, Pierre. *Race and Racism: A Comparative Perspective.* New York: Wiley, 1978.

Whelan, Carol Zapata. "'Do I Contradict Myself?' Progression Through Contraries in Walt Whitman's 'The Sleepers.'" *Walt Whitman Quarterly Review* 10, no. 1 (Summer 1992): 25–39.

Whitman, Thomas Jefferson. *Dear Brother Walt: The Letters of Thomas Jefferson Whitman.* Ed. Dennis Berthold and Kenneth M. Price. Kent, Ohio: The Kent State University Press, 1984.

Whitman, Walt. *Complete Poetry and Collected Prose.* Ed. Justin Kaplan. New York: Library of America, 1982.

———. *The Correspondence.* Vol. 1. Ed. Edwin Haviland Miller. New York: New York University Press, 1961.

———. *The Early Poems and the Fiction.* Ed. Thomas L. Brasher. New York: New York University Press, 1963.

———. *The Gathering of the Forces.* Ed. Cleveland Rodgers and John Black. 2 vols. New York: G. P. Putnam's Sons, 1920.

———. *I Sit and Look Out: Editorials from the Brooklyn Daily Times.* Ed. Emory Holloway and Vernolian Schwarz. New York: Columbia University Press, 1932.

———. *Leaves of Grass.* Ed. Sculley Bradley and Harold W. Blodgett. New York: W. W. Norton, 1973.

———. *Notebooks and Unpublished Prose Manuscripts.* Ed. Edward F. Grier. 6 vols. New York: New York University Press, 1984.

———. *The Uncollected Poetry and Prose of Walt Whitman.* Ed. Emory Holloway. 2 vols. Garden City, N.J.: Doubleday, Page & Company, 1921.

———. *Walt Whitman of the New York Aurora.* Ed. Joseph J. Rubin and Charles H. Brown. State College, Pa.: Bald Eagle Press, 1950.

Whittier, John Greenleaf. "Ichabod." *The Complete Poetical Works of John Greenleaf Whittier.* Boston: Houghton Mifflin, 1894. 186–87.

Wilentz, Sean. *Chants Democratic: New York City and the Rise of the American Working Class, 1788–1850.* New York: Oxford University Press, 1984.

Yannella, Donald. *Ralph Waldo Emerson*. Boston: Twayne Publishers, 1982.
Zanger, Jules. "The 'Tragic Octoroon' in Pre–Civil War Fiction." *American Quarterly* 18 (1966): 63–70.
Zweig, Paul. *Walt Whitman: The Making of the Poet*. New York: Basic Books, 1984.

Index